Exploring Desert Stone

"The Cathedral" as seen from
Camp 39 Sept 17th 1859

EXPLORING DESERT STONE

JOHN N. MACOMB'S 1859 EXPEDITION TO
THE CANYONLANDS OF THE COLORADO

Steven K. Madsen

Logan, Utah
Utah State University Press

Utah State University Press
Logan, Utah 84319-7800
USUPress.org

978-0-87421-707-0 (cloth)
978-0-87421-708-7 (e-book)

The National Trails-Intermountain Region of the National Park Service funded development of the facsimile of the 1864 *Map of Explorations and Surveys in New Mexico and Utah made under the direction of the Secretary of War by Capt. J. N. Macomb, Topographical Engineers, assisted by C. H. Dimmock, C. Engineer,* by Frederick W. von Egloffstein.

Manufactured in China
Printed on acid-free, recycled paper

Library of Congress Cataloging-in-Publication Data

Madsen, Steven K.
  Exploring desert stone : John N. Macomb's 1859 expedition to the canyonlands of the Colorado / Steven K. Madsen.
       p. cm.
  Includes bibliographical references and index.
  ISBN 978-0-87421-707-0 (cloth : alk. paper) – ISBN 978-0-87421-708-7 (e-book)
  1. Geological surveys–Four Corners Region–History–19th century. 2. Geological surveys–Four Corners Region–History–19th century–Sources. 3. Scientific expeditions–Four Corners Region–History–19th century. 4. Canyons–Four Corners Region–History–19th century. 5. Paleontology–Four Corners Region–History–19th century. 6. Macomb, J. N. (John N.), 1810 or 11-1889–Travel–Four Corners Region. 7. United States. Army. Corps of Topographical Engineers. 8. Four Corners Region–Geography. 9. Four Corners Region–Discovery and exploration. 10. Colorado River (Colo.-Mexico)–Discovery and exploration. I. Title.

  QE79.5.M33 2010
  557.92'59–dc22

                            2009031474

To the noble ladies,

Margaret Jones Perritt and the late Mary M. "Terby" Barnes,

who helped make this work possible.

CONTENTS

Illustrations and Maps

LANDSCAPE VIEWS

Plate I. Abiquiu Peak [or Cerro del Pedernal], looking westerly
Plate II. Near Vado del Chama, upper Cretaceous mesa
Plate III. La Piedra Parada [Chimney Rock], looking west
Plate IV. The Pagosa & San Juan River, looking easterly
Plate V. Rio Dolores & Sierra de la Plata. From near Camp 21
Plate VI. Casa Colorado & La Sal Mountains, looking northerly
Plate VII. Head of Labyrinth Creek [Lower Indian Creek], looking
   south-easterly
Plate VIII. Head of Cañon Colorado [Sixshooter Peaks]. Erosion of Triassic
   series
Plate IX. Lower San Juan, looking west. From near Camp 35
Plate X. The Needles [Ship Rock], looking south-westerly
Plate XI. The Cabazon. From near Camp 54
Trap Dyke, Pope's Well, south of Santa Fé, New Mexico
The Pagosa, S.W. Colorado
Ruins of stone houses on Cliffs, Labyrinth Canon

ACKNOWLEDGMENTS

I express heartfelt thanks to my sister, Lucinda, and her husband, Richard Craven, for helping to facilitate my research visits to the National Archives, the Library of Congress, and the Smithsonian Institution Archives in Washington, D.C., and to the Virginia Historical Society in Richmond. With their support many documents were found that added depth to the story of the Macomb expedition. Following the document-trail of the exploring expedition with Richard and Lucinda, and my wife, Adrienne, made the adventure enjoyable. The four of us also shared a travel adventure along the Macomb route at Santa Fé, Abiquiu, Ghost Ranch, Dulce, Farmington, and Shiprock, New Mexico; and at Pagosa Springs, Colorado.

I am very grateful to three "oil men"—Leo Pacheco, Tom Roberts, and Freddie Frausto—who more than once dug my vehicle out of the bottomless sands of Cañon Largo and towed it to firmer ground. On a hot, dusty day in August, opposite the mouth of Tapicito Creek, in northern New Mexico, Leo and Tom shared with me the history of the canyon. Leo's grandfather, Manuel C. Pacheco, patented land in the canyon in 1934. Tom told stories of the route when it became a stage road and a cattle trail. Both of them pointed out interesting aspects of the archaeologically rich canyon, now peppered with gas and oil lines and pumping stations.

I wish to express my appreciation to my longtime friend John L. Jackson, for his professional competence and insightful suggestions that have aided me in the writing of this work.

I acknowledge the tremendous help from Dan Cassidy, owner of Five Quail Books, Prescott, Arizona. Dan graciously allowed me to copy his original Egloffstein map for inclusion in this volume. (The originals in the National Archives and at the University of Utah are damaged and torn.) Thank you to Aaron Mahr Yañez, superintendent, and the National Trails-Intermountain Region of the National Parks service, which funded development of the map.

C. Gregory Crampton introduced me to the topic of the Macomb expedition when we launched our research on the Old Spanish Trail in the mid-1970s. From that work came the publication *In Search of the Spanish Trail: Santa Fe to Los Angeles, 1829–1848*, the first study to locate and map the historic trail.

I extend appreciation to my friend, Jicarilla Apache guide Lambert Callado, who assisted me in pinpointing where Dimmock in 1859 sketched Horse Lake, in northern New Mexico. With his help, I also located the Macomb expedition campsite immediately south of the lake's outlet, in the shadow of a cliff overhang.

A warm thank you goes to Dosha Dee Dee Bradley and her brother Will Curley, for permission to publish her photograph taken in the shadow of Ship Rock. And to Jerry Garza, resident of Tecoloté, New Mexico, for showing me the "cornerstone" of the historic village church along the Santa Fe Trail.

The good people at Pecos National Historical Park, New Mexico, proved helpful: Don Pettijohn, Lorenzo Vigil, and Eluterio Valera, Jr. David Reynolds, retired aerospace engineer from Lawrence, Kansas, helped me photograph the ruins of the Spanish mission church at Pecos Pueblo from the approximate spot where Dimmock made his pencil sketch.

The Dolores *Star* staff helped me scout out a favorable place to photograph the Dolores River Valley. Donald Martinez, employee at the Ghost Ranch Museum, helped me in my search for Dimmock's "Cachucha," dubbed "Orphan Rock" by locals. My son Thomas helped me explore by jeep and by foot Macomb's wilderness route in the Indian Creek Canyon area, immediately east of Canyonlands National Park. We glimpsed the enormous challenges faced by the Macomb team. Alternately deep sands and rock-studded primitive roads, sheer cliffs, and a dizzying array of desert stone blocked our path. On our return trip we scouted the broken terrain from Needles Overlook, anticipating a future expedition to Canyonlands.

My deepest thanks go to my brother, Gordon C. Madsen, who offered to take me back to the Indian Creek area in his jeep. We followed a ten-mile bumpy road to the head of Rustler Canyon, where we launched a grueling hike to the place where Macomb's 1859 expedition culminated. Equipped with camel packs full of water, broad-brimmed hats, hiking poles, good boots, and fruit and protein snacks, we trudged down the lower canyon of Indian Creek to the "perpendicular fall," a 40- to 50-foot pour-off, which had blocked the progress of Macomb's team. Undeterred, we found a way around the obstacle and ascended the first tier of Newberry Butte, the formation that Macomb's explorers ultimately surmounted. Limited water, hot temperatures (at least ninety-four degrees Fahrenheit), and spent energy prompted us to return to the jeep. Near the end of the twelve-mile hike, I ran out of water and suffered from heat exhaustion and leg cramps. Each of us had consumed a gallon and a half of water and Gatorade, but that wasn't enough. My brother gave me the rest of his water and hiked back to the jeep (some 40 minutes away). When he returned with more water and fruit and rescued me, he succumbed to heat exhaustion and a leg cramp. I waited for him to recover and together we made our way out of the desert, thankful to be safe and sound.

Valuable aid was rendered by staff members of the Library of Congress; National Archives; Utah State Historical Society; University of Utah's Marriott Library; Bancroft Library, University of California, Berkeley; Yale University Library; University of Utah Natural History Museum; College of Physicians of Philadelphia; Kansas State Historical Society; Virginia Historical Society; Rio Grande County Museum; Ohio Department of Natural Resources, Division of Geological Survey. The following individuals and institutions deserve special mention: Irisha Corral at New Mexico Highlands University; Ann Oldham, Pagosa Springs Museum; Tomas Jaehn, Fray Angelico Chavez History Library, Palace of the Governors, Santa Fé; T. Juliette Arai, Old Military and Civil Records, National Archives, Washington, D.C.; John McClure, Virginia Historical Society, Richmond; James A. Steed, Smithsonian Institution Archives; David G. Smith, National Museum of Natural History, Smithsonian Institution; Tara C. Craig, Butler Library, Columbia University; Anne Johnson, Special Collections Research Center, Swem Library, College of William and Mary; Mark Emmons, University of New Mexico Libraries; Martha C. Hayden, Utah Geological Survey; Lisa Van Doren, Ohio Geological Society; Michelle Gachette, Harvard University Library; Susan Lintelmann, Manuscripts Curator, Special Collections, United States Military Academy Library; and Lt. Col. Sherman L. Fleek, historian, West Point Military Academy.

I also acknowledge the professional help provided by Robert Behra, Karen Carver, Paul Mogren, Walter Jones, Roy Webb, and Gregory C. Thompson at the Marriott Library. In addition, thanks go to Rick Grapes, Lauren Cowles, and Dusty White of the Harold B. Lee Library, Brigham Young University.

Moreover, recognition is due the Virginia Historical Society for its stewardship of the Charles H. Dimmock Papers. The Society has given a great deal of care to the preservation of the Dimmock documents.

Thanks to John B. Krygier, associate professor of geography, Ohio Wesleyan University, who provided valuable information on Egloffstein. And to Bill Cole, North Cape May, New Jersey, who provided useful information on Dimmock.

I'm grateful to my good friend "Tom" W. B. Sutton, Utah State Office of Education Social Studies specialist, who provided enormous encouragement throughout the project. In addition, I thank the following people, who in a number of ways encouraged this work: David W. Dietering, Kenn Carpenter, Lorraine Carpenter, W. L. "Bud" Rusho, Phil Stevens, Lucille M. Nielsen, RuthAnn M. Therkelsen, Craig Emery, Diana Emery, Max Bylund, Lauré Holland, Joan Y. Hanson, Rick Payne, Dale Pitkin, Karen Harrison, Mike Nelson, Jonathan Lever, my friends at the Wentworth Branch—Blaine and Diane Anderson, Lloyd Larrimore, John Mazanis, Tony and Debbie Mitchell, E. "Woody" Gurney, Rick Black, Bill McKee, Chuck Dew, and Kent Ogaard—and the Granite Peaks High School staff, particularly Dayanne Coombs and Michele R. Callahan, principal. I tip my pith helmet to fellow members of the Utah Westerners Association and to my team leaders Celia Powell and Cindy Moyle in Granite School District's Instructional Technology Department—Dr. James H. Henderson, director—for their encouraging words.

Special thanks are due John R. Alley, Utah State University Press editor, for his advice and support. Thanks also go to historian Will Bagley for his valuable suggestions. I congratulate my wife, Adrienne, and my children Belinda, Heather, and Tom, and son-in-law, Bryce, for their contributions in the research and writing phases of this work.

With utmost respect and admiration, I acknowledge the kind support of two very important individuals, the late Mary M. "Terby" Barnes and Margaret Jones Perritt, to whom I dedicate this work.

Much of the early archival work for this book took place in the library of Fran and Terby Barnes of Moab, Utah. Terby kindly shared her Macomb expedition research with me. As this book was going to press, she died following a long bout with cancer. I will greatly miss her friendship.

I also express deep gratitude to Margaret Jones Perritt, owner of the Charles H. Dimmock Papers, who graciously authorized the publication of Dimmock's diary and the illustrations from his sketchbook. She made available valuable information that stitched together the historic patchwork of numerous fragmentary records. With Margaret's help, I was able to put flesh on the bones of this work.

INTRODUCTION

To the casual observer the Macomb expedition report may appear typical of other government-issued survey reports of the time, but a closer look reveals much more. It is a classic of frontier literature. Army historian Frank N. Schubert explains that the geographical and geological depictions in the report "revealed a new and unknown region" to Americans. Its authors "gave the nation a substantial amount of information about the Colorado" and "made significant contributions to the development of science." (See Schubert's *Vanguard of Expansion*.) In addition, the report's color illustrations and romantic narrative offered new vistas for Americans seeking a national identity following the Civil War.

Furthermore, the Macomb report chronicled a surprising event—the historically important discovery of petrified bones on the Old Spanish Trail. (Among the paleobiology collections of today's Smithsonian Institution are the famous vertebrate fossils discovered by the expedition. The Museum of Natural History publicizes the specimens as the first significant fossils of their kind added to its collections.)

Printed in large format, the title in gold leaf on the spine of the Macomb report reads: *Exploring Expedition from Santa Fé to Junction of Grand and Green Rivers. 1859. Macomb. Geological Report. Newberry.* The gilt shield of the Corps of Topographical Engineers, with the national spread eagle perched on a crest, wrapped with a wreath of oak leaves and laurel foliage, adorns the bottom of the spine. Within this volume are eleven beautifully rendered, full-page color plates of landscape vistas, three black-and-white landscape lithographs, and eight plates of fossils. Tipped into the back of the book is a large folding map depicting the frontier region examined by the expedition.

Inexpensive reprint editions of the Macomb report and free online copies of the publication render another reissue of the report unnecessary. Nevertheless, none of the online versions comes with a reproduction of the superb folding map, and only one Web site includes the color plates in its file. The quality of lithographs contained in the Internet collection ranges from adequate to poor. Even the reprint of the report by the University of Michigan Library's Scholarly Publishing Office lacks the color lithographs and the large-scale map. This book showcases both historical gems.

In 1859, the U.S. War Department charged Captain John N. Macomb, Jr., with finding a practicable route for military supplies from Santa Fé, New Mexico, to the southern settlements of Utah Territory—in the event of future conflicts with its inhabitants. In addition, it directed him to locate the confluence of the Green and Colorado rivers, fill a great gap in the geographical knowledge of the American West, survey the region transected by the Old Spanish Trail, and conduct a scientific study of the Four Corners region, particularly the canyonlands of the Colorado Plateau.

The Macomb report, delayed until 1876 because of Civil War conditions and apparent problems with finishing the illustrations, contained a summary of the expedition's travels by the leader of the expedition, an eminent military engineer. The prominent physician/geologist Dr. John S. Newberry wrote the eloquent scientific study of the geology and natural resources of the region. Newberry had been with the Joseph C. Ives expedition in 1858. The Ives party ascended the Colorado River to determine the extent of its navigability for steamboat travel. In addition, the U.S. Army sought to use the Colorado as a waterway from which to dispatch troops and supplies to inland military posts, particularly Camp Floyd in central Utah. During the survey, Newberry became the first scientist to reach the floor of the Grand Canyon. His geological study, issued in the Ives report, complemented his work with the Macomb expedition. Newberry and the noted paleontologist Ferdinand B. Meek compiled important fossil reports for Macomb. Frederick W. von Egloffstein, who had also served with Ives, pioneered a new technique in cartography and perfected it with the survey map that accompanied the Macomb report. In addition, civil engineer Charles H. Dimmock provided a splendid field map from which Egloffstein built his masterful representation of the Four Corners region, where four southwestern states merge.

The region mapped by Captain Macomb's command encompasses a diverse landscape of majestic alpine mountains, desert badlands cut by impassable canyons and studded with massive rock monuments, plateaus blanketed in sagebrush and grasses, and juniper and piñon forests. Much of the country, sparsely dotted by modern towns and transected by rib-bons of highway, remains barely touched by the onrush of civilization.

At its heart lies one of the largest uninhabited and undeveloped landscapes in the American West. A myriad of fanciful shapes, captured in stone, greet the eye. Moreover, two of the largest streams of North America—the Colorado and Green rivers—flow through it. The area is rugged, scenic, and remote. (The high desert can also be a dangerous and deadly place. Modern adventurers need to take adequate precau-tions when visiting the route of the expedition, particularly away from the pavement.) The luxury of time, and advanced technology, allows today's travelers to pause and soak in its natural beauty.

The views in these settings stimulate literary flights of fancy, a common nineteenth-century activity among scientists and explorers. Both the ex-pedition's geologist and topographer engaged in it. For this writer, the allure of the Colorado Plateau's heartland also proved unavoidable. It is a wildly contorted land, alive with color and harmonious features; even the random visitor feels the magic of the landscape's compelling solitude. A number of vantage points in the pristine air near the confluence of the Green and Colorado rivers reveal panoramas magnificently diverse yet unified by a succession of rocks standing upright—temples of sandstone and flat-topped monuments. Rock sentinels, gleaming in the hot sun, provide a grand color-fest for the artist's palette. Clouds shift to create new intensities of light and shadow on another precipice, another can-yon, another view. A haunting wind scrapes the desert floor and whispers as it circles cliffs and passes through eroded canyons and stone notches. Soft talus slopes form broad, apron-like bases below sheer stone walls—a pattern that echoes across a vibrant landscape. Upthrust rocks, while retreating from erosion, retain their profiles in this "land of living rock."

Most of the landmarks seen by the expedition remain intact and ob-servable—many are accessible from modern highways. Besides a descrip-tion of the expedition's general route of travel, this book tells its long overlooked story with more depth and accuracy than has been possible in the past by using newly discovered historical documents. Many of these, which I have transcribed, appear in part II. Although brief excerpts of a few selections have previously appeared in print, none has been issued in its entirety until now. The recovery of these documents provides a more complete record of the Macomb expedition. In addition, this work in-cludes brief biographical sketches of the key participants and uses ex-cerpts from their contemporary notes and correspondence to complete the picture.

In 1860, John N. Macomb, Jr., the leader of the San Juan Exploring Expedition, submitted a report of the expedition's activities that appeared at the beginning of the final publication. John S. Newberry wrote the geological notes, the substance of the published work, which appeared next. Two reports on fossils collected by the expedition, one written by noted geologist Fielding Bradford Meek and the other by Newberry, appear at the end of the book. A map drawn by Baron Frederick Wilhelm von Egloffstein, a Prussian aristocrat, completed the work. (Neither Egloffstein nor Meek, however, had participated in the expedition.)

Paleontologist Edward D. Cope issued a report on Newberry's dinosaur fossil find in volume 4 of the 1877 George M. Wheeler Survey Report. Cope's report and the lithographic plate illustrating the dinosaur bones are in the second part of the volume on paleontology; this book includes a copy of the plate.

Some notes about the source materials printed in this volume: Both Newberry and Charles H. Dimmock, the expedition's topographer and cartographer, kept diaries of their experiences in the field. In addition, Dimmock kept a sketchbook and a separate portfolio of pencil sketches illustrating the people and landscapes he encountered on the journey. Recently, I discovered Dimmock's diary and sketchbook at the Virginia Historical Society in Richmond. Thanks to the owner, Margaret Jones Perritt, Dimmock's diary entries and sketches appear in print for the first time. I also located Dimmock's portfolio in the College of William and Mary in Williamsburg. Nearly all of Dimmock's foxed and yellowed pencil sketches are shown in part I.

In addition to his drawings, Dimmock submitted a topographical memoir to Macomb, which was not included in the expedition's official manuscript collection. Instead, Macomb's wife placed it in a collection of family papers, now in the Library of Congress. My transcription of the complete memoir appears in part II.

Newberry's lengthy diary constituted another primary source; although referenced numerous times in the Macomb report, the original manuscript has not been found. Perhaps, since he had included several of his diary entries in the published report, Newberry did not bother to preserve the manuscript. Instead, he submitted an abridged diary, written in telegraphic style, which I have transcribed and included here; only a microfilm version of this document has been found. The National Archives is unable to locate Newberry's original abridged diary and several other expedition materials that appear in their microfilm collections. My search in the National Archives failed to locate many of the materials shown on microfilm. At least two other searches by previous researchers also proved fruitless.

Newberry also drew pencil sketches of the wilderness landscapes he encountered, many of which were subsequently rendered in color and black-and-white plates by lithographer J. J. Young for publication in the Macomb report. The location of Newberry's original drawings and other personal papers remains one of the unsolved mysteries of this study. We can only hope that, some day, someone will find a rich cache of Newberry's lost papers in the National Archives or among the scattered materials of Young or in some obscure collection.

Macomb apparently did not keep a journal of the expedition. His summary of the venture, printed in the final report, is a compilation of information he appears to have gleaned from his own personal letters to his wife and his correspondence with the topographical bureau.

Little else remains to fill in the remaining historical gaps of the expedition. This is perhaps because expedition members faced strict guidelines in terms of notes, sketches, and other material they collected. The policy read: "an established rule of the [War] Department requires that each assistant shall distinctly understand, in accepting his appointment, that the specimens, notes, sketches, memoranda, and all of the material collected & prepared by him in the field, shall be considered the property of the government, and shall be turned over to the Chief of the Expedition at the conclusion of the work, & that he shall not publish, nor furnish to any parties for publication, either during the progress of the expedition or after its conclusion, any of the information or results which he may have procured while engaged upon the duty."

Unfortunately, some members of the Macomb expedition made ethnocentric and sometimes racist remarks in their descriptions of Hispanics, African Americans, and American Indians. I do not excuse their statements, but they reflect the times and the explorers' backgrounds.

A note about the nomenclature found in the report: Some of the place names encountered by the expedition no longer appear on maps of the region. Tunecha Mountain is now Chuska Mountain. Locals call the Abajo Mountains the Blue Mountains. Sierra de los Valles, or Vias Mountain, is presently known as Valles Calderas. Cañon Pintado, or Cañon de las Pañitas, is today's East Canyon. La Piedra Parada is now Chimney Rock. The Needles is present-day Ship Rock. The Cerro del Pedernal is now Abiquiu Peak. At least two names have disappeared and their identity remains a mystery: El Alto de la Utah and Lagoon des Chavias.

Historic names that tend to cling to the landscape include Cañon Largo, Casa Colorado, Rio Puerco, La Plata Mountains, Nacimiento Mountain, La Sal Mountains, Mesa Verde, Great Sage Plain, Colorado Plateau, Arroyo Seco, Abiquiu, Rio Grande, and Old Spanish Trail.

The colorful names of streams along the route of the Old Spanish Trail preserve the flavor of the times. Spanish colonial exploring and trading parties, notably the Dominguez-Escalante and Juan Maria de Rivera expeditions, applied lyrical names to the San Juan (Saint John), Rio Piedra (Stone River), Rio de los Pinos (River of Pines), Rio de la Plata (The Silver River), Rio Florida (Flower River), Rio Mancos (Cripple River), and Rio de las Animas (River of the Souls). Many if not most of these and other Spanish names in that area remain in use today.

Macomb's party followed much of the Old Spanish Trail route, a trade artery extending from Santa Fé, New Mexico, to Los Angeles, California, today a federally recognized National Historic Trail. Since 2002, the National Park Service and the Bureau of Land Management jointly administer the Old Spanish National Historic Trail.

Far to the northeast of Macomb's route and the Old Spanish Trail, in a seemingly different world at the time, prospectors and miners played out the drama of the 1859 Pike's Peak gold rush in the environs of modern Denver, Colorado. Two of Macomb's assistants, Newberry and Dimmock, witnessed the homeward stream of miners whose prospects had "busted" as they traveled the Santa Fe Trail. But the rush played no role in the outcome of Macomb's survey of the desert Southwest.

Not finding any water was among the "chief fears" "Nannie" Macomb had for her husband's safety as he set out to explore America's frontier. During the trip, topographer Charles H. Dimmock wrote, "Heavy clouds this evening & soon [a]n increase of rain which falls as if the windows of heaven were opened." Macomb, a religious man, assured his wife, "I feel so well that I often think I must be profiting by your prayers for my well being." At journey's end, Macomb noted that since his arrival in New Mexico two years earlier, he had never seen so much wet weather. He reported, "We had plenty of water, for where there was no water usually we were bountifully rained upon and thus spared all suffering in that score throughout our 77 days of absence." In fact, it had rained more than fifty days.

The expedition discovered a downside to all the moisture. Damp conditions prevented geologist John S. Newberry from protecting all of the natural history specimens he had collected.

Newberry's brilliant mind enabled him to sort out the pieces of the geologic puzzle splayed across the Colorado Plateau region and form sweeping scientific conclusions. Additions to the report's scientific studies would do little to improve it; therefore, I have chosen not to annotate his notes on geology and paleontology.

Unfortunately, many of the dozens of scientific names contained in the official report have been superseded. In addition, a number of classifications appear to have changed over time. (Numerous searches of the scientific names to determine their common names have proven mostly unproductive.) Much of the scientific methodology and corresponding data is now obsolete. Moreover, only a few of the natural history specimens that Newberry collected have been studied and the findings published.[1]

Even Newberry questioned the idea of updating his own work, and he presented his reasons in the Prefatory Note: "The observations made fifteen years ago, if accurately made, have equal value now as then; if inaccurate, it is only right that the credit of the correction of errors should belong to those who make such corrections. . . .It is evident that to modify the report so as to conform to all the conclusions more recently reached, would be to falsify the record and greatly impair the independence and value of the statements it includes. The truth or error of these statements will soon be demonstrated by the extension of the explorations of other parties into this field."

Newberry divided his geological report into six chapters, each covering a specific geographic range. He devotes three chapters of his report to the topography, geology, and natural history he encountered during the expedition. Chapter 4 commences the trip up the Rio Grande. Chapter 5 describes the geology of the Great Sage Plain and the valley of the Colorado. Chapter 6 examines the geology of the banks of the San Juan and across the Continental Divide. The narrative in chapter 6 follows the expedition as it reenters the Rio Grande Valley via the pueblos of Jemez and Santo Domingo.

With Newberry's scientific findings, eloquently written and splendidly illustrated, the Macomb expedition produced a classic of frontier literature. Seized by spectacular landscapes and marvelous geology and paleontology, as well as important archaeological finds, the Macomb explorers aesthetically interpreted the Four Corners region. The survey laid the groundwork for future scientific studies, and specimens gathered by the team, including historically significant vertebrate fossils, became part of the collections of the Smithsonian Institution.

---

1.   For those who wish to read an analysis of Newberry's geologic studies, see A. M. Celâl Şengör, *The Large Wavelength Deformations of the Lithosphere*, pp. 185–95. Another excellent source on Newberry is Stephen J. Pyne's *How the Canyon Became Grand.*

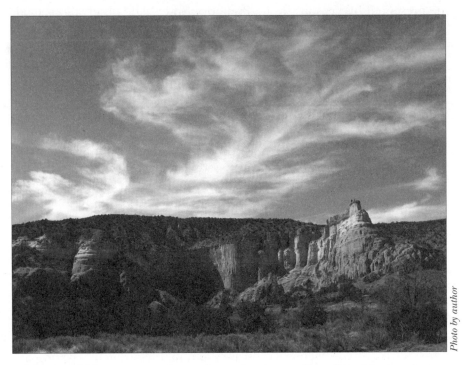

Echo Amphitheater, a sandstone formation in northern New Mexico along the Arroyo Seco on the route followed by the Macomb party.

PART I

The Story of the Macomb San Juan Exploring Expedition

The houses of these Indians present usually the
appearance of exceeding neatness, while in their
persons there is a want of cleanliness objectionable
beyond measure.

Courtesy of Margaret Jones Perritt and the Virginia Historical Society

Sketch of a Pueblo Indian house, by Charles H. Dimmock.

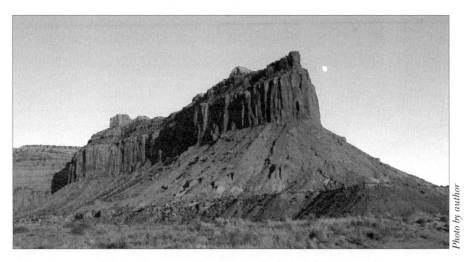

A close-up view of a sandstone butte near Canyonlands National Park seen by the Macomb Expedition and sketched by Charles Dimmock (see page 76).

Organizing the Expedition

August 5, 1859. Camp No. 16 at the Rio Florida, 220 miles northwest of Santa Fé, New Mexico:

We have just heard rumors of a fight between our soldiers & the Mormons in the Salt Lake City—these rumors are brought in by Indian traders who came into our camp yesterday on their return from the great rivers we expect to visit—the reports are so extravagant we can scarcely believe them—they speak of battering down houses & killing women & children—so unusual a course for us that I cannot credit the reports—yet the description of the effects of the great guns so accurately given by the Indian reporters would seem to give a color of truth to the story after all—for without witnessing such scenes the Indians could hardly contrive such a story.[1]

So wrote Capt. John N. Macomb, Jr., to his wife, "Nannie," as he led an Army exploring expedition into the wilds of Utah Territory.

In the years before Captain Macomb's survey, Utah Territory was administered by federally appointed officials who frequently clashed with a powerful governor, Brigham Young, over Indian policies, mail contracts, land surveys, and probate courts. Since Young served also as the prophetic leader of the Church of Jesus Christ of Latter-day Saints, dubbed the Mormon Church, federal appointees feared the power he exercised. Furthermore, Utah's populace overwhelmingly supported Young. Ultimately, open conflict intensified between federal

---

1. Captain John N. Macomb, Jr., Santa Fé, New Mexico, to Ann Minerva "Nannie" Rodgers Macomb, Washington, D.C., August 5, 1859, Rodgers Family, Papers, Library of Congress. (Hereafter LOC.)

and local officials and complaints reached Washington. In the spring
of 1857, when James Buchanan became president, he acted on these
complaints by sending an expeditionary force commanded by Albert
Sidney Johnston to Utah to replace the governor and insure allegiance
to federal authority.

During 1857–1858, the clashes between the United States and the
Mormons, known as the Utah War, accelerated the exploration of the
Mountain West by the Army's topographical engineers. Historian C.
Gregory Crampton wrote, "The success of the Mormon resistance to
Johnston's Army in 1857 and the logistical isolation of the federal troops
at Camp Floyd [some forty miles from Salt Lake City] made it imperative
that the War Department seek new supply routes into Utah."[2]

Prompted by the conflict, the War Department directed the U.S. Army
Corps of Topographical Engineers during the years 1857–1859 to survey
the Mormon territory and find new approaches to Utah. They launched
a three-pronged effort: From the Gulf of California Lt. Joseph C. Ives
steamed up the Colorado River in the USS *Explorer*, a fifty-four-foot iron
sternwheeler, to Black Canyon, where Hoover Dam now stands. Before
turning back, he continued overland with a small party of men to explore the Grand Canyon. From Camp Floyd Capt. J. H. Simpson marched
westward across the Great Basin to Genoa, Nevada, and beyond—on
existing roads—over the Sierra Nevada Mountains to Placerville, near
Sacramento. On the return march from Genoa he followed yet another
path across the great interior basin, thereby discovering a shorter route
to California, which the Pony Express and mail and stage lines would
later follow. From Santa Fé Capt. John N. Macomb plotted a course into
Utah's canyon country and attempted to find a military route through
the legendary sandstone labyrinth near the junction of the Green and
Colorado rivers.

With their tents pitched in the San Juan River drainage along a wilderness trail, the men of the Macomb expedition, also known as the San Juan
Exploring Expedition, seemed "inclined to believe" the reports that "our
troops had bombarded Salt Lake City."[3] Though the reports later proved
false, Macomb's adventure into the West's raw frontier moved forward.

Following the survey, Macomb commissioned a famous cartographer
to create a map of the region his party explored. With the outbreak of the
Civil War, the government delayed publication of the expedition's report,

2.   C. Gregory Crampton, "Mormon Colonization in Southern Utah and in adjacent parts of
      Arizona and Nevada," unpublished manuscript, 1965, 74.
3.   Charles H. Dimmock, Papers, 1850–1873, Diary, August 4, 1859, Virginia Historical Society,
      Richmond. (Hereafter cited as Dimmock, Diary, VHS.)

United States Military Academy Library Special Collections

John N. Macomb, Jr.

which cost its members and its cartographer, the recognition due them. A number of biographies of the leading men still overlook the venture, or they ignore its important achievements.

The following narrative history represents the first detailed study of the Macomb expedition. Publication of this volume highlights the Macomb report's beautiful color plates and the magnificent map of the region. It also features an interesting selection of the newly discovered official records, personal correspondence and diaries, raw pencil sketches, and other primary materials related to the frontier survey and its men. These documents provide fresh insights and new interpretations into the lives and contributions of Macomb and his companions.

In the course of their exploration of the West's interior, the ambitious John S. Newberry launched a series of excursions to closely examine the region's geography and natural history, particularly its paleontology, geology, and anthropology. As a civilian geologist, Doctor Newberry's duties involved collecting scientific specimens, including zoological and botanical samples, for the Smithsonian Institution and providing a full report on the geology and mineralogy of the area. If necessary, he was required to supply

Courtesy of the Library of Congress

Ann Minerva "Nannie" Rodgers Macomb.

medical and surgical attention to the men and to produce a report on the natural history of the region he examined. Determining the region's natural resources for later exploitation by miners, cattle and sheep ranchers, railroaders, and settlers, was an implied task assigned to the team.

Just as Newberry made short jaunts to study the area, I make tangential journeys to depict more fully the activities and personal lives of Macomb and his companions. We will find an ambitious scientist and physician possessing great vision and intelligence and a tendency to see the beauty and potential in nature. We will also learn of the visual sensitivity of the expedition's homesick topographer, who depicted wilderness scenes in pencil drawings and romantic word pictures. And we will discover both a loving family man and a task-oriented commander, with little imagination or landscape appreciation, who despised the desert Southwest.

Born April 9, 1811, in New York City, John Navarre Macomb, Jr., was the great grandson of Philip Livingston, a signer of the Declaration of Independence. In 1838, John married his cousin, Czarina Carolina

Macomb, the daughter of General Alexander Macomb, Jr. She died in 1846. Four years later, he married Ann Minerva Rodgers, kin to a long military line. From the two marriages came eight children.[4]

Macomb launched his military career from West Point, where in 1832 he graduated from the military academy. That same year he served in the Black Hawk Expedition in the Midwest. Assigned to artillery units and engineering duty over the next several years, he rose through the ranks. Among his many duties, he made a hydrographic survey of the Straits of Detroit, took charge of seven military roads in Michigan, and made the preliminary surveys of the Manitou Islands and Grand Traverse Bay. Promoted to captain of the Topographical Engineers in 1851, he took charge of the survey of the northern and northwestern lakes. During that period, he began the survey of the Straits of Mackinac. Near the close of his surveys of the Great Lakes in 1856, the War Department assigned him to serve as the chief topographical engineer in the Military Department of New Mexico.[5]

The Army sent Macomb to New Mexico to replace a fiscally incompetent officer and repair the budgetary mess he had created. More importantly, the Army directed him to construct five vital military roads in the district. Macomb arrived in May 1857, and by July 1858 he had constructed and improved the "roads which formed the basis for New Mexico's highway and railway system." According to historian David Remley, Macomb's work won the praise of the *Santa Fé Gazette* and of New Mexico's governor. In addition, along the Taos to Santa Fé wagon route, the people of New Mexico erected a memorial pole in honor of Macomb, "who by aid of the government greatly improved the road."[6] In 1859, Macomb was a forty-eight-year-old career officer. His wife and family resided at 361 H Street in Washington, D.C.

---

4.   See "John Navarre Macomb, Jr., Colonel, United States Army," Arlington National Cemetery Web site, http://www.arlingtoncemetery.net/jnmacomb.htm (accessed August 14, 2003). Macomb's children by his first wife included John Navarre Macomb and John Navarre Macomb, III. (Apparently, the first son died in infancy.) From his second wife came William Henry Macomb, Montgomery Meigs Macomb, Augustus "Gus" Canfield Macomb, Minerva Henry Rodgers Macomb, Christina Livingston Macomb, and Nanny Rodgers Macomb. See "Family of Marshall Davies Lloyd: John Navarre Macomb, Jr.," by Marshall Davies Lloyd, http://www.gencircles.com/users/mlloyd/3/data/1038 (accessed September 15, 2004).

5.   Macomb to Col. J. J. Abert, October 30, 1858, Letters Received, Bureau of Topographical Engineers, War Department Records, National Archives, Washington, D.C. (Hereafter NA.) Other officers who graduated with Macomb included James H. Simpson and Randolph B. Marcy.

6.   David Remley, "*Adios Nuevo Mexico:*" *The Santa Fé Journal of John Watts in 1859* (Las Cruces, New Mexico: Yucca Tree, 1999), 136, 155; Frank N. Schubert, *Vanguard of Expansion: Army Engineers in the Trans-Mississippi West, 1819–1879* ([Washington, D.C.]: Historical Division, Office of Administrative Services, Office of the Chief of Engineers, [1980]), 79. See also Egloffstein to Macomb, June 12, 1861, NA. For a full account of Macomb's federal road projects in New Mexico, see W. Turrentine Jackson, *Wagon Roads West: A Study of Federal Road Surveys and Construction in the Trans-Mississippi West, 1846–1869* (Berkeley: University of California Press, 1952), 112–20.

Despite its military and political origins, the San Juan Exploring Expedition culminated in a quintessential scientific endeavor that collected rare and unique specimens for the Smithsonian Institution and made important contributions to America's scientific foundation. With a prime objective "to examine especially . . . the region . . . traversed by the old Spanish Trail," the reconnaissance would explore more than two hundred miles of the historic trace and fill a great gap in the geographical knowledge of the American West. Another important objective was "to fix also in position the lower portions and the mouths of the Green and Grand rivers"—to locate the junction of the Colorado and Green rivers.[7]

Until recently, the results of the Macomb expedition have remained largely ignored. The conditions of the Civil War delayed the publication of the final report for more than fifteen years. When issued in 1876 the report drew little public attention since America's frontier exploration focus was set on the Great Surveys—those of Ferdinand V. Hayden, Clarence King, George M. Wheeler, and John Wesley Powell.

Nevertheless, the contributions of the San Juan Exploring Expedition deserve our attention. The Macomb survey eloquently described and splendidly illustrated its scientific work. The surveyors studied the region's resources, assembled topographic information, and gathered important natural history specimens. Enraptured by spectacular landscapes and marvelous fields of archaeology, geology, and paleontology, the Macomb explorers poetically interpreted the frontier region transected by their team.

The expedition's assistant topographer and geologist both were prone to adopt the nineteenth-century tendency to romanticize red rock erosion as cyclopean cities and Gothic cathedrals. However, they yielded to a stronger and more modern impulse for fact gathering, attention to detail, and astute observations of geologic wonders. The keen and often poetic observations of the geologist, the expedition's key player, went beyond the typical topographical studies of the period to make "a significant contribution on erosion to world geology."[8] Furthermore, he would make a startling discovery while en route to the inner reaches of today's Canyonlands National Park.

In 1987, following twelve years of investigative field work, Moab naturalists and writers Fran and Terby Barnes scaled a multicolored sandstone cliff in southeastern Utah's "Canyon Pintado" and rediscovered the long-lost site of the first sauropod dinosaur bones found in the western

7.   Capt. A. A. Humphreys, Washington, D.C., to Capt. John N. Macomb, Santa Fé, New Mexico, April 6, 1859, NA.
8.   Newberry helped revise American geology with his scientific studies of the Colorado Plateau region. See James M. Aton and Robert S. McPherson, *River Flowing from the Sunrise: An Environmental History of the Lower San Juan* (Logan: Utah State University Press, 2000), 50.

hemisphere. (This sauropod, a giant, long-necked, long-tailed, plant eater from the Jurassic Period, may be the ancestor of all North American sauropods.) John S. Newberry in 1859 had originally located the bones some 250 feet above the canyon floor and excavated several samples for the Smithsonian Institution. Newberry reported that he made the discovery "directly on the Old Spanish trail." He pulled from the site a femur, a humerus, portions of the ribs, and some toes of the "monster." But he complained that he had been compelled to stop the dig after excavating about two hundred pounds of the fossils.[9] The find was an unexpected outcome of an expedition whose mission included the acquiring of "good results for the great map of our country."[10] At that time, large blank spaces and numerous representations of mythical natural features riddled frontier maps.

For example, the widely circulated commercial map issued by J. H. Colton & Co. in 1855 charting Utah and New Mexico territories carried two glaring geographical fictions: The great Colorado and Green rivers merged far below the confluence of the San Juan and Colorado rivers. Both river junctions appeared incorrectly deep inside New Mexico Territory.[11]

Before 1858, the Grand Canyon region and the remote heartland of the Colorado Plateau (named by geologist Newberry), a highland region drained by the Colorado River and its affluents, remained largely unknown, an immense mysterious land in America's interior West. This *terra incognita* appeared as a large blank on the "Map of the Utah Territory showing Routes connecting it with California and the East," issued in 1858 by the Corps of Topographical Engineers. Bold letters swept across the map's white space proclaiming it a "Region Unexplored Scientifically." This same map showed a mythical, wild variant of the Old Spanish Trail, labeled as the "South Trail in Winter Season," crossing the Green and Colorado not far above their confluence. B. A. M. Froiseth copied this fiction on his "New Sectional and Mineral Map of Utah," published in 1878.

The collective efforts of the U.S. Topographical Engineers and the Pacific Railroad surveys, contemporary to the Macomb expedition, had

9.   John S. Newberry to Dr. Joseph Leidy, January 17, 1860; John S. Newberry to Dr. Joseph Leidy, February 8, 1860, Historical Collections, Library, College of Physicians of Philadelphia. See also John N. Macomb, *Report of the San Juan Exploring Expedition, from Santa Fé, New Mexico, to the Junction of the Grand and Green Rivers of the Great Colorado River of the West, in 1859, . . . with Geological Report by Prof. J. S. Newberry* (Washington, D.C.: Government Printing Office, 1876), 91. (Hereafter Macomb, *Report.*)

10. Macomb to Humphreys, July 7, 1859, "Monthly Report of June 1859," NA.

11. J. H. Colton & Co., *Territories of New Mexico and Utah* (New York: J. H. Colton, 1855). These same errors reappeared on A. P. Wilbar's "Sketch of Public Surveys in New Mexico, 1860," in U.S. Congress, *Report of the Secretary of War*, 36th Cong., 2d sess., Senate Executive Document 1, vol. 2, serial no. 1081 (Washington, D.C., 1860).

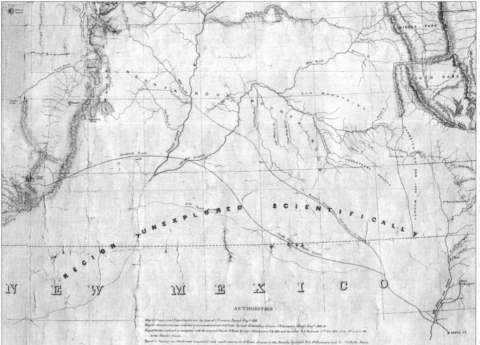

Section of "Map of Utah Territory showing the Routes connecting it with California and the East," 1858.

filled many of the blanks on the map of the western United States and greatly increased the geographical and geological knowledge of the region. Miners, farmers, cattlemen, and lumbermen who studied the government publications and maps resulting from these surveys easily accessed the unexploited areas of the West along well-defined pathways.

Beyond plotting the easiest routes into the West, the publications helped debunk the geographical myths, including El Dorados and fictitious lakes, streams, and mountain ranges. But the challenge of completing the scientific explorations in the remaining unknown lands of the West persisted. With the Utah War came a new urgency to explore the enormous extent of uncharted ground and led Capt. Macomb to plot a course from Santa Fé into Utah's canyon country and attempt to penetrate its intricate landscape near the confluence of the Green and Colorado rivers.

The natural wonderland that surrounds the legendary junction of these two mighty rivers possesses a geographic unity. Its immense, jagged landscape has been elaborately sculpted by rushing waters, creating a harmony of colors, erosive cuts, and formations. The physical characteristics of the area played a role in the development of the Old Spanish Trail, which looped northward in a great arch around the more deeply eroded interior of the Colorado Plateau. The rugged features and steep-walled gorges in the heart of the high plateau region formed an insurmountable obstacle to direct east–west travel.

On April 6, 1859, by order of the Secretary of War, Capt. A. A. Humphreys, Chief of the War Department's Office of Explorations and Surveys, sent instructions to Macomb, stationed in Santa Fé, to explore the San Juan River basin and the "lower courses of the head-tributaries of the Colorado of the West." In addition, he directed Macomb "to determine the most direct and practicable route that may be through the region between the Rio Grande and the southern settlements of Utah." Furthermore, Humphreys ordered Macomb "to examine *especially* the part of the region in question traversed by the 'Old Spanish Trail' from Abiquiu N.M. to California, with a view to ascertain if there be a practicable route, in the neighbourhood of the San Juan River, between New Mexico and Utah."[12] [Emphasis mine.]

Before the reconnaissance, Humphreys furnished Macomb with a map and explanatory notes "summarizing the total knowledge of the War Department in 1859 of the topography of the region."[13] In the explanatory notes to Macomb we read:

> The position of the "Old Spanish trail" is represented on the compiled map of Lt. Parke, Top. Eng., near the 37th parallel. By Captain Beckwith it was moved more than a degree further north, as the trail was believed to cross Green and Grand Rivers some distance above their junction. Both positions are laid down on the accompanying map under the supposition that Capt. Beckwith'[s] map is correct, it seems difficult to imagine why the early Spanish travellers from Santa Fé to Los Angeles should have taken so great a circuit to the north, instead of following the practicable line of country along the 35th parallel.[14]

---

12.   Humphreys to Macomb, April 6, 1859, NA. In August 1858 Lt. Henry L. Abbott, in charge of the Office of Explorations and Surveys, notified Captain Macomb that the War Department contemplated the idea of exploring the region along the Old Spanish Trail to the settlements northwest of Santa Fe, beyond the San Juan River. Secretary of War John B. Floyd directed Abbott to transmit an estimate of the travel time and costs to Macomb and to get his input. Macomb responded that, with an escort of three hundred men, he could thoroughly explore the region in ninety days, but the cost would be nearly $20,000 instead of the proposed $12,000. See Macomb to Humphreys, October 26, 1858, NA.

13.   As quoted in Steven K. Madsen, "The 1859 San Juan Exploring Expedition along the Old Spanish Trail," *Spanish Traces* 12, no. 3 (Fall 2006): 18.

14.   [Lt. Joseph C. Ives] to Macomb, "Memorandum to accompany a map furnished to Captain J. N. Macomb, Topl. Engs., for his assistance in the exploration of the San Juan River &c.," [April 1859], NA.

The Old Spanish Trail, 1829–1848, a trade and emigrant route, spanned the greater part of the American Southwest and linked the frontier settlements on the upper Rio Grande to the Spanish-built settlements in southern California. New Mexican wool merchants hauled woolen goods—raw wool and locally woven fabrics—on the backs of mules from Santa Fé, New Mexico, to Los Angeles, California. In California, they exchanged their woolen products for horses and mules and drove them back to Santa Fé, where they made a handsome profit. Horse dealers also found a ready market among American Indians and fur trappers in the mountain wilderness.

In 1829, Antonio Maria Armijo blazed the southern route (the Armijo Route) of the Old Spanish Trail. One segment of his pioneering path crossed the San Juan River and ran the length of New Mexico's Cañon Largo where Macomb's command later marched.

Another alternate route of the Old Spanish Trail—the North Branch—followed a path with ample room for wagon traffic. Captain John W. Gunnison in 1853 followed this branch via Taos, New Mexico, as well as Colorado's Cochetopa Pass and Grand Junction, to rejoin the "Main Route" of the Old Spanish Trail near Green River, Utah.

Fur traders William Wolfskill and George C. Yount in 1830–1831 developed the trail's Main Route. Their path looped northward into present-day central Utah to avoid hostile tribes in the region to the south. In addition, the long, waterless stretches south of Utah hindered direct east–west travel. Macomb and his companions later followed the Main Route of the Old Spanish Trail to reach their destination.

Macomb wrote his wife about his forthcoming trip, "I expect to trust myself in the care of experienced travellers of this country and to plod along absorbed with my Survey & astronomizing." Additionally he assured his wife, "I expect to go out by way of Ca[ñ]ada and Abiquiu where I was working a road last summer. My first route is to be over a part of the old "Spanish trail," which I have heard very favourably spoken of in regard to supply of grass, water and fuel."[15]

To aid Macomb in his exploratory survey of the uncharted land crossed by the Old Spanish Trail, the War Department authorized him to employ four assistants: one physician/naturalist, one topographer, one assistant astronomer and meteorologist, and one guide, plus the necessary number of packers, herders, and camp men.

Macomb focused on one position in particular. He quickly sent a letter to the noted trapper Antoine Leroux of Taos, New Mexico, asking him to pilot the expedition. Leroux, a skilled trail guide, possessed extensive

---

15. John Macomb to "Nannie" Macomb, June 19, 1859, LOC.

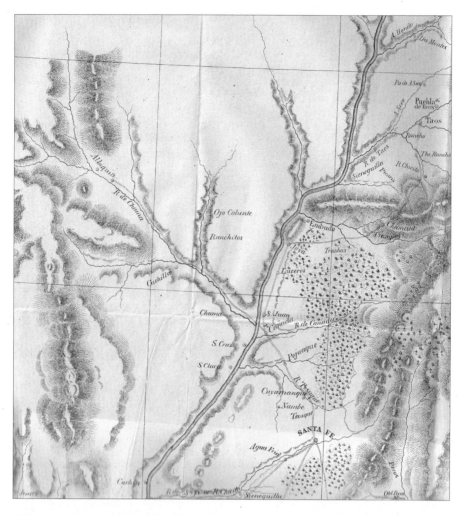

Section of "Map of the Territory of New Mexico . . . 1844–47," by J. W. Abert and W. G. Peck. The Macomb Expedition followed generally the historic road from Santa Fé to Abiquiu. See Wm. H. Emory, *Notes of a Military Reconnaissance*, 1848.

knowledge of the Old Spanish Trail route. But Leroux either declined the offer or was unavailable at the time.[16]

Macomb immediately rushed another letter to the commander of the New Mexico Military Department requesting a military escort "to protect my party during the tour of duty"; the Navajo were presently at war in the region. In determining the strength of the escort, Macomb asked the

16.   Macomb to Leroux, May 28, 1859, NA.

department to consider "the necessity of frequently sending all detachments to the right and left from the main party; and also the very unsettled state of affairs at this time in the Navajo country across the northern lands of which this expedition will pass."[17]

Taking precautions to safeguard his outfit, Macomb asked the military department of New Mexico for three hundred men. The soldiers would furnish "safe escort through a wild and inhospitable tract of country, partly occupied by hostile and treacherous Indians."[18]

For subsistence, New Mexico's military department suggested that the detachment "carry some Bacon" and supply itself with "Beef Cattle for the first few days, and for the remainder sheep, . . . at a rate of three to each man, having the sheep sheared to facilitate their traveling." The commanding officer of Fort Defiance, in present-day Arizona, was ordered to "furnish Captain Macomb with any supplies, you have on hand, that can be spared from the public service." Macomb, however, was required to pay for any provisions shared with "the civil employees."[19]

Macomb began at once assembling an entourage of civil employees and other important people to carry out a scientific study of the southeastern approach to Utah Territory. Besides Newberry and Dimmock, his personnel included Albert H. Pfeiffer, "sub-agent for the Utah Indians," who facilitated Macomb's passage through the country of the Capotes and other bands of Ute Indians; Nepomuceno Valdez, Ute interpreter; Armijo (or Jaramillo), the guide; John Campeau and Juan P. Martin, who

---

17. Macomb to Lt. John D. Wilkins, Military Department of New Mexico, May 28, 1859, NA. Macomb took precautions to avoid the disasters faced by John W. Gunnison and John C. Fremont on their overland expeditions. He set out on his expedition in the summer season to prevent entrapment in heavy snow. He also took along a military escort to protect them from attack by indigenous tribes.

18. "The escort for passing through the region to the North and West of Fort Defiance should not be less than three hundred men. There should accompany the expedition an experienced "mountain man" as a guide, in addition to the persons enumerated in the preliminary estimate." Macomb to Humphreys, October 26, 1858, NA. On his arrival in Santa Fé, Newberry wrote Spencer F. Baird, assistant secretary of the Smithsonian Institution: "Macomb has made application for 300 men as escort so we shall probably be safe, but will be restricted in our movements." John S. Newberry, Santa Fé, New Mexico, to Spencer F. Baird, Washington D.C., June 4, 1859, Record Unit 7002, Box 30, Smithsonian Institution Archives. (Hereafter SIA); F. A. Barnes, *The 1859 Macomb Expedition into Utah Territory* (Moab, Utah: Canyon Country Publications, 2003), 79. Dimmock blamed the reduction in troops on Col. Benjamin L. E. Bonneville. See Dimmock, Diary, July 5, 1859, VHS.

19. The expedition ultimately purchased the sheep and "experiment[ed] in subsistence," said Newberry. Newberry, Abridged Diary, July 18, 1859, Letters Received, N unentered 1861, Bureau of Topographical Engineers, War Department Records, NA; John D. Wilkins, to "Officer Commanding Fort Defiance, New Mexico," July 8, 1859, Department of New Mexico Letters, vol. 10, p. 351, Record Group 98, NA, in Arrott's Fort Union Collection, Thomas C. Donnelly Library, New Mexico Highlands University. (Hereafter Arrott's Fort Union Collection.) See also J. N. Macomb correspondence, 1858–1860, Part II of BANC MSS P-E 219, Bancroft Library, University of California, Berkeley. Fort Defiance was originally chosen as the starting point for the Macomb expedition. It is unknown why Santa Fé was subsequently selected.

served as scouts; some unnamed Indian guides; and three assistants—
Louis Wm. Dorsey of Washington, D.C., Francis P. Fisher of New York,
and James H. Vail of Virginia. Fisher assisted Macomb with astronomical
observation; Dorsey and Vail carried barometers and thermometers and
kept daily records of their readings. Dorsey also assisted Newberry in collecting natural history specimens.[20]

Several camp followers apparently joined Macomb's group as cooks
and common laborers. Including the military escort, the exploratory
party totaled "not less than sixty men."[21] Macomb's party also comprised
a small group of men he had hired to establish a camp at a mountain
pasture twelve miles east of Santa Fé as a recruiting place for the animals
that would be used on the march.[22] (Among the unidentified members
named in the Macomb expedition were Stephen Conroy, Joseph Dély,
Benjamin Lepard, James McGrace, a Mr. Hathaway, a Mr. Lawlep, a Mr.
Ferry, and a Mr. Johnston or Johnson.)[23]

To transport supplies, survey instruments,[24] and specimens, Macomb
purchased pack animals from a nearby road construction team and

20. Macomb, *Report*, 5, 7, 97; Charles H. Dimmock, Topographical Memoir, Series I, Box 21,
     Rodgers Family, Papers, Manuscripts Division, LOC; See also F. A. Barnes, *The 1859 Macomb
     Expedition into Utah Territory*, 85; F. A. Barnes, "Early Explorations of Utah," *Canyon Legacy*
     9 (Spring 1991): 3–4. Macomb, Newberry, and Dimmock tripped over the spelling of
     Nepomuceno Valdez. Macomb spelled his name Neponocino, Newberry referred to him as
     "Ponocino," and Dimmock called him "Pomosima," "Pomosamia," and "Tomasonia." In 1867,
     E. H. Bergman correctly spelled his name when he listed Nepomuceno Valdez as his "Mexican
     guide." See E. H. Bergman, Commander of Camp Plummer, to J. H. Carleton, Commander
     of New Mexico Military District, Santa Fé, "Report of a Reconnaissance to the Animas River
     to Locate a Site for a Military Post," unpublished manuscript, March 15, 1867. Armijo, or
     Jaramillo, has not been identified. Nevertheless, one José Miguel Jaramillo served as a guide
     for a command of mounted riflemen sent from Fort Craig, New Mexico, to pursue more than
     one hundred Navajos who had stolen large numbers of sheep. In February 1860, they engaged
     a Navajo party in battle, "killing and wounding sixteen Indians." See S. Cooper, "Report of the
     Adjutant General," No. 12, in *Report of the Secretary of War*, 36th Cong., 2d sess., Senate Executive
     Document 1, vol. 2, serial no. 1079 (Washington, D.C., 1860), 202–203. At age 20, in 1848,
     Francis Porter Fisher graduated from Harvard, then married Ann Eliza Crane of New York five
     years later. Following his service with the Macomb expedition, he worked as a civil engineer for
     the Texas and New Orleans Railroad. In 1861 he joined the 55th Illinois Infantry and partici-
     pated in the Civil War. After the war he moved to Chicago, where he and his brother Frederic
     started the Fisher Bros. fire insurance firm. He died in Chicago in 1907. "Francis Porter Fisher,"
     in Charles T. Rothermel and Company, *Portraits and Biographies of the Fire Underwriters of the City
     of Chicago*. (Chicago: Charles T. Rothermel and Company, 1895). http://www.archive.org/
     stream/portraitsbiograp00chas/portraitsbiograp00chas_djvu.txt (accessed May 23, 2009).
21. John D. Wilkins, to "Officer Commanding Fort Defiance, New Mexico," July 8, 1859, in
     Arrott's Fort Union Collection.
22. Macomb's account of June 21, 1859, Letterbook, 64, Letters Received, Bureau of Topographical
     Engineers, War Department Records, NA.
23. Macomb bought two mules from "A. D. Johnson" on June 23, 1859. It is possible that Johnson
     accompanied the expedition. In later years, he became a steamboat captain on the lower
     Colorado River.
24. Humphreys to Secretary of War John B. Floyd, April 6, 1859, NA.

from private individuals. Of the sixty-nine mules and eight burros, "to say nothing of Donkeys," that he acquired for the march, thirty-two mules and one bell mare came "from the caballada of Don V. S. St. Vrain."[25] Furthermore, Macomb noted that "the escort has as many more" animals.[26]

Nevertheless, the challenge of finding enough pack animals to supply Macomb's outfit caused him "unexpected delays." The large number of animals required to launch the Utah War effort had depleted local herds in New Mexico. He wrote, "There has been an unusual scarcity of mules in this section of the country for the last eighteen months; that is since the purchases were made for the use of the Army in Utah. This has greatly delayed me in that essential part of my outfit."[27] In late November 1857, Col. Albert Sidney Johnston had sent Capt. Randolph B. Marcy with a small force from Camp Scott in what is now Bridger Valley, Wyoming, to Fort Union, New Mexico, to purchase 1,500 horses and mules for the U.S. Army. Marcy's command followed a course "through an almost trackless wilderness, in the very depth of winter" to obtain the necessary animals, returning the next June with almost 1,000 mules, 160 horses, and a few sheep. It was a heroic march.[28]

The scarcity of stock animals in New Mexico concerned Macomb who worried about equipping his own expedition. But he faced stubborn resistance from mule owners: "There are some 20 mules and a few donkeys to be purchased yet—and the holders think that we want them more than they Do & charge for them accordingly."[29] Nevertheless, Macomb had acquired up to this point six thousand pounds of provisions. He could afford to relax a little.[30]

Total appropriations for the federally funded survey amounted to $20,000. Of that amount, $500 could be spent to purchase, "for the purpose of trafficking with Indians, and compensating them for services, such articles of Indian goods as may be more desirable." In outfitting his

25. "Mules or other Public Animals, Santa Fé, N.M., June 1859, San Juan Expedn," Letterbook, 64, Letters Received, Bureau of Topographical Engineers, War Department Records, NA. Vincent St. Vrain was "a member of the famous family of traders originally from Missouri, lived in Mora." Remley, "Adios Nuevo Mexico," 217 n. 4. As kin to Taos trader Céran St. Vrain, Vincent served as executor of his will when he died in 1870. Ceran, the more famous frontiersman, was a wealthy merchant, land grant owner, and political figure in New Mexico. "Bent, St. Vrain & Company," http://www.sangres.com/history/bentstvrain.htm (accessed May 10, 2007).

26. John Macomb to "Nannie" Macomb, August 5, 1859, LOC.

27. Macomb to Humphreys, July 7, 1859, NA.

28. A. H. Guernsey, "Army Life on the Border," Harper's New Monthly Magazine 33, no. 196 (September 1866): 437; Charles P. Roland, Albert Sidney Johnston: Soldier of Three Republics (Austin: University of Texas Press, 1964), 211.

29. John Macomb to "Nannie" Macomb, July 3, 1859, LOC.

30. Ibid.

party, Macomb complained that the limited resources around Santa Fé drove up prices and rapidly exhausted many of the funds that had been appropriated for the expedition.[31] He also noted that "the expedition can only last a certain length of time on account of the limited supply of money, by wh[ich] entirely I am to govern my movements."[32]

The War Department placed Macomb under strict orders to balance the expedition's financial accounts. Nevertheless, without any input from Macomb, Lt. Joseph C. Ives, officiating in the War Department's Office of Explorations and Surveys, deducted $1,500 from the total appropriations "to defray charges for transportation" of Macomb's assistants and the survey instruments from Washington to Santa Fé. In addition, Ives appointed the five technical assistants for the expedition—Dorsey, Fisher, Vail, Newberry, and Dimmock. Macomb received copies of each appointment, "with instructions," in Santa Fé.[33]

A retelling of the travel experiences of Macomb's civil assistants to and from Santa Fé, and their sojourn in the city, gives us fresh insights into overland travel and frontier conditions. In addition, we may view the expedition and its members through a more powerful lens by using the newly discovered depictions of diarist Charles Henry Dimmock.

Dimmock possessed a rare quality among the men of his day: literary skills to eloquently depict the American frontier. His writing style alternates between the recording of detail—including the mundane chronicling of mileages, temperatures, time schedules, and weather conditions—and the poetic and literary grand style of the period, characteristically Victorian and full of embellishment.

Dimmock's professional skills as a civil engineer and surveyor contributed greatly to the success of the Macomb expedition. He drew "an excellent sketch of the [Macomb] route . . . in one large map" at a scale of "half an inch to the mile." Moreover, as assistant topographer of the expedition, he wrote a topographical memoir of the route and mileages

---

31. Humphreys to Macomb, April 6, 1859, NA; Macomb to Humphreys, July 7, 1859, NA. Much of the money appropriated for the reconnaissance covered salaries. The War Department allocated a $125 monthly salary for each of Macomb's assistants. Newberry's salary, however, amounted to $150 per month. Along with the other assistants, he was entitled to travel expenses. While on duty in the field, they could get one army ration per day. As a civilian geologist, Dr. Newberry's duties involved collecting scientific specimens, including samples of zoology and botany, for the Smithsonian Institution and providing a full report on the geology and mineralogy of the region explored by the party. If necessary, he was required to supply medical and surgical attention to the men and to produce a report on the natural history of the region he examined.

32. John Macomb to "Nannie" Macomb, June 19, 1859, LOC.

33. Ives to Floyd, April 28, 1859, NA; Ives to Charles H. Dimmock, April 25, 1859, NA; Ives to Louis William Dorsey, April 25, 1859, NA; Ives to Francis P. Fisher, April 25, 1859, NA; Ives to John S. Newberry, April 28, 1859, NA; Ives to James H. Vail, April 25, 1859, NA.

Courtesy of Margaret Jones Perritt

Charles H. Dimmock.

traveled by the pack train.[34] (A close examination of Dimmock's exceptional field map enables modern explorers to accurately locate the eastern leg of the Old Spanish Trail.)

More important, perhaps, were his artistic skills—his pencil drawings
of people, landscapes, architecture, and other subjects—and his diary account of the expedition, that provide rare first glimpses of the wild, Far
West and help verify the travel route of Macomb.

34.   Dimmock explained his qualifications: "In ten years experience, as a Civil Engineer, I have
      been enabled to become familiar with every department of that profession. What talent I
      may naturally have possessed has been cultivated by Map drawing & Topographical sketch-
      ing. If credentials of proficiency are desired, they will be presented." Dimmock, Baltimore,
      Maryland, to Mr. R. Drinkard, Esq., April 25, 1859, NA. Dimmock, was twenty-seven years
      old in the summer of 1859. It appears that the War Department regulation that prevented
      Dimmock and his associates from publishing their findings or experiences in the field may
      have orginated from a policy applied by John C. Fremont in 1845.

Born October 18, 1831, in Baltimore, Maryland, Dimmock at an early age moved with his parents to Virginia where he enrolled in the Richmond Academy under Col. Claude Cozet. Dimmock's father, a West Point graduate, served as a military officer in the commonwealth and, before the Civil War, took charge of the Richmond Armory. At age sixteen, Charles entered the field as a civil engineer and worked several years surveying the line on the Virginia and Tennessee Railroad. The Baltimore and Philadelphia Railroad subsequently hired him, and he worked on that line under the direction of J. Ridgeway Trimble (later a general of the Confederate States of America).[35]

In 1858, Dimmock moved back to Baltimore to study law. There he married Emily Moale, whom he affectionately called "Emmy." In 1859, he and Emmy had a baby son, Charly, and were expecting a second child. In the office of S. Teakle Wallace, Dimmock read law and passed the Maryland bar. During his tenure with the law firm Lt. Joseph C. Ives, representing the War Department's Bureau of Topographical Engineers, apparently contacted him to serve with the Macomb expedition.[36]

The government directed Dimmock to travel to Santa Fé with another civil assistant, Francis P. Fisher. In early May of 1859, Dimmock departed his residence in Baltimore and boarded the train for New York to pick up Fisher, who would accompany him to Independence, Missouri, via St. Louis. The War Department's Office of Explorations and Surveys had allotted $80 for their travel expenses to Independence, not enough to pay for the entire trip. So Dimmock fronted some of the expenses until he could be reimbursed. Most of their trek was on the Baltimore and Ohio Railroad with stops at Martinsburg, Grafton, Bellaire, Zanesville, Cincinnati, Vincennes, and St. Louis.

At St. Louis Dimmock hired a carriage to visit the nearby arsenal, perhaps to get information and ideas for his father who later served as Virginia's chief of ordnance works. From St. Louis, Dimmock and Fisher traveled to Jefferson City and boarded the Missouri steamboat South Wester, bound for Independence. Card playing and gambling seemed to be the only recreation on board ship. The Missouri River appeared "wretchedly muddy," noted Dimmock. He observed that the restless passengers complained about the number of landings the boat made. One of those on board, land speculator J. T. Watkins paced the deck nervously. (Watkins had purchased property in nearby Beattie, Kansas, in anticipation of the coming railroad.)[37]

35. Charles H. Dimmock, Papers, 1850–1873, Section 11, Obituaries, VHS.
36. Ibid.
37. Dimmock, Diary, May 14, 1859, VHS; "History of Beattie," Beattie, Kansas, Web site, http://www.marshallco.net/beattie/history1.html (accessed June 24, 2007).

Courtesy of the Smithsonian Institution Archives

Dr. John S. Newberry.

When they reached Independence, the head of the Santa Fe Trail, they found Newberry and the expedition's other civilian assistants, Louis Wm. Dorsey and James H. Vail. Newberry immediately paid Dimmock $14.50 for his additional travel expenses.

Independence, with a population of about three thousand, the last city on the edge of the American frontier, served as the terminus of the Santa Fe Trail. Here Dimmock, Newberry, Dorsey, and Vail boarded the Santa Fé-bound stage. Fisher remained behind for a week to await the arrival of a freight of survey instruments, slowly making its way from Washington, D.C.

Between May 16 and June 4, 1859, Macomb's assistants traveled the Santa Fe Trail via the Cimarron Cutoff. The trip gave Dimmock an opportunity to engage in a scientific exploration with Newberry. The thirty-six-year-old scientist and physician had previously explored the West with two other government parties.

Newberry was born December 22, 1822, in Windsor, Connecticut, and reared in Ohio. In his youth, his father opened and operated a number of coal mines not far from present-day Cleveland. Newberry discovered fish and plant fossils from the shale that saturated the "fossiliferous strata" of his father's mines. His studies in natural science eventually gave him the skills needed for his later career. He became well versed in paleontology and the abundant fossils found in "coal-measures." Nevertheless, he entered Western Reserve College and "pursued studies in medicine." Later, in 1848, he graduated from Cleveland Medical School, began practicing medicine, and married Sarah Brownell Gaylord of Cleveland. The following year he and Sarah traveled to Paris, France, where he continued his medical education and studied botany at the Jardin des Plantes. After returning to Cleveland in 1851, he went back to his medical practice. Four years later, the government appointed him to serve with Lt. R. S. Williamson's exploration of the West Coast between San Francisco and the Columbia River. In 1857–1858, he served with Lt. Joseph C. Ives in his exploration of the lower Colorado River.[38]

With the Ives expedition, Newberry explored the Colorado River upstream to the head of navigation and beyond, into the Grand Canyon. In January 1858, Ives assembled his expedition at Fort Yuma, near the U.S.-Mexico border, about 150 miles upstream from the Gulf of California. Over the next two months, his team ascended the Colorado by steamboat—the USS *Explorer*—to Black Canyon, where they struck rock. Undeterred, he proceeded in a skiff to the mouth of Las Vegas Wash. Ives then sent the steamboat back to Yuma and, with a small exploring party, continued his survey of the Colorado by land. From Diamond Creek to Havasu Canyon, Ives, Newberry, and others examined the Grand Canyon. They crossed the Painted Desert to the Hopi villages and disbanded the expedition at Fort Defiance, in what is now Arizona. (Since both the Ives and Macomb expeditions explored the canyons of the Colorado and scientifically studied the geography and geology of the Colorado Plateau, they are considered complementary surveys.)[39]

Newberry's astute observations contributed greatly to the emerging school of thought in American geology known as fluvialism.[40] (Fluvialism

---

38. Charles A. White, "Biographical Memoir of John Strong Newberry, 1822–1892," in National Academy of Sciences, *Biographical Memoirs*, 1909, 5–7.

39. C. Gregory Crampton, *Land of Living Rock: The Grand Canyon and the High Plateaus: Arizona, Utah, Nevada* (New York: Knopf, 1972), 96–100.

40. Aton and McPherson, *River Flowing from the Sunrise*, 50.

Lithograph of the USS *Explorer*, illustrated in the report
of the Ives Expedition.

is the study of landform changes produced by the action of streams.)
Exploring deep inside the lower gorge, Newberry saw firsthand the clear
evidence of fluvial erosion over time. In his published report, he described the erosive power of the Colorado River.

In 1869, when John Wesley Powell launched his famous voyage of discovery down the Colorado River, Newberry resented the news story "that
nothing is known of the grand cañon of the Colorado." He reminded
readers of Denver's *Daily Rocky Mountain News* of the Ives expedition
that "entered the mouth of the big cañon, and afterwards explored its
source two hundred miles further by land, or to the junction of the Little
Colorado." Furthermore, he had served as "geologist to another expedition in 1859, Capt. MaComb [*sic*], which explored the country around
the junction of the Grand and Green rivers, and traversed the valley of
the San Juan[,] . . . a stream as large as the Connecticut 'whose banks,
lined with ruins, and once supporting a hundred thousand people, are
now entirely deserted.'"[41]

The Ives expedition never completed the survey of the great canyon. However, one publication claims that Newberry actually convinced
Powell "that an expedition by boat down the Colorado River through

---

41.   Denver, Colorado, *Daily Rocky Mountain News*, June 23, 1869, 1. The newspaper responded, "It
appears from Prof. Newberry's statement that the portion of the cañon between the mouth of
the San Juan and the Little Colorado, a stretch of over two hundred miles, has not yet been
explored. . . . and Prof. Powell's party have virtually a new field for discovery."

the Grand Canyon would be worth the risk in order to complete the survey."[42]

Historians James M. Aton and Robert S. McPherson have explained the significance of Newberry's achievements. They wrote that Newberry's landmark case study, in which he eloquently described the river systems of the Colorado and the San Juan as major agents of landscape change, ultimately drew international attention to the region, particularly among geologists. Aton and McPherson added that Newberry's arguments for the fluvial theory of landform development strengthened the Darwinian view of earth's antiquity. Newberry's "study of erosion helped geologists push back the age of the earth and rethink geomorphology."[43]

On the road to Santa Fé in 1859, Newberry continued his study of landscapes and erosion, and examined the geology of the land bordering the Santa Fe Trail. The journey allowed him to confirm many of his conclusions from the previous year on his homeward journey following the Ives expedition. "I am happy to say that the conclusions arrived at in my former report on the geology of this region, in regard to the relative position of the various strata noticed, were fully confirmed by our later observations," he wrote.[44] Some of the scientific specimens gathered by Newberry would become compositions for Dimmock's drawings. During his travels, however, Dimmock failed to sketch any mules, the chief mode of transporation used by the expedition.

"Mules wretched and roads fearful," griped Dimmock as they started their journey. The mules often became unruly, one "hard to get in ranks; kicking out of traces." Sleeping in the cold wind one night, Dimmock witnessed "mules getting away from their pickets crowded around the wagons for protection from wind. One dropped its manure upon Dorsey's bed."

If and when stage stations offered food to passengers, the generally poor meals didn't help matters any. At the Little Muddy, Dimmock noted, "Branch justified its title. A mud puddle! Such a breakfast! Cooked by teamsters with unwashed hands. Bill of fare—Fried Bacon, Crackers & Coffee, muddier than the Little Muddy." But Dimmock's experience at Martin Kozlowski's stage station near Pecos, New Mexico, proved an exception to the rule. "Our host a Pole (Kousloski) gave us a first rate supper and admirable beds." The historic station still stands along the Santa Fe Trail.

To augment their stage fare, the men shot at wild game. "Dr. Newberry shot wild Goose . . . [and] killed 4 snipe. Self 2 wild ducks," noted Dimmock. At another location, "one of the Teamsters (Mexican) shot

42. Ann G. Harris, Esther Tuttle, Sherwood D. Tuttle, *Geology of National Parks*, 6th ed. (Dubuque, Iowa: Kendall/Hunt, 2004), 8.
43. Aton and McPherson, *River Flowing from the Sunrise*, 50.
44. Macomb, *Report*, 15.

Photo by author

Martin Kozlowski's stage station on the Santa Fe Trail, in today's Pecos National Historical Park, New Mexico.

two Antelopes near us, in pursuit of which [Vail] had gone. Bough[t] the hind quarters." At one camp, an oyster can placed too close to the cook's fire burst, "filling Dorsey & self with fragments."

In addition to wild geese, ducks, and snipe, Dimmock and his fellow travelers observed plovers, antelope, grey wolves, sheep, and "myriads" of prairie dogs. They also passed a "train of Burrows (Donkeys), ladened [*sic*] for the Indian trade." Near the Little Arkansas River, they found "innumerable" buffalo.

Along the way, the party contended with sulky teamsters, high winds, rain, mist, heat, dust, and parched conditions. In the valley of the Cimarron, insects pestered everyone. Newberry apparently took advantage of the situation and at one point resorted to "bug bottling."

The men faced challenges ranging from water leakage in the stage to abominable sleeping arrangements—men forced at times to sleep inside the coach, on the floor, or on the makeshift bunks of stage stations or outdoors, where heavy dew wet their blankets.

Passing through the Shawnee and Kaw reservations, they met a number of Kaws and Kiowas on the road. When Dimmock gave money to a Kaw Indian chief, he became "indignant because he received so little." The "Road passes about 35 miles through I[ndian] T[erritory]," noted

Dimmock as they traveled across the panhandle of Oklahoma. Dimmock was repulsed to see an American Indian lady, "with two very pretty girls," who "amuses herself *eating* the lice from the head of the younger."

Bouncing about inside the stage, Dimmock and his associates noticed a stream of prospectors trudging up the Santa Fe Trail returning from the Pike's Peak gold rush, "foot sore & disgusted." Dimmock recorded one miner's experience. "Could make 10¢ a day & d[amne]d hard work at that! Good chance to starve unless you steal & if you steal your[*sic*] certain to be hung."[45]

At "Whetstone Spring," along the Overland Trail, "stone fused by volcanic action" caught Newberry's eye. Among the large number of geologic remnants at the site, he collected the "fossils of plants in the sandstone around the spring." One narrow leaf fossil appeared similar to "one obtained at Smoky Hill," noted Newberry. He also found "a re-markable fissure" that had "been opened by volcanic force in the rocks containing these plants." Here he discovered "five species of fossil plants, three of which were new." Attempting to pinpoint the locality of the whetstone fossil plant, modern scientists in 1987 found a leaf similar to Newberry's *Salix foliosa* along Palo Blanco Creek in Union County, New Mexico. They also discovered quartzose, which could "serve as an excel-lent grinding stone, hence the name Whetstone."[46]

While examining Whetstone Spring, Dimmock paused to measure and sketch an antelope horn that, for him, seemed remarkable. At an-other paleontological site, Dimmock sketched an "Apus," or fossilized crustacean "allied to the horse shoe crab."

At regular intervals, the stage stopped in a number of impoverished New Mexican villages scattered along the trail. In his cursory obser-vations, Dimmock seemed inclined to record their squalid conditions and paint a poor image of their inhabitants. He was especially critical of the Santa Fe Trail town of Tecoloté, where he paused to sketch the local church.[47]

Stopping at Fort Union, a military station built to protect overland travelers, Dimmock briefly described the location. "Queer looking clus-ter of cabins, built of round pine logs & 'adobes.' Saw several officers & were invited to drink the meanest possible whiskey, as we found it. Country around a Sodom—No rain having fallen for more than six months. Hot! Very hot!"

45. Dimmock, Diary, May 22, 1859, VHS.
46. Macomb, *Report*, 32; Spencer G. Lucas, Adrian P. Hunt, Kim Martini, "Newberry's Locality for Cretaceous Plant Fossils at Whetstone Creek, New Mexico," *New Mexico Journal of Science* 27, no. 2 (December 1987): 97.
47. Dimmock, Diary, June 2–3, 1859, VHS.

Photo by author

The renovated adobe church in Tecoloté, New Mexico.

Nineteen days out of Independence, dust-covered and hungry, they reached Santa Fé and stepped off the stage near the historic plaza or public square. That evening, Dimmock and his companions enjoyed "a good dinner & comfortable rooms" at the Exchange Hotel, dubbed "the Fonda, the American hotel of the city." The present La Fonda, built in the early twentieth century, sits on the spot of the former inn, at the end of the Santa Fe Trail, opposite the downtown plaza.[48]

Settled by Spaniards on the site of abandoned Pueblo ruins overlooking the northern Rio Grande Valley, at the western base of the Sangre de Cristo Mountains, Santa Fé in 1610 became the capital of New Mexico. Laid out around the plaza, Santa Fé emerged as an important trading hub for merchants using the Camino Real, the Old Spanish Trail, and the Santa Fe Trail. When northern Mexico fell to the United States in 1848, American troops occupied the city and established Fort Marcy north of the Palace of the Governors, the seat of government facing the city center. Perhaps because of the limited capacity of the army post, or his officer

---

48. Today's La Fonda, or "inn," was built in 1922 on the site of the former one-story hostelry, constructed in the 1840s. The hotel claims that the original building existed as early as 1821, when Capt. William Becknell opened the Santa Fe Trail from Missouri. On his arrival in Santa Fé Dimmock wrote, "Stopping at the Fonda, the American hotel of the city. Gave us a good dinner & in comfortable rooms we feel like taking 'mine ease in mine Inn.'" Dimmock, Diary, June 4, 1859, VHS.

Lithograph of Santa Fé, ca. 1846. Issued in Wm. H. Emory's
Notes of a Military Reconnaissance, 1848.

status, Macomb resided in privileged conditions—in the quarters of the
Catholic bishop near the end of the trail.

At first sight, Macomb expressed satisfaction with his government-
appointed assistants. He recorded: "The stage came in about noon and
I have seen and conversed with Dr. Newberry and Mr. Dimmock—with
whom I feel well pleased, and I trust that we shall go smoothly through
the season and think none worse of one another at the close up of it."[49]

Dimmock felt positively impressed by Macomb, whom he described as
"an unostentatious, cultivated gentleman." On meeting the captain, he
drew his salary and promptly sent it to his wife Emmy.[50]

After meeting Macomb, Newberry felt that the captain needed to do
more homework before entering the field. Newberry wrote the assistant
secretary of the Smithsonian, "Have seen Macomb, and like him very
much, but as we suspect he might be slightly improved. If you had him
at the Smithsonian for a half day and could talk zoology into him all the
time, I think he would be better prepared to go into the field than he now
is." "His interest in natural science is no[t] quite decided but general &
abstract," he added.[51]

Newberry's inquisitive, scholarly nature caused him to accept the appointment to join the Macomb expedition and explore the Colorado

49. John Macomb to "Nannie" Macomb, June 4, 1859, LOC.
50. Dimmock, Diary, June 5, 1859, VHS.
51. Newberry to Baird, June 4, 1859, SIA; Cited in F. A. Barnes, *Canyonlands National Park: Early
      History and First Descriptions* (Moab, Utah: Canyon Country Publications, 1988), 114.

Plateau region close to the Grand Canyon area. For Newberry, the great, unexplored region ahead offered a "repository of truth which we might gather and add to the sum total of human knowledge."[52] He was firmly determined to explore the innermost reaches of the Colorado Plateau.

Macomb, on the other hand, grew anxious as the starting date of the expedition neared. Harassed with the problems of outfitting his expedition he wrote his wife, "I could not help feeling rather overpowered . . . in relation to the outfit for this exploration with but little prospect of discovering any thing worth knowing—but Dr. Newberry says the country must be explored & the Govt. *ought* to pay for the expense so I have given myself less anxiety on the subject of late."[53]

With help from a military insider who had the ear of the Secretary of War, Macomb would be released from his assignment in New Mexico following the expedition. He now could bear the task of conducting the survey. He wrote, "I feel very much indebted to Major [Henry Hopkins] Sibley for his timely suggestions to the Secretary [of War] for without the homeward tendency of the expedition the whole thing would be utterly distasteful to me. I look upon all of this region, I have yet seen[,] as being worth less than the cost of examining it."[54]

In the field, the surveyors would carefully record the Hispanic and Native American names of physical features, locate prehistoric ruins, and study and collect specimens of the geology, botany, mineral resources, and fossil remains of the trail landscape. In addition, they would sketch the wild and beautiful scenery along the Old Spanish Trail, take barometer readings, make careful triangulations, and map the expedition's course.

The War Department authorized the shipment of several fragile and expensive U.S. Topographical Bureau survey instruments to Santa Fé for the expedition. The instruments included portable transit, telescope, sextant and artificial horizon, pocket and sidereal box chronometers, prismatic and pocket compasses, odometers, reconnoitering or "spy" glass, and cistern and "syphon" barometers. The expedition also had access to the following tools and useful items: pocket and spirit levels, thermometers, surveyors' compasses, drawing instruments, triangles and rulers, colors, scales, surveyors' chains and sets of pins, measuring tape, target, camera lucida, theodolite, nautical almanacs, barometer tubes, and a bottle of mercury—presumably for use in the levels. In addition, they had

---

52. Macomb, *Report*, 84.
53. John Macomb to "Nannie" Macomb, July 10, 1859, NA.
54. Ibid., July 19, 1859, NA. Major Henry Hopkins Sibley, inventor of the famous "Sibley tent," had served in the Utah War. In the Civil War, he lost New Mexico for the South, thus ending the Confederacy's expansionist dreams.

"an ambulance to carry inst[rument]s."[55] They did not however take the ambulance with them on their wilderness survey.

No stranger to survey equipment, Macomb made good use of the tools shipped to Santa Fé. As a member of the elite Corps of Topographical Engineers, he possessed exceptional surveying skills. He also immersed himself in military life.

Aside from his military career, Macomb was a devoted family man and husband. His letters to his wife, Nannie, illustrate his affection and sensitivity: "With love to all I remain your devoted husband" and "ever your own devoted husband." He lovingly called Nannie "my dear wife" or "wifey." And he regularly showed concern for his children's education and hoped for his family's good health. In addition to routinely sending his wife and children support money, Macomb gathered flowers on the expedition and sent them home. He displayed a lively interest in Nannie's newsy letters and responded by elaborating on the daily activities related to his survey work.[56]

Dimmock's diary reveals that he, too, was loyal to his family. During his absence from home, he forwarded his salary to his wife, Emmy. While stationed in Santa Fé, he bought a Navajo tilma, or cloak, for his infant son, Charly. He also commissioned a local jeweler to fashion a set of "Aztec" earrings that he designed for Emmy. On the night before the expedition's journey into the field he somberly wrote, "Home sick to night, horribly." Dimmock spent a great deal of his leisure time writing to Emmy and his mother, Henrietta. He anxiously awaited the arrival in Santa Fé of the eastern and southern mail stages to get the news from home.[57]

We know very little of Newberry's personal life. His former associate, Gen. William Birney, recalled Newberry's "virtue of human kindness." He often "bestowed alms" to beggars "because it grieved him to witness even seeming distress without trying to relieve it." From his marriage to wife Sarah, came seven children. Newberry characterized himself and his wife as "fondest parents." In his correspondence to Spencer F. Baird, his mentor at the Smithsonian, we discover that he christened his third son "Spencer Baird" in the church to which Newberry belonged. In 1859, Newberry purchased a set of earrings as a gift for his wife before heading home to Cleveland.[58]

55. Humphreys to Floyd, April 6, 1859, NA; "Instr. on return 30th Sep. 1859," Letters Received, Bureau of Topographical Engineers, War Department Records, NA.
56. See John N. Macomb's Correspondence in part II.
57. See Charles H. Dimmock's Diary in part II.
58. *Selected Families and Individuals: John Strong Newberry.* See http://members.cox.net/paradiseoc1/pafg140.htm (accessed February 16, 2008); Charles A. White, "Biographical Memoir of John Strong Newberry, 1822–1892," in National Academy of Sciences, *Biographical Memoirs* 6 (1909): 13.

Charles Dimmock Papers, Special Collections Research Center, College of William and Mary

The hills south of Galisteo, New Mexico, near Captain John Pope's
artesian well. Sketch by Charles H. Dimmock.

Beginning in May 1859, when his civil assistants were traveling overland to Santa Fé, Macomb commenced taking astronomical and barometrical observations to prepare for his expedition. But he "found no
chance to observe" on "cloudy & windy" evenings. When his men finally
arrived in Santa Fé, particularly Dimmock, Macomb began conducting
"simultaneous" cistern barometric readings in Albuquerque and Santa Fé
to determine the accuracy of the instruments.

Dimmock also assisted Macomb "in placing the Transit table" as well as
"in time observations" and in calculating "the Barometrical elevations of
Santa Fé & Algadones." Moreover, Dimmock helped Macomb calculate
the difference in height, barometrically, between Santa Fé and Galisteo,
New Mexico. The determination: 917.3 feet.

Galisteo was near Capt. John Pope's artesian well drilling site, visited by
Newberry, Dimmock, and Fisher on June 28. Captain Pope bored the well
"in the hope of obtaining water that should spontaneously rise above the
surface." He drilled the well in anticipation of possible railroad construction through the valley. Newberry noted that the valley of Galisteo Creek
formed "a natural pass from the plains to the valley of the Rio Grande,
affording a practicable and convenient railroad route."[59] In later years,

59. Dimmock, Diary, June 6, 16, 22, 28, 1859, July 1, 1859, VHS; Macomb to Humphreys, July 7,
     1859, NA; Macomb, *Report*, 38.

Photo by author

Hills south of Galisteo, New Mexico, dubbed by locals "Dinosaur Back."
The Placer Mountains appear in the background.

the Atchison, Topeka and Santa Fé built its line along a route not very far from Pope's well water.

Near Galisteo, likely in the Placer Mountains, Newberry and Dimmock made a failed attempt to find gold.[60] Newberry paused here to sketch the landscape's most dominant feature, the dike of igneous rock, later illustrated in his report.[61] Dimmock drew a nearly identical sketch of the terrain.

Earlier in the year, New Mexico's Bishop Jean Baptiste Lamy had invited Macomb and another Army officer to accompany him on an excursion from Santa Fé to Captain Pope's artesian well "to see the . . . boring in progress." Macomb quipped, "So we are going with the Roman Catholic Bishop to see a Pope, if not *the* Pope."[62]

---

60. Macomb, *Report*, 51; Dimmock, Diary, June 28–29, 1859, VHS. Newberry described the Placer as a group rather than a chain of mountains. He noted, "The Placer Mountains have received their name from the [great quanities of] gold which they furnish." He added, "The 'Old Placer' has been worked by the Mexican population since the first occupation of the country by the Spaniards, and probably was a place of resort by their predecessors the Pueblo Indians. . . . An American company has recently purchased a proprietorship at the Old Placer." Here Newberry obtained "very beautiful specimens of the sulphides of copper and iron." He also noticed "many large masses of magnetic iron ore" near the Old Placer. Macomb, *Report*, 39–40.
61. Ibid., lithograph between pp. 50–51.
62. John Macomb to "Nannie" Macomb, February 6, 1859, LOC.

The captain stirred some excitement in Santa Fé at one point when he brought out his telescope and exhibited its capacity to the townsfolk, including the governor of New Mexico, Abraham Rencher, and his wife. Among the party appeared nineteen-year-old John Watts, a student on leave from college in Bloomington, Indiana. Watts kept a diary of his sojourn in Santa Fé in 1859. Among the entries is a record of his encounter with Macomb. He enjoyed peering through Macomb's telescope, "the first one I ever looked through." Watts noted, "We looked at Saturn—the moon and several other of the stars—looking time about. I noticed a broken uneven [edge?] on the lower portion of the moon which the Captain says are mountains." Macomb also displayed "a sextant he had to measure the distances between the stars," wrote Watts.[63]

The following evening Macomb and Dimmock "were beset by the city gamblers," presumably from the Fonda Hotel, desiring to engage in "moon gazing." Dimmock wrote, "They all saw in the moon something of their avocation—one silver, another a woman's dress &c."[64]

Apart from impressing local crowds, Macomb engaged his assistants, Dimmock and Fisher, in meticulous surveys and measurements. Dimmock took responsibility for training Fisher "in reading [the] vernier," a device used for making finer measurements with survey instruments. Ultimately, their most reliable tools would be James Green's cistern barometer, William Würdemann's sextant no. 12, and sidereal chronometer no. 217. (The numbers apparently relate to the inventory of the U.S. Topographical Bureau.) In the field the observers noted, "After leaving Camp No. 7 Chrom. No. 217 was used for all observations where it is not otherwise specified." The surveyors also used pocket chronometer no. 8632, sidereal chronometer no. 225, and Jurgenson watch no. 6960. In measuring the distances of the march, they also had the use of chains and sets of pins and other surveying equipment.[65]

On one occasion, Dimmock called into question Macomb's instrument readings, since their barometric observations were nearly identical. So he "ran over the ground with the levelling instrument" from the courthouse to Fort Marcy, the old post located on the hill above Santa Fé, 664 yards north of the plaza, and found that it "agreed with a former line run by the Capt[ain]."[66]

In addition to his survey work, Macomb faced heavy demands as the leader of the expedition since he held many roles, including commissary,

63. David Remley, "*Adios Nuevo Mexico*," 123–24.
64. Dimmock, Diary, July 7, 1859, VHS.
65. Ibid., June 13, 1859; "San Juan River Survey: Astronomical and Barometrical Observation, 1859," Bureau of Topographical Engineers, War Department Records, NA.
66. Macomb to Humphreys, July 7, 1859, NA; Dimmock, Diary, June 25, 1859, VHS.

Photo by author

Modern survey marker at old Fort Marcy in Santa Fé.

and endured many interruptions in the course of a day. Sunday July 3, 1859, he writes: "I had no sooner seized the pen again than in came my *hostler* with 'Captn. I cant get any waterhole to soak them rawhides in.'" Macomb finally gained access to a muddy corral pond and before he could toss in the hides, he faced "various other interruptions," including a shipment of "all my provisions & camp equipage" for the expedition. "These had to be received and stowed away at once! I have now some of my young gentlemen keeping guard over these stores and shall have until we can depart from this City for there is not a reliable lock in the Castle I have rented, on the other side of the Parroquia from my quarters, to keep these things in until the day of my departure from this City."[67]

As noted earlier, Macomb resided in Bishop Lamy's quarters, adjacent to the adobe parish church, La Parroquia, at the end of San Francisco Street. The present St. Francis Cathedral, built of stone under the direction of the Catholic bishop rests on the site of the former structures.[68]

(Dimmock had the good fortune to meet the famed bishop, who "insisted upon our visiting his flower garden & gave us a boquet [*sic*] of very delicate construction.") While stationed in Santa Fé, Macomb's men attended the local Catholic services held there. Dimmock also attended the

---

67. John Macomb to "Nannie" Macomb, July 3, 1859, LOC; See also Dimmock, Diary, July 3, 1859, VHS.
68. John Macomb to "Nannie" Macomb, July 3, 1859, LOC. Bishop Lamy built the Romanesque style cathedral in 1869. Lamy was Macomb's "landlord." Macomb referred to his residence as "the Bishop's *palace.*" See also Dimmock's Sketchbook in Charles H. Dimmock, Papers, 1850–1873, Section 6, Sketchbook, 1859, VHS.

Courtesy of Margaret Jones Perritt and the Virginia Historical Society

La Parroquia. The adobe cathedral in Santa Fé, New Mexico, 1859. Pencil
sketch by Charles H. Dimmock.

local Baptist church and listened to a good sermon but refused to return.
"Such singing as would delight an ear attuned to board sawing," he pro-
tested. (In his diary, Dimmock held tight to the reins of his beliefs and
never revealed his religious affiliation.)

In this frontier setting, he encountered the typical languor of nineteenth-century Santa Fé, interrupted at times by pulses of excitement,
such as lively concerts on the plaza by the Army regimental band,
political campaigns (particularly the Miguel Antonio Otero race for
Congress), circus activities, the arrivals and departures of both the
eastern and the southern mail stages, and Catholic festivals and pro-
cessions. Dimmock chronicled the events on Corpus Christie Sunday.
"Observed by the Catholics with much form. Morning the Host carried
from Shrine to Shrine by the Bishop & his assistants, followed by the
girls from the Convent in white & men in the rear shooting blank cartridges to scare the Devil." In addition, he recorded the local Masonic
Order's observance of St. Juan's Day with a procession and oration.

Photo by author

St. Francis Cathedral, built on site of La Parroquia in Santa Fé.

More important, Dimmock gave an account of a grand political reception. Congressman John S. Phelps of Springfield, Missouri, was "met by an escort & band" and "received by the Gov.," New Mexico's Governor Rencher. The reception included "Many Speeches." According to Dimmock, "Hon. Mr. Phelps" came to town to promote "this route for the Pacific R[ail] R[oad]."

Dimmock spent much of his leisure time sketching scenes in and about the city. On one occasion, he captured in pencil the indigent "flower boy of Santa Fé adorned with the old military cap of Capt. Macomb." Macomb considered him "one of my pet beggars." He enjoyed the "sweet parfum" [*sic*] of the "bruised rose leaves which after the fashion of the Country, he dignifies as 'Rosas de la Castilla!'"[69]

69. Charles H. Dimmock, Papers, 1850–1873, Section 6, Sketchbook, 1859, VHS; John Macomb to "Nannie" Macomb, June 4 1859, LOC. It appears that Dimmock's "flower boy," Faustin Ortéga Ortiz, was murdered in March 1890. Locals found his brutally beaten remains, with bullet wounds, in an arroyo, according to *(Santa Fé) New Mexican.* Cited in Paul Weideman's "Fort Marcy Area Holds History," *(Santa Fé) New Mexican,* http://www.freenewmexican.com/sfguide/114.html (accessed May 31, 2007).

Dimmock also attended bailés (dances), read books from the library of Fort Marcy, met and dined with military officers, visited with political figures (including Governor Rencher), waited for the mail stages that carried news to and from home, and played cards. He also spent a great deal of time writing letters.

One of the highlights of Dimmock's stay in Santa Fé included meeting Kit Carson. "Was introduced and had a conversation with Kit Carson. He has a broad, german head, do. face, hair long & in elf locks, eyes small & restless, colour gray. Mouth broad & decided, filled with strong, irregular teeth. Body heavy & shoulders broad. Lower limbs comparatively slight & a little bowed. Height about 5ft. 9 in. Age 48 years."[70]

In preparing for the survey, Dimmock spent much of his time helping Macomb. He assisted Macomb "in Sextant observations & adjusting Barometers"and several other technical duties.[71] In addition, Dimmock "aided the Capt. in packing" and noted, "Much depends on the docility of the mules." On the day they were to set out, Dimmock reported on the stubborn behavior of the animals. "Some of them . . . exhibit decided indications of dislike for the packs," he wrote. On the journey, Dimmock observed "while unpacking a wild mule with Cook's tripods & axes kicked herself free of her load, cutting her legs severely."[72]

Just days before the expedition embarked on their journey into Ute and Navajo country, Col. Benjamin L. E. Bonneville, New Mexico's military commander, limited their escort to forty infantry soldiers and one officer. Macomb responded "in great disgust" at the number of men supplied by the military. On hearing the news, Dimmock unfairly characterized the colonel as "an old woman."[73] He complained that the force was "entirely inadequate for our trip....We will be much circumscribed it is feared in our operations."[74]

---

70. Dimmock, Diary, June 23, 1859, VHS.
71. Ibid., June 6, 1859, VHS.
72. Ibid., July 12, 13, 14, 1859, VHS.
73. Ibid., July 5, 1859, VHS. Lt. Milton M. Cogswell (1825-1882) would command Macomb's escort. He graduated from West Point in 1849 and served with the U.S. Infantry. In 1855 the Army assigned him to duty in New Mexico. At the outbreak of the Civil War he commanded the New York Volunteer Infantry. During the war he was captured at the battle of Ball's Bluff, Virginia, and held prisoner until released in a prisoner exchange. In 1865 the Army brevetted him a colonel for his "gallant and meritorious service" during the war. Following the war he served in various capacities, including military governor in South Carolina. From 1869 until his retirement in 1871 he served with the 21st Infantry in Arizona. Near the close of his life, he served "under President Hayes at the Soldier's Home in Washington, D.C." *Selected Biographical Sketches: Milton Cogswell.* http://www.arlingtoncemetery.net/milton-cogswell. htm. Accessed May 8, 2007.
74. Dimmock, Diary, July 5, 1859, VHS; John D. Wilkins, First Lt., Third Infantry, to "Officer Commanding Fort Defiance, New Mexico," July 8, 1859, in Arrott's Fort Union Collection.

Courtesy of Margaret Jones Perritt and the Virginia Historical Society

Sketch of the "flower boy" of Santa Fé, by Charles H. Dimmock.

THE EXPEDITION

On July 13 the Macomb command commenced its adventure into unmapped territory to reach the junction of the Colorado and Green rivers. Briefly, their journey beyond Santa Fé took them up the headwaters of the Rio Grande and across the Continental Divide into the upper drainage of the San Juan, a major tributary of the Colorado River. After they crossed the 37th parallel into today's Colorado, they entered the eastern limits of Utah Territory, formed in 1850, with this area ceded to Colorado in 1861. They followed a west and northwest course across the headstreams of the San Juan and dropped into the sandstone wilderness of Utah's canyonlands, south of present-day Moab. From the Colorado River, their homeward path ran southward to the San Juan, which drainage they followed back into New Mexico. They finally reached the upper Rio Grande Valley and returned to Santa Fé two and one-half months later, a journey of eight hundred miles.

On the day of departure, presumably near the east end of the plaza in Santa Fé, Macomb's men loaded mule packs with bedrolls, tents, and other camp equipment, as well as survey instruments and provisions, to begin the long journey northward. Charles H. Dimmock noted "the starting point of our Pack train" on a pencil sketch he had drawn of "the House of Padres," an adobe Spanish colonial building similar to one that still stands on East Palace Avenue.

Like a scene out of a Wild West story, reminiscent of the Old Spanish Trail era, Hispanic packers and herders launched the seventy-mule train, led by a bell mare, with several sheep in tow. Some twenty men, including the cook and the common laborers, accompanied the train as it

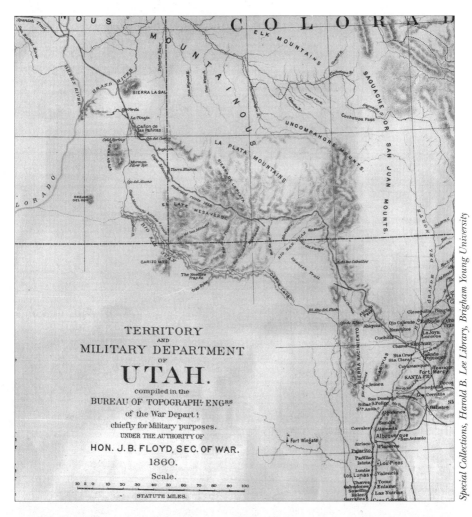

Section of map of the "Territory and Military Department of Utah," 1860,
showing the outward and homeward route of Macomb's party.
Note the "Spanish Trail," which, in part, the Macomb Expedition
followed to reach the Grand (Colorado) River.

Special Collections, Harold B. Lee Library, Brigham Young University

lumbered out of the city and, in all likelihood, commenced a steady gait
up the Santa Fé to Taos Road via Bishop's Lodge Road.

Macomb, Dimmock, and Newberry apparently gave the pack train a
good head start before they mounted their sure-footed walking mules.
Dimmock recorded that they "visited with Gov. Rensher [*sic*] & lady, took
a glass of wine & bade them good bye. The Capt[ain] dined at the Fonda
with us." Following dinner, they set out for their short tour of duty. (The
Army had arranged for their military escort to join them later.) They

The starting point of our Pack train
Santa Fe July 14th 1859

"House of the Padres": Santa Fé.
Built of Adobes.

Sketch of the "House of Padres" by Charles H. Dimmock. The adobe building marked "the starting point of our Pack train," wrote Dimmock.

Spanish colonial structure on East Palace Avenue in Santa Fé.

The Scotchman, between Santa Fé & the Nambé

New Mexico. 15 miles from Santa Fé
July 13th 1859.

Sketch of the "Scotchman," today's Camel Rock, by Charles H. Dimmock.

The landmark Camel Rock, in Tesuque, New Mexico.

Courtesy of Margaret Jones Perritt and the Virginia Historical Society

Singularly poised Rocks, one mile from Abiquiu

Sketch of "Singularly Poised Rocks," twenty-five feet high and one mile from Abiquiu, New Mexico, by Charles H. Dimmock.

Photo by Richard Craven

Balanced rock, near Abiquiu Elementary School, one mile north of the town of Abiquiu, New Mexico.

traveled eighteen miles up the wide dirt road to Pojoaque Pueblo, via Tesuque, where they set up their first camp.[1]

They made their second night's camp near San Juan Pueblo, now Ohkay Owinge Pueblo, just above the confluence of the Chama and Rio Grande rivers. The following day they pushed up the valley of the Chama to the village of Abiquiu, some fifty miles north of Santa Fé. Here they met Ute Sub-agent Albert H. Pfeiffer and his guide Nepomuceno Valdez, who would accompany them through Ute country. They also met the Capote Ute leader Temuché, whom Dimmock portrayed unfavorably.

Historically, the village of Abiquiu, founded by *genizaros*, or Hispanicized Indians, had served as a buffer between the Spanish cities on the upper Rio Grande and the American Indian tribal region beyond. Outside Abiquiu, the existing wagon road ended. Beyond this point, the path entered the Old Spanish Trail, a horse and mule trail leading to California. En route to their destination, Macomb's men traced more than two hundred miles of the historic trail.

At Abiquiu, the infantry soldiers under the command of Lieutenant Cogswell joined them. Since the Macomb expedition crossed a region simmering with tribal hostilities, it was important they have a military escort. In the beginning stretch, and at the tail end of their journey, their route ran through peaceful tribal pueblos. Much of their wilderness course, however, passed over the main route of the Old Spanish Trail through the homelands of the Ute and Navajo, or Dineh, tribes. Growing tensions among the various native groups threatened to spark widespread armed conflict.

About the initial trail segment, Dimmock stated, "Between Santa Fé—the rendezvous and starting point of the Expedition & Abiquiu, the distance and topographical features were so fully known, that it was deemed Superfluous to begin the notes of the expedition until after leaving the latter place." On Dimmock's field map, however, he penciled in the exact route taken by the party. Furthermore, in his diary, he provided additional details of the route.[2]

Throughout the reconnaissance, Newberry made several side trips to explore geologic wonders and gain a broader perspective of the region. In these excursions, he engaged in scientific pursuits with matchless zeal. (Newberry had worried before the expedition that the presence of the military escort assigned to the expedition would restrict his

1.   Dimmock, Diary, July 13, 1859, VHS. The starting point of the pack train may have been in front of the house built by Maj. Jose Sena, the home of today's Casa Sena Restaurant. The old plaza in Santa Fé originally extended farther east than it does today and may have encompassed the historic house. See Charles H. Dimmock, Sketchbook, 1859, VHS.

2.   Dimmock, Topographical Memoir, 1, LOC.

Sketch of an American Indian boy from San Juan Pueblo, by
Charles H. Dimmock.

movements.) Near Abiquiu Newberry undertook his first exploratory
journey away from the main party. With Indian Sub-agent Albert H.
Pfeiffer, he trekked nine miles beyond the Rio Chama to the ancient
Cobre copper mines and gathered several fossil specimens to add to the
Smithsonian collections.

Newberry's account of the Cobre mines reads: "To reach the most important of the ancient mines of this vicinity, we climbed up the face of the
southern cliffs of the valley. . . . Here we found an entrance five by six feet
in dimensions, which led to a series of galleries, having a combined length
of perhaps a hundred yards. The work exhibits considerable skills in the
use of tools, and with a familiarity with the business of mining. The roof is
carefully braced where weak, and old galleries are closed by well-laid walls

Cerro del Pedernal or Abiquiu Peak, New Mexico

of masonry. From the style in which the excavation is done, and from the perfect preservation of the woodwork, I attribute this and other similar mines in this region to the earlier Spanish explorers." Newberry adds, "The most interesting incident of our visit to this copper-mine was the discovery in the shale roof-stone of thousands of impressions of plants, of which abundant species were procured."[3]

Another excursion took Newberry and his fellow travelers to Cerro del Pedernal (Flint Mountain), or Abiquiu Peak, a prominent flat-topped landmark, which they mostly accomplished on muleback. "When we arrived within 500 feet of the summit, we left our mules and commenced the ascent on foot. This part of the mountain is very steep, and the upper 200 feet is a perpendicular wall of trap-rock."[4] They climbed to its top (elevation 9,862 feet) and examined the Pueblo ruins nearby.

3.   Macomb, *Report*, 68–69.
4.   Macomb, *Report*, 70. On Abiquiu Peak on July 20, 1859, Dimmock made the following notations in his sketchbook:

Magnetic Reading of Compass	Object
53°—N. 53° E.	Santa Fé Mountains, The Bald
16°—"16"".	Taos' Mountains, behind Taos
1°—"1"".	The Spanish Peaks or "Wachatojas"
92°—S. 88° E.	The "Valles" (The North Western Peak)

Course of the Summit of Abiquiu Peak 60° = N. 60 E.
Length of Summit about ½ mile, top a "chuchilla" & notched.

On the road between Abiquiu & the Arroyo Seco
July 20th 1859

The "Cachucha" or Cap.
Alternate strata of Red & Yellow Sandstone

Courtesy of Margaret Jones Perritt and the Virginia Historical Society

Sketch of the "Cachucha" (cap) rock formation, by Charles H. Dimmock.

Of the scenery alongside the Old Spanish Trail near Abiquiu, Dimmock lavishly gave the following observation: "The magical variety of outline & shape to be seen in the Sandstone formations around Abiquiu—from a distorted Titan, to the minute vagaries of a Chinese fancy; from the castellated towers of architecture run mad, to the shadowy traceries of a Fairy's home—must lead every traveller to wander awhile from the beaten trail."[5] In the twentieth century, nationally famous artist Georgia O'Keeffe made this area her home and the subject of many desert landscape paintings.

Beyond Abiquiu the survey team pursued the Old Spanish Trail pathway more than thirty miles to reach the Rio Cebolla. En route, they stopped at the historic crossing of the Rio Chama, "in a beautiful locality . . . about 100 miles from Santa Fé," wrote Dimmock. Rain set in and prevented them from moving on to the next camp. At the Chama River ford, Dimmock "gathered at least 20 different varieties of most delicately beautiful flowers." The men also "occupied [themselves] in mending rents & adding patches" to the tents.[6]

5.   Dimmock, Topographical Memoir, 1, LOC.
6.   Dimmock, Diary, July 22, 23, 1859, VHS.

Landmark formation Orphan Rock, near Ghost Ranch, New Mexico.

At this camp, Cogswell made a favorable impression on Macomb's men. Dimmock wrote, "Lieut. Cogswell dined with us & amused all by his punning proclivity." Over time, however, their opinion of the commander began to deteriorate. Macomb, on the other hand, considered him a friend. "We have messed together ever since I came into Santa Fé . . . and I wish very much he could go with me into the states after our summer[']s journey."[7]

After a two-day delay the expedition pushed on through intermittent rain and followed the Rio Cebolla three miles until Macomb decided to detour from the historic route and take his command northward to Pagosa Springs. Dimmock noted, "the old Spanish Trail thus far travelled is diverged from." On their field map Dimmock carefully marked the parting of the ways.[8]

7. Ibid., July 23, 1859, VHS; John Macomb to "Nannie" Macomb, August 5, 1859, LOC. David Remley noted that Cogswell served as "post commander at Fort Marcy . . . for several months in 1859." He explained that the "active military post, Fort Marcy, [was] situated north of the governor's palace and east of the old Baptist Church." David Remley, "*Adios Nuevo Mexico*," 95, n. 15 and n. 17.

8. Dimmock, Topographical Memoir, p. 2, LOC; Charles H. Dimmock, "Map of Explorations

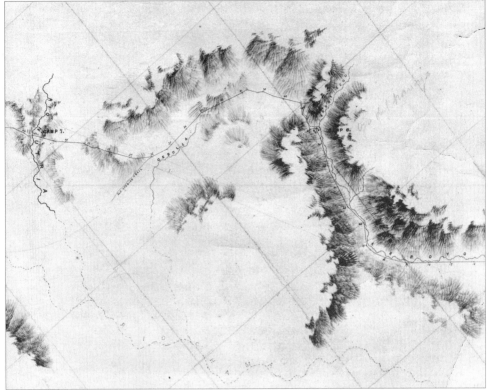

National Archives, Washington, D.C.

Section of Dimmock's topographical field map showing the
Old Spanish Trail at the Rio Cebolla.

(The historical record provides no solid evidence to explain why
Macomb diverted from the Old Spanish Trail. Possibly, since the Ute Sub-
agent Albert H. Pfeiffer had accompanied the expedition, the party decided to visit the Ute bands along the San Juan and negotiate peace with
them and their Navajo neighbors.)

Marching northward, they passed over the Continental Divide at
Laguna de los Caballos (Horse Lake), elevation 7,600 feet, straddling the
eastern edge of today's Jicarilla Apache Indian Reservation. The lake de-
rived its name "from the drowning of some traders' horses which were
swamped in its margins in an effort to cross it," reported Newberry. On
the lake's south side, near its outlet, they pitched their tents. Dimmock
wrote, "Scarcely in camp before a heavy thunderstorm came up driving us

and Surveys in New Mexico and Utah, made under the Direction of the Hon. John B. Floyd,
Secretary of War by Capt. J. N. Macomb, Topographical Engineers," 1859, Manuscript Map,
Record Group 77, NA.

Sketch of the "Laguna de los Caballos," or Horse Lake, in New Mexico, by Charles H. Dimmock.

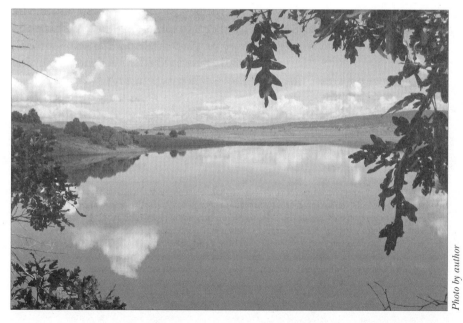

Modern view of Horse Lake, in the Jicarilla Apache Nation, from Charles H. Dimmock's perspective in 1859.

& dinner tables into tents. Lightening struck the cliff just above us." Here Macomb's men killed "a half dozen Rattle Snakes around camp."[9]

Beyond Horse Lake the party continued to the Rio del Navajo and camped just below "a magnificent wooded gorge" through which the stream flowed "in its exit from the mountains." Encamped in an idyllic setting, the men feasted on the now-endangered "Gila Trout." But not everyone experienced the sublime. Something triggered resentment among the herders that day. The expedition's chroniclers failed to explain why. "Stamped[e] of Mexican sheep herders," according to Newberry. Dimmock wrote, "Mexicans discontented & threaten to leave."[10]

"Mule travelled well," reported Dimmock the next day as the survey party moved on to the Rito Blanco (Little White River). "A detachment of Utes" visited their camp, "received tobacco & were off," he noted.[11]

The following day Macomb's command marched to the San Juan River, near today's Pagosa Springs. Men and animals, including sheep, faced a hazardous crossing. Newberry stated, "San Juan forded with difficulty. Soldier narrowly Escaped drowning."[12]

Above the crossing, the river emerges in Colorado's San Juan Mountains on the Pacific side of the Continental Divide. In its upper reaches, the San Juan (and this includes its major branches—Los Pinos, Animas, and La Plata rivers) is a typical mountain stream. From Pagosa Springs, it flows southwesterly into New Mexico where it turns to the west and northwest, and its character changes. Crossing northern New Mexico the river occupies a broad, winding channel in an arid valley bordered by low, terraced mesas. In the Four Corners area the waterway enters the southwestern edge of Colorado before reaching Utah. Near Bluff, Utah, the San Juan runs into a deeply entrenched canyon through which it flows to the Colorado River some fifty miles distant.

Camped on the upper San Juan, Newberry described Pagosa as "one of the most remarkable hot springs on the continent, well known, even famous, among the Indian tribes, but, up to the time of our visit never having been seen by the whites." For Newberry, "scarcely a more beautiful place [existed] on the face of the earth." He accurately predicted that in the future "it will become a celebrated resort."[13]

---

9.   Newberry, Abridged Diary, July 25, 1859, NA; Dimmock, Diary, July 25, 26, 1859, VHS. The Jicarilla reservation, created in 1887, is generally wooded, rough, and possesses few distinguishing landmarks. The Jicarilla Apache once occupied the Dry Cimarron Valley and nearby mesas in northeastern New Mexico. Comanche raids in the eighteenth century forced them onto colonial New Mexico's outskirts.

10.   Newberry, Abridged Diary, July 26, 1859, NA; Dimmock, Diary, 26 July 1859, VHS.

11.   Ibid., July 27, 1859.

12.   Newberry, Abridged Diary, July 28, 1859, NA.

13.   Macomb, *Report*, 74.

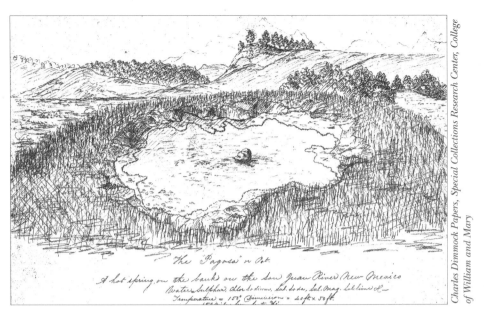

Sketch of Pagosa Spring, by Charles H. Dimmock.

The hot spring at Pagosa Springs, Colorado, surrounded by modern development.

Tasting the water, Newberry wrote, "When cooled, the water has a strong mineral taste, though rather agreeable than otherwise. It was freely drank [*sic*] by all our party while in this vicinity with no unpleasant effects, but, on the contrary, a decided sharpening of the appetite."[14] Drinking from the spring, Dimmock reported, "Water strongly impregnated with sulphur, magnesia &c." Macomb's party pulled out a thermometer to determine the spring's temperature—150 degrees Fahrenheit. Its basin measured "40 by 50 feet in diameter" and was "of unfathomable depth." "The deep-blue water seethes and surges as in a boiling caldron, giving off a column of vapor which in damp weather is visible for miles."[15]

From the hot springs, the party turned westward twelve miles to their next camp, in the heartland of the Utes. Here "some 30 Utes" visited them. Dimmock reported that they "shot their arrows for a Coat & drove them deeply into an oak block. Gave them all tobacco &c—& bade them adieu. Souvetah [Sowiette], the chief of this attachment, will accompany us to Rio las Animas." (Macomb would later carry the oak block home with him on his return to Washington.) Ironically, by this time Sowiette, the civil head chief of the Northern Ute bands, had joined the Mormon Church and gained the friendship of Brigham Young. Several bands formed the Northern Ute confederation that occupied an area of some 225,000 square miles. With no fixed borders, they inhabited much of northern New Mexico, eastern and southern Utah, and most of Colorado.[16]

The day after their encounter with the Utes, they passed the rock sentinel Piedra Parada—"a singular pinnacle," wrote Dimmock. Newberry described the "well-known landmark" as "a chimney-like column of rock, rising with its base to the height of eight or nine hundred feet above the surrounding country." He and Dimmock stopped long enough to make a sketch of the monolith, near their camp on the Rio Piedra.[17] (Located about seventeen miles west of Pagosa Springs, the stone pillar is visible from today's U.S. Highway 160.)

An interlude of peace appears to have occurred in the San Juan Basin among the Ute bands and the Navajo at this time. On the Rio Piedra, Dimmock recorded the following event: "A delegation of Utes, from one

14. Ibid., 75.
15. Dimmock, Diary, July 28, 1859, VHS; Macomb, *Report*, 74. Macomb had success with his "astronomizing" after he was "aroused by the Sentry when the sky cleared at midnight," stated Dimmock. Dimmock, Diary, July 30, 1859, VHS.
16. Ibid., July 30, 1859; John Alton Peterson, *Utah's Black Hawk War* (Salt Lake City: University of Utah Press, 1998), 90; Clifford Duncan, "The Northern Utes of Utah," in Forrest S. Cuch, *A History of Utah's American Indians* (Salt Lake City: Utah State Division of Indian Affairs and Utah State Division of History, 2000), 173–74.
17. Dimmock, Diary, July 31, 1859, VHS; Macomb, *Report*, 78.

Sketch of "Piedra Parada," by Charles H. Dimmock.

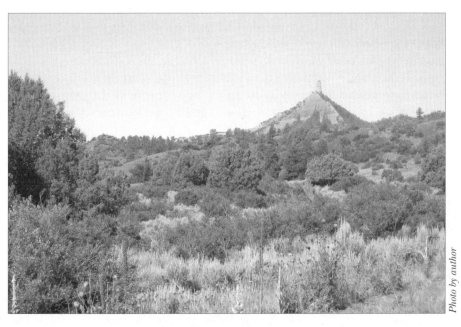

Chimney Rock, west of Pagosa Springs, Colorado.

of the tribes ahead of us, came in to day, headed by Delgarito their great man. Had a long talk professing most friendly relations to the whites. Delgarito dressed beyond measure, a proud supercilious but dashing fellow." To foster warm relations, Albert Pfeiffer and Nepomuceno Valdez apparently orchestrated a meeting of Ute and Navajo leaders that evening. Included in the party were: Capote chief Temuché, Navajo leader Manuelita, and chief of the Northern Ute confederation, Sowiette. Dimmock wrote: "Tamuché, Souvetah[,] P[f]eiffer, Tomasonia [Nepomuceno], & all the party around a cheery fire to night, also Manolita."[18]

Another meeting with tribal leaders occurred the following day, after Macomb passed by "the lodges of Delgarito's tribe." Macomb's men paused and "took a pipe," a token of peace, "with Delgarito who[m] they found shorn of all his yesterday's finery," wrote Dimmock. Later that day, "Delgarito's & Cabazon's tribes" arrived in camp; "by delegates & all received either Blankets[,] Shirts or Cotton."[19]

On the bank of the Rio Florida, Macomb observed "an occultation of a small star near Lower limb of moon on dark part of moon immersion [sic]." Frequent poor weather throughout the march had, however, limited his ability to take astronomical observations and slowed his pace to a crawl. Macomb muttered, "The progress of the march has been very considerably delayed by the necessity of waiting at some points for clear weather to get an opportunity to make the requisite astronomical observations. We have had more rain than I have seen during my whole residence at Santa Fé."[20]

From their camp on the Rio Florida, Newberry launched another side trip, traveling thirty-five to forty miles downstream to "the ruins on the Animas," the site of today's Aztec Ruins National Monument in northern New Mexico. But before he ventured out, he fretted over the possibilities. Writing to his friend Spencer F. Baird at the Smithsonian, Newberry stated, "Tomorrow morning I am off to an ancient Pueblo of great interest—near our present camp—& on our return—if we return, for it is a trip of some danger—Pfeiffer the Indian agent returns to Santa Fé and will take our letters." He continued, "We are now more

---

18. Dimmock, Diary, August 1, 1859, VHS. Manuelita (1816–1894) had become head chief of the Navajo in 1855. Albert H. Pfeiffer (1822–1881) sailed from the Netherlands to America in 1844 and arrived in New Mexico the year it was annexed into the United States. He joined the U.S. Army and rose to the rank of colonel. For several years, he served as an Indian Agent in the region. Pfeiffer later played a controversial role in assisting Kit Carson against the Navajo.
19. Ibid., August 2, 1859.
20. "San Juan River Survey: Astronomical and Barometrical Observation, 1859," Bureau of Topographical Engineers, War Department Records, NA; Macomb to Humphreys, August 5, 1859, NA.

Rio Grande County Museum, Monte Vista, Colorado. Courtesy of Charles O. Elliott

Albert H. Pfeiffer, Sr., Indian agent.

than 200 miles N.W. of Santa Fé in a region never before explored by whites." He further stated, "We are among Indians—but so far all are Utahs & friendly[.] We hear rumors of war from the Indians but hope to get through safely."[21]

The Macomb men, however, heard a more disastrous sounding rumor on August 5 when Hispanic Indian traders spread the unfounded news that the U.S. Army had attacked Salt Lake City and had engaged in house-to-house combat.

With a small exploring party that included Ute Indians, Newberry reached the ancient ruins the next day and gave this description: Pueblo Indians had constructed and occupied the "handsomely built" large pueblos made of well-preserved stone buildings. Their smooth external walls, "unbroken by door or window," stood twenty-five feet high. The building interiors contained numerous small rooms "in a perfect state of preservation and handsomely plastered." "Mounds and fragments of masonry" surrounded the larger structures, "marking the sites of great numbers of subordinate buildings." In the vicinity of the structures, with

---

21.   Newberry to Baird, August 3, 1859, SIA.

a "peculiar style of architecture," Newberry found abundant "fragments of ornamented and glazed pottery" covering the ground.[22]

On his trip to the ruins, Newberry made a geographical discovery. He found that the Rio Florida forms "a branch of the Animas and does not flow directly into the San Juan as was before supposed."[23]

At the Rio Florida camp, Dimmock reported, "Temuché, Rio Vajo, Nutria & another Ute sent to Kyatano, the renegade Navajoe, desiring him to come in." Temuché and Rio Vajo brought the following news: "Last night the rascal Nutria assisted by the other Utes ran off all of Kyatano's horses."[24]

With his small body of men, Newberry "visited the Camp of Kiatano from whom . . . some of our Utes stole several horses with which they escaped to their own country and we saw no more of them." On hearing this news, the expedition immediately took a precautionary step. "Temuche was dispatched with presents to remove any suspicion of a want of good faith on our part which might have been excited in the mind of Kiatano."

Nutria's actions could have had serious consequences in the region. The customary practice of intermarriage among the region's major tribes (Ute, Navajo, Apache, and Hopi), meant that if one band initiated a fight all the others might enter the fray.[25]

Following Newberry's safe return, the expedition struck camp. Less than two miles beyond the Rio Florida, they rejoined the Old Spanish Trail in Utah Territory in what is now southwestern Colorado. Once again, Dimmock carefully recorded the trail route on his field map.[26] From here, the expedition would travel more than 125 miles along the famous pack trail on their approach to the Colorado River.

In his geological notes, Newberry wrote about an exploitable resource in the area: "Below the crossing of the Spanish trail the valley of the Animas is susceptible of cultivation to the junction of the Florid[a], though the belt of arable land is narrow, and, in part at least, can only be cultivated by irrigation."[27]

Macomb's men pitched their tents on the banks of the Animas River "at the point where it is crossed by the old Spanish trail." Newberry wrote that the crossing, located on the southern outskirts of modern Durango, extended "nearly a hundred yards" and ran "deep and rapid, and, at present stage of water, not easily forded." (Upstream from the Old Spanish Trail crossing, near the mouth of Lightner Canyon—a natural opening to the west—the Denver & Rio Grande Railroad established today's city of

22. Macomb, *Report*, 80.
23. Newberry, Abridged Diary, August 4, 1859, NA.
24. Dimmock, Diary, August 5, 1859, VHS.
25. Newberry, Abridged Diary, August 5, 1859, NA; Peterson, *Utah's Black Hawk War*, 82.
26. Dimmock, "Map of Explorations and Surveys in New Mexico and Utah," 1859, NA.
27. Macomb, *Report*, 81.

Sketch of the Sierra La Plata, near Macomb's camp on the
Rio Florida, by Charles H. Dimmock.

The La Plata Mountains near the Florida River, east of Durango, Colorado.

Durango in 1881.) In camp, Dimmock observed the following incident: A party of "4 Mexicans came in to day, most pitiable objects . . . on the eve of starvation. Temuché yesterday extorted from one of them his coat & $16 (all he had) for a piece of dried meat as large as one hand. Just the scoundrel we should have believed & doubtless is an aider [*sic*] in the horse stealing."[28]

Once across the river, Macomb's team climbed an adjacent steep, gravel and boulder terrace, covered by thick foliage, about three hundred feet high. From the terrace top, the party passed through a sparsely wooded, open country for about nine miles to reach the La Plata River near the present site of Ute Junction, an abandoned station on the Denver & Rio Grande Railroad.

At the Rio de la Plata, Dimmock enjoyed a luxurious bath in the "beautifully clear, rock stream," surrounded by "fine grama grass & a waste of flowers upon which we bedded." Nearby, just above the present town of Hesperus, Colorado, he sketched the striking La Plata Mountains.

Newberry found the mountain paradise exhilarating:

> the Rio de la Plata is a beautifully clear, cold, mountain-brook . . . well-stocked with trout. The valley in which it flows, as it issues from the mountains, is exceedingly beautiful, and our camp, one of the most delightful imaginable. Our tents are pitched in the shade of a cluster of gigantic pines, such as are scattered, here and there, singly or in groups, over the surface of the valley, separated by meadows thickly coated with the finest gramma grass. Stretching off southward, a wall of verdure, tinted with the fresh and vivid green of cottonwoods and willows, marks, while it conceals, the course of the sparkling stream whose murmuring flow comes softly to the ear. On either side of the valley rise picturesque wooded hills, which bound the view both east and west; between these on the south an open vista reveals, far in the distance, the blue chains of the Sierra la Carriso and Tunecha [Carrizo and Chuska mountains]. On the north the bold and lofty summits of the Sierra de la Plata look down upon us in this pure atmosphere with an apparent proximity almost startling.[29]

Encamped at the base of the La Plata Mountains—later the area of rich mineral operations—the party ironically found no metallic evidence to suggest that the nearby range merited the Spanish name Sierra de la Plata, or Silver Mountains. Dimmock wrote, "vainly the eye peers among naked, hopeless crags for some gleaming of that metal the name of the

---

28.   Ibid., 80; Dimmock, Diary, August 6, 1859, VHS.
29.   Macomb, *Report*, 81.

Sketch of Temuché, leader of the Capote Utes, by Charles H. Dimmock. Dimmock captioned the sketch with a scathing critique of Temuché: "T[e]muché is a most incorrigible rascal, the husband of five successive wives. . . . His former wives, when sick were attended by . . . Indian medicine men who were killed when failing to cure. The last one T[e]muché put out of the way before his wife died. T[e]muché makes it a religious duty to get drunk whenever the material therefor[e] is accessible. As T[e]muché is to accompany us for the next month this memorandum is but due to him & a just appreciation of his worth."

Charles Dimmock Papers, Special Collections Research Center, College of William and Mary

Sketch of the La Plata Mountains towering over the valley of the La Plata River, by Charles H. Dimmock.

Photo by author

The La Plata River valley near Hesperus, Colorado.

Sierra indicates, until heavy and wearied it sinks in the conviction that the steel-clad Hidalgo must have seen with an eye of faith, strengthened by avarice, the inaccessible hoard deep buried in the bowels of the grand old mountain."[30]

In the La Plata high country, at the present-day hamlet of Hesperus, the expedition turned westward and crossed the divide between the La Plata River and Cherry Creek at an elevation of about 8,330 feet. From the divide, they marched downstream to Thompson Park, a lush, green mountain valley skirting the extreme southern base of the La Plata Mountains. Newberry described the park as "a natural pass, or *puerta*, through which the Spanish trail leads."[31] Their path crossed the upper end of the park, running parallel to the route of modern U.S. Highway 160.

The ridge west of Thompson Park divided the La Plata and Mancos rivers and offered a spectacular viewpoint along the trail. Standing on this threshold in 1859, Newberry described the mountaintop perspective:

> Here we were to leave the lofty sierras of the Rocky Mountain system, which had so long looked down on our camps and marches, the picturesque scenery of the foot hills, their flowery valleys and sparkling streams, the grateful shade of their noble forests, and take our weary way across the arid expanse of the great western plateau; a region whose dreary monotony is only broken by frightful chasms, where alone the weary traveler finds shelter from the burning heat of a cloudless sun, and where he seeks, too often in vain, a cooling draught that shall slake his thirst.[32]

Not long after their luxuriating respite at the La Plata, Lt. Milton Cogswell launched a military routine, sounding the bugle at an early hour. And whenever clear skies appeared, Macomb engaged his men in observations, calculations, and, at times, demanding survey work.

From the La Plata River to Utah's Abajo Mountains, the Macomb expedition passed through the present Four Corners country, a region extending outward from the common point where the boundaries of Utah, Colorado, New Mexico, and Arizona converge. In the Four Corners region, beyond the La Plata-Mancos divide, they followed the geologic trough that separates the La Platas and the great sedimentary tableland of Mesa Verde.

Inhabited by the Ancestral Pueblo people for thousands of years before the arrival of the Spaniards, the region is famous for its prehistoric cultural

---

30. Dimmock, Topographical Memoir, 7, LOC.
31. Macomb, *Report*, 83.
32. Ibid.

resources. Ancestral Puebloans cultivated crops of maize, beans, and squash and resided in villages and in apartment houses, including many imposing cliff dwellings, typified by those in Mesa Verde National Park. They abandoned their homeland in the Four Corners about AD 1300, and their great urban centers at Mesa Verde and elsewhere became the first ghost towns in the Southwest. Some distance south from the Old Spanish Trail, the Ancestral Pueblo ruins at Mesa Verde—the largest archaeological preserve in the United States—was not discovered until the 1870s.[33]

Descending the western slope of the La Plata-Mancos divide in the shadow of Mesa Verde, the Macomb party crossed the main forks of the Mancos River in an open valley two miles above the town of Mancos.[34]

Near this point, Newberry left the main party and hiked to the top of a rampart on the north face of Mesa Verde to investigate the surrounding countryside. He observed, "The Mesa Verde is, geologically, but a portion of the high table-lands which border the Upper San Juan; the northern margin of which is followed by our route from the ford of the Chama to the Mancos." He added, "This mesa we completely encircled; examined it at a thousand points, and can speak of its structure and extent with confidence."[35] However, Newberry, who recorded the Hispanic name of the high tableland, failed to discover the celebrated ruins of the present park.

Although he missed the famous cliff dwellings, Newberry found important prehistoric sites throughout the San Juan River Basin. He wrote the first scientific descriptions of the crumbling remains near the Rio Dolores and the Yellowjacket Pueblo Ruins in Colorado, as well as the ancient ruins of Aztec Ruins National Monument in New Mexico.

From the headwaters of the Mancos, the Macomb party continued west-northwest, closely following the modern route of Colorado Highway 184 to the Big Bend of the Dolores River. Where Macomb's command reached the Dolores, the river makes a broad bend to the north. Puzzled by the name "Rio Dolores" (River of Sorrow), Dimmock observed, "The Rio Dolores sparkling & clear, 70 feet in width, flowing in a rapid shallow & winding stream, through flowery meadows & rich green cotton-woods, bending in leafy exuberance, seems but illy named, as too fair a scene for one to 'come to grief.'"[36]

---

33. Madsen, "Retracing the Spanish Trail: Across Colorado's San Juan Basin," *Spanish Traces* 2, no. 2 (Fall 1996): 6.

34. Ibid.

35. Macomb, *Report*, 85. In this vicinity, Newberry observed the effects of fluvial erosion: "An unbroken table-land once stretched from the base of the Sierra de la Plata all the way across to the mountain chains west of the Colorado, and . . . from this plateau, grain by grain, the sedimentary materials which once filled the broad and deep valleys of the Colorado and San Juan have been removed by the currents of these streams." Macomb, *Report*, 84.

36. Dimmock, Topographical Memoir, 8, LOC.

Sketch of the Rio Dolores near Macomb's Camp 21, in present Colorado, by Charles H. Dimmock.

The Dolores River valley west of Dolores, Colorado, from the hills overlooking McPhee Reservoir.

En route to the Dolores, Newberry found the area "everywhere covered with fragments of broken pottery, showing its former occupation by a considerable number of inhabitants." South across the stream from the present town of Dolores, on the rim overlooking the Dolores River, the party halted. "Our Camp a noted stopping place on the Spanish trail," stated Newberry. Here he observed "extensive ruins of Stone structures on the hills overlooking Camp, (the same mentioned by Padre Escalante in 1774 [sic].)" The 1776 Dominguez-Escalante expedition had explored the ruins near the river's Big Bend.

After setting up camp, "Dr. N[ewberry] & Fisher [set] off to visit an old Pueblo some two miles up the river," noted Dimmock. Newberry apparently rediscovered and explored the Escalante Pueblo, built during the AD 1100s, on the hilltop above today's Anasazi Heritage Center within the Canyons of the Ancients National Monument. The U.S. Bureau of Land Management has curated at the museum millions of artifacts from the surrounding area.[37]

Macomb's men also found other ruins near their camp. According to Dimmock, "All went to the top of the m[e]sa adjacent to see an old Pueblo & enjoy the view. Found ruins indicative of greater antiquity than any we have seen. Mingled with the stone is much pottery, broken & of a ruder stamp than previously collected."[38]

Back in camp, the pack train's bell mare gave birth to a colt. "This induces hesitation as to moving to day," reported Dimmock. He continued, "Capt. finally resolves to kill the young one & move on. The Ute with us prevents this cruel necessity by making his squaw take it, with her, on her horse."[39] (Tragically, the following morning the party awoke to discover that the pack mules had bitten the colt to death.)

Dimmock noted that the route beyond the Dolores River passes "over a gently broken sage plain, spreading far to the right interspersed with stunted pinons." Tired by the "monotonous Cretaceous geology" along the route, Newberry named the plateau the "Great Sage Plain," a name that prevails on modern maps.[40] The entire area dips to the south, which allows for additional warm weather during the winter—a kind of oasis that the Ancestral Puebloans exploited in their dry farming. Off to the

---

37. The Bureau of Land Management claims that "this area has the highest known archaeological site density" in the United States. Thousands of archaeological sites occupy the nearly 164,000-acre area within the Canyons of the Ancients National Monument in southwestern Colorado. Artifacts collected from Ancestral Puebloan sites on the Great Sage Plain in Colorado are preserved at the Anasazi Heritage Center, near Dolores.

38. Macomb, *Report*, 86; Newberry, Abridged Diary, August 10, 1859, NA; Dimmock, Diary, August 12, 1859, VHS.

39. Dimmock, Diary, August 13, 1859, VHS.

40. Dimmock, Topographical Memoir, 8, LOC; Macomb, *Report*, 84, 90.

Photo by author

Escalante Pueblo, on the hill above the Anasazi Heritage
Center, Dolores, Colorado.

south, Ute Mountain, vaguely resembling a recumbent woman, relieves
the monotony of the Great Sage Plain.

Today the route followed by Macomb over the Great Sage Plain crosses
an extensive dry farming region—open, rolling country consisting of dry
farms interspersed with scrub pine and sagebrush. Much of the land is
under cultivation, which has obliterated most traces of the Old Spanish
Trail Macomb followed. Cultivation may have also stirred many of the
"thousands and millions" of fossils scattered across the plain. Newberry
noted that the fossils provided "conclusive evidence that the Middle
Cretaceous shales once covered the sandstone floor of the Sage-plain
from which they have been nearly removed by aqueous [watery] action."[41]

Standing on this elevated plain, Newberry caught a sweeping glance of
the countryside. "Directly west the Sage-plain stretches out nearly hori-
zontal, unmarked by any prominent feature, to the distance of a hundred
miles. There the island-like mountains, the Sierra Abajo and Sierra LaSal,
rise from its surface. South of these is the little double-peaked mountain,
called by the Mexicans Las Orejas del Oso—the bear's ears."[42]

41. Macomb, *Report*, 84.
42. Ibid., 85.

From Dolores the expedition continued on to the head of a canyon, watered by a bountiful spring, called Yellow Jacket by those in modern times who found the place to be the preferred habitat of wasps. Here the group passed to the right of acres of crumbling Ancestral Pueblo ruins. In prehistoric times, Yellow Jacket was one of the important regional centers of the Ancestral Pueblo culture north of the San Juan River. Newberry first described the ruin, located on a flat stretch of land north and west of Yellow Jacket Creek, and labeled it "Surouaro," a Ute word meaning desolation. (The name of the site appears today on the National Register as a subtle reminder of the Macomb expedition.)

Newberry examined the "ruined town" and speculated about its former inhabitants. Evidence suggested that a large Pueblo population had inhabited the ruins over centuries and abandoned them "several hundred years ago." Newberry puzzled over "how they managed to exist" and "how their town was depopulated." He found abundant "remains of metates (corn-mills)," corn obviously the "staple article of their existence." Acequias or ditches, "through which water was brought perhaps from a great distance," led to "several large reservoirs, built of masonry." Here had lived ancient Pueblo Indians—"peaceful, industrious, and agricultural"—residing in large houses "built of stone, hammer-dressed" on their surfaces. Numerous fragments of pottery "like the buildings, show great age."[43]

From the ruins at Yellow Jacket, their route took them along a narrow, flat strip of land, crossing a number of intermittent streams flowing southwest to the San Juan River. Just south of present-day Dove Creek, Colorado, they camped at a large tributary, Cross Canyon, which contained good water, trickling from the base of a low sandstone cliff, whitened by mineral salts. The Macomb expedition named the place Tierra Blanca (White Land), due to the presence of alkali in a tributary stream.

Beyond Tierra Blanca, Macomb crossed into what is now Utah on a sloping plain near today's Ucolo, a community of farms some fifteen miles east of Monticello. His party camped at a spillway on Piute Draw, which they identified as Guajalotes, meaning salamanders.[44] Here the overflow from Piute Spring, upstream from the spillway, formed pools in a "canyon slimy with water-lizards," noted Dimmock.[45]

Leaving behind the pools of "water lizards," Macomb ascended the sage and grass-carpeted Great Sage Plain to a spring near a long gash furrowed into its northwestern rim. In camp, Dimmock reported, "To our surprise Souvetah (the dispatch from Santa Fé & Pfeiffer) came in." He

---

43. Ibid., 88–89.
44. See Ruben Cobos, *A Dictionary of New Mexico and Southern Colorado Spanish* (Santa Fé: Museum of New Mexico Press, 1983), 78.
45. Dimmock, Topographical Memoir, 9, LOC.

Courtesy of Margaret Jones Perritt and the Virginia Historical Society

Sketch of a scorpion, by Charles H. Dimmock.

added: "Souvetah given presents, with which he seemed much pleased, & bidding us adieu took the back trail." (Sowiette was quite familiar with the Old Spanish Trail route that Macomb's men were following. The historic path led northward to the La Sal Mountains, or "Elk Mountains" as the Mormons called them, and beyond. Historian John Alton Peterson writes, "Sowiette's Northern Utes spent so many winters near the Elk [La Sal] Mountains that Colorado whites often referred to them as 'Elk Mountain Utes.'" Around the camp, the men caught a rattlesnake and a scorpion.[46]

Dimmock later depicted the venomous desert arachnid in his drawing book and minimized the threat it posed. "These little fellows evince an amount of spirit worthy of a larger & sharper sting. A stick thrust at them they seize with their claws & endeavour, time after time, to let it feel the venom of their tails. Failing in this they open their pinchers & stand prepared for the approach of something more vulnerable. Their sting has much the power & effect of that of the Bee."

46. Dimmock, Diary, August 16–17, 1859; Peterson, *Utah's Black Hawk War*, 196.

From the Great Sage Plain the expedition plunged into South Canyon, dropping a thousand feet in about three miles to the floor of East Canyon—a long, narrow canyon opening out into Dry Valley. Newberry recorded the name of the canyon of vividly colored rock as Cañon Pintado, or Painted Canyon. Dimmock called the canyon Cañon de las Pañitas—a canyon of little rocks.

In the midst of the canyon, Newberry made history. Referring to himself in the third person, Newberry modestly noted, "Dr. N. finds bones in cliff." Awed by the discovery, Dimmock recorded the following: "Dr. N. up in the wall of the cañon excavating a fossil Icthyosaurus, whose gigantic bones are our wonder."[47] (In the geologic deposits of the Morrison Formation, high on the cliff face one quarter of a mile from Camp No. 26, Newberry had found a massive fossilized dinosaur encased in sandstone. He would return to the quarry ten days later to continue digging.) Using the inadequate tools at hand, he began removing the bones. "Our start somewhat retarded by this," wrote Dimmock.

Down the wash from Newberry's dinosaur discovery site, the San Juan Exploring Expedition made its abrupt entry into the wild, red rock country east of today's Canyonlands National Park, a region typified by scattered monuments of bald sandstone domes, wind-shaped into fanciful forms. The men were awed by the "intricate mass of irregular bluffs, detached buttes & sinuous canyons" whittled by nature's forces.[48]

Following the Old Spanish Trail to the upper end of Dry Valley, Macomb's command halted at the intricately carved landmark rock, Casa Colorado (Red House), jutting up more than two hundred feet from its broad, undulating base. The deeply grooved alcoves cut into the southern wall of this "detached butte" of Entrada sandstone reminded passersby of the windows of a massive house. Although nineteenth-century travelers seldom appreciated the natural allurements alongside the Old Spanish Trail, Newberry described Casa Colorado as "one of the most striking [formations] seen from our route." Both Newberry and Dimmock stopped to sketch the "immense mass of sedimentary rocks."[49]

At the richly contoured slickrock base of Casa Colorado, the expedition found large tanks carved into a sandstone surface. Newberry recorded the name of the site, El Tenejal, the Place of the Tanks. In the heart of the

47. Newberry, Abridged Diary, August 17, 1859, SIA; Dimmock, Diary, August 18 1859, VHS. In his topographical memoir Dimmock noted: "Saurian fossils of exceeding interest were exhumed—with most inadequate implements—by the indefatigable order of an enthusiastic & accomplished Geologist* (*Dr. John S. Newberry)."

48. Dimmock, Topographical Memoir, 10, LOC.

49. Macomb, *Report*, 92; Steven K. Madsen, "Retracing the Spanish Trail: Across the Colorado Plateau," *Spanish Traces* 4, no. 1 (Spring 1998): 7.

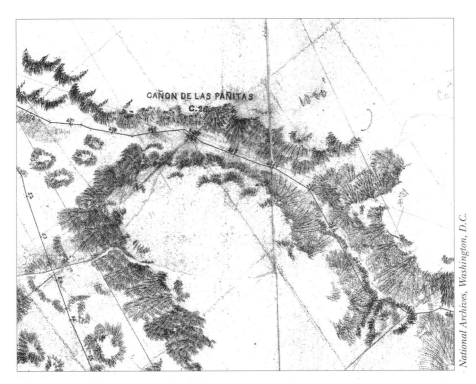

CAÑON DE LAS PAÑITAS
C.26

National Archives, Washington, D.C.

Detail of Dimmock's topographical field map showing Camp 26 in Cañon de
las Pañitas, or Cañon Pintado. In this canyon Dr. John S. Newberry discovered
in 1859 "Fossils," noted on the map, of a giant sauropod dinosaur.

expansive slickrock mass below Casa Colorado was La Tinaja (The Tank),
an enormous pothole—having a capacity of about two thousand gallons
of water—formed by erosion and surrounded by several natural basins.
Newberry described it as "a deep excavation in the red sandstone, which
retains so large a quantity of surface-water, and for so long a time, as to
become an important watering-place on the Spanish trail." Dimmock recorded, "Walked to the top of an adjacent sandstone hill where we had an
extensive but sterile view."[50]

From La Tinaja, Macomb sent three men—a Shiberetch Ute chief,
John Campeau, and Armijo—to scout out a suitable route to the west.
(It is possible that Sowiette had arranged for the Elk Mountain, or
Shiberetch, Ute chief to guide the Macomb party to their destination.)
Juan P. Martin led another team of scouts headed south. (In 1855, a
Mormon scouting party, sent to explore the region south of Moab,

50. Macomb, *Report*, 92; Dimmock, Diary, August 18, 1859, VHS. Dimmock reported that the
men used kegs to obtain water from sandstone waterholes nearby. Dimmock, Diary, August
19, 1859, VHS.

Sketch of Casa Colorado, by Charles H. Dimmock.

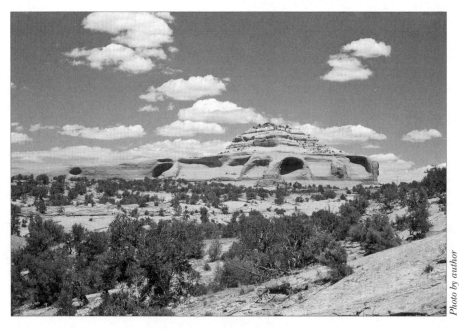

Casa Colorado, south of Moab, Utah.

had traversed Dry Valley and southward along the route followed by Macomb's second team of scouts.) In addition, "Sargent [Hathaway?] & Stephen [Conroy?]" struck out through the desert to find "a favourable camp ground." They returned and reported on a "good Camp 10 miles west," said Newberry., Following an easy grade below La Tinaja, the Macomb expedition crossed the "dry barren country to Ojo Verde" (Green Spring), a "fine spring" with "good grass," said Newberry. The historic spring was located in present Hatch Ranch Canyon, one and a half miles from its junction with Hatch Wash. ("Massive erosional cutting into the alluvium" has drastically altered the site, according to Fran Barnes. Barnes provides us with its precise location: NW ¼ of SE ¼ of Section 35, T29S, R22E, Salt Lake Meridian.)[51]

Five miles west of Casa Colorado, they diverged from the Old Spanish Trail route. (Again, the War Department had instructed Macomb to locate the junction of the Colorado and Green rivers along with a supply route suitable for wagons. Since the Old Spanish Trail northwest of Casa Colorado could not accommodate much more than pack animals, certainly not military wagons, Macomb veered from the trail to find an alternate route.) About the Old Spanish Trail, Macomb said, "The greater part of our journey from Abiquiu to this point was by the old Spanish trail, which has not heretofore been accurately laid down upon any map. This trail is much talked of as having been the route of commerce between California and Mexico in the days of the old Spanish rule, but it seems to have been superseded by the routes to the north and south of it, which have been opened to modern enterprise."[52]

At Ojo Verde, Macomb established a depot camp from which to explore the wild canyonlands to the west in hope of finding the confluence of the Colorado and Green rivers. The scouting party, led by the Shiberetch Ute chief, came into camp here and reported its findings. The trail leading to the Grand River was "utterly impracticable for our packs. Distance about 55 miles to the junction, which they did not reach. They report fresh Indian signs."[53] With that information, Macomb prepared for his exploratory adventure.

Leaving the main body including the military escort in camp, nine armed men embarked on a reconnaissance to the rivers' confluence. In the party

51. Dimmock Diary, August 19, 1859, VHS; Newberry, Abridged Diary, August 19, 25, 1859, NA; Barnes, *The 1859 Macomb Expedition into Utah Territory*, 82, 83.

52. Macomb, *Report*, 5–6. Macomb's manuscript map of 1860 clearly shows the Old Spanish Trail bypassing Ojo Verde as it curves to the north. "Map of Explorations and Surveys in New Mexico made under the direction of Hon. J. B. Floyd, Sec. of War by Capt. J. N. Macomb, Topl. Engrs. assisted by C. H. Dimmick [*sic*], C. Engr, &c. 1860," scale 1:800,000, NA.

53. Dimmock, Diary, August 21, 1859, VHS.

Courtesy of Margaret Jones Perritt and the Virginia Historical Society

Sketch of a "Horn of the Rocky Mountain Sheep," at
"El Ojo Verde," Utah Territory, August 26, 1859, by
Charles H. Dimmock. The length of the horn's outer
curve measured 30 inches, recorded Dimmock.

were Macomb, Lieutenant Cogswell, Dimmock, Newberry, Campeau,
Hathaway, Armijo, and "two Mexicans." (The latter were probably "cooks
&c" that Dimmock had indicated would join the party.) The ride was "hot
& fatiguing," wrote Dimmock. Moreover, the route was so treacherous
that Newberry wrote of their "horrible time generally." Thickets, quick-
sand, and rocks slowed their march. Along the way, Newberry found a
"ca[ñ]on formerly inhabited," containing "ruined stone houses in cliffs."[54]

---

54. Ibid., August 22, 1859. See also Dimmock's entry for August 21, 1859; Newberry, Abridged
     Diary, August 22, 1859, NA.

Dimmock noted that the route to the confluence was "by a path the trembling mule hesitates to pursue."[55] Macomb added, "it is fortunate that no attempt was made to bring forward our pack train as we must have lost many mules by it, and moreover there was not sufficient pasture for the few animals that we had with us."[56]

Newberry described the route to their next camp: "On leaving camp we struck southwest, gradually ascending for six miles, when we reached the brink of a magnificent cañon twelve hundred feet in depth, called, from the prevailing color of its walls, Cañon Colorado, into which with great difficulty we descended."[57] According to Barnes, Cañon Colorado is today's Hart's Draw.[58]

Downstream from the junction of Hart's Draw and Indian Creek Canyon, "in the lower stretch of Indian Creek Canyon," the Macomb party arrived at their Camp No. 29. In lower Indian Creek Canyon, Newberry's "Labyrinth Cañon," they "reached a point where water was found in holes at 4:15 PM where we conclude to stop for the night," stated Dimmock. That night, Dimmock "aided the Capt. in observations by light of a newspaper lantern."[59]

From their camp, the scouting party, reduced seemingly to six men—Macomb, Newberry, Dimmock, Cogswell, Campeau, and Armijo—proceeded on toward the Colorado. Heading for today's Canyonlands National Park, Dimmock wrote of the challenges the party faced: "Plodding down through the mazes of the Cañon Colorado, through which passes, at times, a rapid, muddy stream, we find our journey most arduous from the steepness of the bank & frequency of crossing the stream. The banks of the stream vary from ten to fifteen feet in height & are so perpendicular that when our mules slide down we cling by the cantle of the saddle to avoid going over their heads. This stream, going & coming, we crossed 270 times."[60] Dimmock kept a count of the crossings since he had to run a surveyor's line of measurements to the next campsite.

Newberry and his companions paused to embrace the red rock wonderland as they approached the heart of today's Canyonlands National Park. He wrote, "[Its] appearance was so strange and beautiful as to call out exclamation and delight from our party."[61]

55. Dimmock, Topographical Memoir, 11, LOC.
56. Macomb, *Report*, 6.
57. Ibid., 93.
58. Barnes, *The 1859 Macomb Expedition into Utah Territory*, 85.
59. Ibid.,88, 89; Dimmock, Diary, August 22, 1859, VHS. At Camp 29, they were eleven and a half miles upstream from the mouth of Indian Creek.
60. Dimmock, Diary, August 23, 1859.
61. Macomb, *Report*, 94.

Sketch of the North and South Sixshooter Peaks, by Charles H. Dimmock.

North and South Sixshooter Peaks near Canyonlands
National Park in southern Utah.

Macomb, however, took a contrary view. Repulsed by the wild land-scape, apparently since it lacked exploitable resources, Macomb wrote, "I cannot conceive of a more worthless and impracticable region than the one we now found ourselves in. I doubt not there are repetitions and *varieties* of it for hundreds of miles down the canon of the Great Colorado."[62]

A seemingly insurmountable challenge awaited Macomb's men as they continued down Indian Creek Canyon. Within two miles of the Colorado River, a high pour-off or "perpendicular fall" blocked the explorers' passage. Arrested in their attempt to reach the river, they decided to obtain a vantage point to survey the stone wilderness that surrounded them. On reaching a high butte overlooking the Colorado, Newberry, Dimmock, and Cogswell "resolved to climb" it to "see the Grand River" and "its junction with the Green." Macomb "attempted to follow but failed."[63]

On August 23, a "perfectly clear and intensely hot" day, Macomb's intrepid explorers began their approximately 1,200–foot ascent of the "pinnacle overhanging [the] river" near the confluence of the Green and Colorado rivers. The temperature reached ninety-two degrees Fahrenheit in the shade. "Stripping off nearly all our clothing," said Newberry, the party continued to scale the steep sandstone slope. He added: "After two hours of most arduous labor, we succeeded in reaching the summit."[64] Dimmock wrote, "[The] difficulties of ascent soon forced us to shed by degrees article after article, until at last the summit was reached & exultingly stood upon, by three men stripped to shirts, draws & boots."[65]

After surmounting the high promontory, Dimmock discovered a land of stunning grandeur. Amazed at the depth of the canyons and the exceeding beauty of the wilderness of massive upright rocks, he wrote, "looking around there met our eyes such a view as is not to be seen elsewhere on earth. But few, if any other whites, were ever the beholders of so magical a variety of towering sierra-like m[e]sas, deep cut by canons, penetrating in all directions, into whose depths the rays of the sun at mid day can only fall. In the distance—to the south—the m[e]sas, broken into isolated pinnacles & clustered, castled, summits gave the effect of a grander city than dream land contains."[66]

Newberry wrote of the astonishing scene that "burst upon us": "It baffles description." He later reflected that the area was the wildest and most fantastic scenery on the surface of the globe." The Grand Canyon, he reported,

---

62. Ibid., 6.
63. Dimmock, Diary, August 23, 1859, VHS.
64. Macomb, *Report*, 96; Newberry, Abridged Diary, August 23, 1859, NA.
65. Dimmock, Diary, August 23, 1859, VHS.
66. Ibid.

Sketch of sandstone formations near the Abajo
Mountains, by Charles H. Dimmock.

Sandstone formations east of Canyonlands National Park.

had "far less variety and beauty of detail than this." His "eye swept over an area some fifty miles in diameter. Not a particle of vegetation was any-where discernible; nothing but bare and barren rocks of rich and varied colors shimmering in the sunlight. Scattered over the plain were thousands of . . . fantastically formed buttes . . . pyramids, domes, towers, columns, spires, of every conceivable form and size. Among these by far the most remarkable was the forest of Gothic spires." His was the first written de-scription of the Needles in present-day Canyonlands National Park, and he struggled to capture its essence: "Nothing in nature or in art offers a parallel to these singular objects, but some idea of their appearance may be gained by imagining the island of New York thickly set with spires like that of Trinity church, but many of them full twice its height. Scarcely less striking features in the landscape were the innumerable cañons by which the plain is cut. In every direction they ran and ramified deep, dark, and ragged."[67]

Ahead, an enormous tangle of sandstone, intricately carved by wind and water, created an insurmountable obstacle for the explorers. They could see that the vertical sandstone walls, lining the Colorado River, ef-fectively blocked further travel. From his vantage point atop the butte, Dimmock was able to plot the distance down Labyrinth Creek, today's Indian Creek, to its junction with the Colorado River.

Ever the topographer, Dimmock took sightings of "the courses to vari-ous points." He recorded in his topographical memoir that the total dis-tance from Santa Fé to the Colorado River by the route the expedition had followed was 375.75 miles, from Abiquiu 323.75 miles. (Perched high above the canyons, Dimmock visually carried his surveyor line to the Colorado River. And he discovered that "the perpendicular breaks in the bottom of the [Colorado River] gorge, preclude the possibility of any farther advance.") To the south, Macomb's explorers thought they saw "another great chasm coming in from the northwest, said by the Indians to be that of Green River." Instead, they saw "The Loop," the goosenecks of the Colorado River some four miles distant.[68]

Unable to shield themselves from the merciless sun as they stood atop the butte (elevation 4,899 feet), which towered more than one thousand feet above the Colorado River, Newberry and Cogswell both suffered "from heat and over exertion." As the heat radiated off the sandstone, Newberry busied himself with making a panoramic sketch of the area. (Unfortunately, his sketch is now lost to history.) Wilted by the scorch-ing sun, he nearly collapsed. He reported. "Before I completed the cir-cle of the horizon I was seized with dreadful headache, giddiness, and

67. Macomb, *Report*, 96–97; Newberry to Baird, October 1, 1859, 51A.
68. Dimmock, Diary, August 23, 1859, VHS; Macomb, *Report*, 97; Barnes, *The 1859 Macomb Expedition into Utah Territory*, 93; Dimmock, Topographical Memoir, 12.

nausea, and, alone as I then was, had the greatest difficulty in rejoining my companions."[69]

Defeated in their attempt to reach the mighty confluence of the Colorado and Green rivers, Newberry stoically recorded in his field notes, "Junction inaccessible from our position—so with Grand river." Having traveled so far, the men failed to express their disappointment at missing the mark. From their lofty perch on August 23, 1859, the labyrinth of stone monuments, mesas, spires, and needles in today's Canyonlands National Park blocked the expedition's path to their final destination by a mere eight and a half miles. Cut off from reaching his goal, a disappointed Macomb would report that "no direct supply routes through to southern Utah suitable for military purposes" existed.[70] As Newberry so eloquently put it, the deep river canyons were "impassable to everything but the winged bird."[71]

With the aid of two writers/backpackers—Raymond Wheeler and Thomas Budlong—Fran Barnes in the late 1980s pinpointed in his publications the high pinnacle, presently dubbed "Newberry Butte," where Macomb's men stood in 1859 to view what they thought, incorrectly, was the confluence. It is precisely in the SW ¼ of the NW ¼ of Section 13, T29S R19E, Salt Lake Meridian.[72] (The GPS coordinates are N 38° 16' 46" W 109° 47' 15".) Today's explorers, who wish to hike the expedition's route firsthand, will find precise locations through this rugged and dangerous terrain in Fran Barnes's publications *Hiking the Historic Route of the 1859 Macomb Expedition* and *The 1859 Macomb Expedition into Utah Territory*, based largely on Terby Barnes's yeoman research.[73] Permission to hike and camp along the Macomb route in today's Canyonlands National Park must first be obtained from the National Park Service.

Descending to the foot of the butte, "composed of alternate layers of chocolate-colored sandstone and shale," the exploratory team paused for a few hours of rest. Then with their strength restored, the men turned their mules' heads eastward, "making our first steps on our homeward march." A homesick Dimmock noted, "To me this was the greatest pleasure of our expedition."[74] That evening with ample time to contemplate

69. Newberry, Abridged Diary, August 23, 1859, NA; Macomb, *Report*, 97. See also Barnes, *Canyonlands National Park*, 40.

70. Newberry, Abridged Diary, August 23 1859, NA; Barnes, *Canyonlands National Park*, 130; Macomb, as quoted in Barnes, *The 1859 Macomb Expedition into Utah Territory*, 20.

71. Macomb, *Report*, 97.

72. Barnes, *The 1859 Macomb Expedition into Utah Territory*, 90.

73. Using "TerraServer," at www.terraserver.com, Thomas G. Madsen pinpointed for the author the GPS coordinates. See F. A. Barnes, *Hiking the Historic Route of the 1859 Macomb Expedition* (Moab, Utah: Canyon Country Publications, 1989); Barnes, *Canyonlands National Park*; Barnes, *The 1859 Macomb Expedition into Utah Territory*.

74. Macomb, *Report*, 96; Dimmock, Diary, August 23, 1859, VHS.

Dimmock's topographical field map showing the
Macomb Expedition route from Ojo Verde
to the Colorado River.

"the future with wife and baby," Dimmock's "mind grew [as] weary as my body in scheming & suggesting."

Back in Camp No. 29, Dimmock stood guard, "my first . . . in an Indian country." But Indians were not Dimmock's greatest danger. He was about to witness something far more menacing: a flash flood. "At the time I first took my watch the discharge of water upon the Abajo [Mountains] came thundering along giving for a time much uneasiness as we were in a position where the water might have reached & troubled us; these fears soon subsided with the torrent, whose rise was in one big wave which fell, with a cessation of the supply, as promptly."[75]

Trudging back to the base camp at Ojo Verde, Dimmock reported that his mule, as with the others, "sank deeply into quick sand from which with mighty struggles she could barely extricate herself." On reaching camp with the other explorers, the "tired & heated" topographer felt "glad as possible to get safely back, having happ[i]ly met with no Indians." That

75. Dimmock, Diary, August 23, 1859.

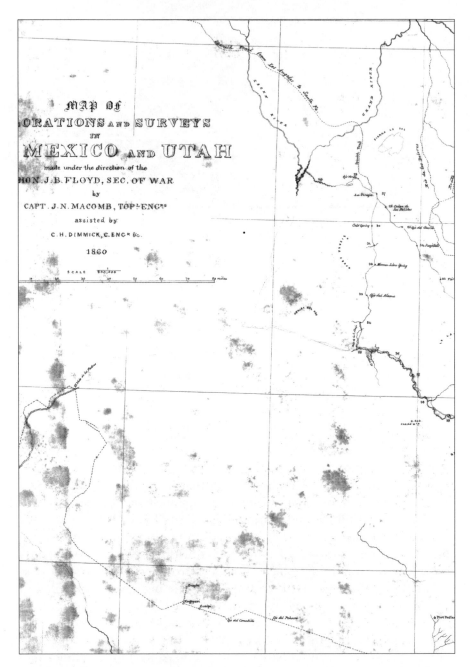

Part of "Map of Explorations and Surveys in New Mexico and Utah made under the direction of Hon. J[ohn] B. Floyd, Sec. of War," by Captain John N. Macomb and Charles H. Dimmock, 1860. Egloffstein based his map of the region encompassing the expedition route on this map. It shows Macomb's route stretching from Tierra Blanca near present Cahone, Colorado, to the Grand

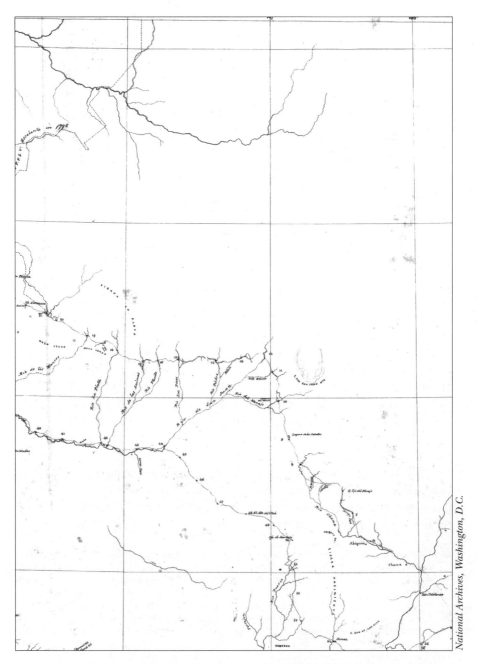

(Colorado) River in southern Utah. Macomb's homeward route led from "La Tinaja" southward along the eastern base of the Abajo Mountains. Note: The Old Spanish Trail bypasses Ojo Verde as it swings northward to reach the crossing of the Grand River, near present Moab, Utah. Macomb also delineates a section of the 1776 Dominguez-Escalante Trail route.

evening, the sentinel stopped "a party of 18 Utes," headed by the father of their Indian scout, from entering camp. Newberry noted that they were "*Savariches*? [Shiberetch] Utes encamped near Sierra la Sal."[76]

To get "a fair understanding" of the Ute party, "we cannot move camp to day," said Dimmock. On their arrival in camp, the expedition distributed presents to them "which they think to be hardly their due." Newberry wrote of "their insolence & importunity dissatisfaction with the presents given them." The Utes told them that "other Americans" had given them "*heaps* of tobacco."[77]

One of the scouts whom Macomb had sent to find a "practicable" route to the south returned with favorable news, but they were unable to strike camp the next day. Sitting at their tables for breakfast, "big drops began to rattle a roll-call on our tin plates & cups," said Dimmock. They donned "India rubber coats" and "got quite comfortably through, though an infusion of rain water does not improve tea nor wetting add to the edibility of biscuit," observed Dimmock. That evening the sky cleared, and they engaged in horse racing, a favorite sport of the Northern Utes.[78]

Departing Ojo Verde and riding back to their former camp at El Tenejal, Dimmock relaxed. "[It was] the first comfortable ride I've had for a month," he said. There was "no necessity for again taking the topography," which he had previously "secured in passing to the Ojo Verde." He spent the evening, however, completing the topography, probably on his field map and in his notes, of the trail to the Colorado River.[79]

On their homeward march, Newberry spent another day "with several assistants" feverishly extricating fossils at the sauropod dinosaur site "in the face of the cliff," high "above its base." Handicapped by tools that "were too light for such heavy work," Newberry lamented that they "were compelled to leave [behind] many bones." Nevertheless, Newberry's party had extracted a substantial amount of the bones, which men packed on the backs of mules that hauled them back to Santa Fé.[80] From there,

---

76. Ibid., August 24, 25, 1859; Newberry, Abridged Diary, August 25, 1859, NA. The Shiberetches, also spelled Sheberetches, were a "desert oriented" band of Utes that lived in southeastern Utah. Duncan, "The Northern Utes of Utah," 176. Another source states that they lived "north of the Spanish trail and west of Green River." Peterson, *Utah's Black Hawk War*, 210. (Although desert oriented, the Shiberetches quite likely depended on subsistence from the nearby LaSal and Abajo mountains.) "By the 1870s, the Sheberetch had been reduced by disease and war. It seems probable that the survivors joined the Uncompahgre, Weeminuche, and Uinta bands." Duncan, "The Northern Utes of Utah," 176.

77. Dimmock, Diary, August 25, 1859, VHS; Newberry, Abridged Diary, 25 August 1859, NA.

78. Dimmock, Diary, August 26, 1859, VHS; Peterson, *Utah's Black Hawk War*, 91.

79. Dimmock, Diary, August 27, 1859, VHS.

80. Macomb, *Report*, 91; Newberry to Dr. Joseph Leidy, February 8, 1860, College of Physicians of Philadelphia. Dimmock reported that "Dr. N, Fisher, Dorsey, Steve [Conroy?], Delis [Joseph Dély?] & a Mex." left immediately after breakfast "to take another pick at the old petrified monster in the m[e]sa's bluff." Dimmock, Diary, August 28, 1859, VHS.

Newberry placed them in boxes. Macomb later carried the boxes in his transit to Washington, D.C. via Fort Leavenworth. Unfortunately, the expedition's published report lacked information on the bone fossils. Paleontologist Edward D. Cope submitted a study of Newberry's dinosaur find, including a lithographic plate illustrating the fossils, which in 1877 was buried in a ponderous volume of the Wheeler Survey publications. The discovery eventually faded in history. (Today the partial skeleton, dubbed *Dystrophaeus viaemalae*, is in the paleontology collection of the Smithsonian Institution. Since its rediscovery by Fran and Terby Barnes, Utah's state paleontologist has recovered more of the dinosaur to study its scientific significance.)[81]

Between their camp at El Tenejal and the San Juan River, 72.5 miles distant, the party found few distinguishing characteristics marking the countryside and encountered little that was noteworthy. The exception was Church Rock, the prominent sandstone monolith on Macomb's route. Beyond El Tenejal, not far from the dinosaur quarry, the expedition's return trip veered from the Old Spanish Trail and encountered the rock, which Dimmock sketched in his drawing book. From Church Rock the route ran through Peters Canyon along present U.S. Highway 191 and up onto the "Sage-plain." About thirty-two miles south of Casa Colorado and nearly six miles east of the Abajo (or Blue) Mountains, Macomb's men gave the name "Mormon or Silver Spring" to the campsite. Newberry had discovered two silver coins nearby, "proving the white man to have been here before us."[82] Earlier Mormon explorations into the region probably accounts for Newberry's find. In 1854, the W. D. Huntington expedition passed through the area. And the following year, the Elk Mountain Mission, led by Alfred N. Billings, explored the highway route south of Moab.

81. E. D. Cope, "Report upon the extinct Vertebrata obtained in New Mexico by Parties of the Expedition of 1874, Chapter XI, Fossils of the Mesozoic Periods and Tertiary Beds," in George M. Wheeler, *Report upon United States Geographical Surveys west of the One Hundredth Meridian*, vol. 4 (Washington, D.C.: Government Printing Office, 1877), 31–36B, plate 83; E. D. Cope, "On a Dinosaurian from the Trias of Utah," *Proceedings of the American Philosophical Society* 16 (1877): 579–85; F. von Huene, "Dystrophaeus viaemalae Cope in neur Beleuchtung," *Separat-Abdruck aus dem Neuen Jahrbuch für Mineralogie, Geologie und Palaeontologie*, Stuttgart, Germany 19 (1904): 319–33; F. A. Barnes, "Utah's Early Place in Paleontogical History," *Canyon Legacy* 6 (Summer 1990): 12. Ultimately the Smithsonian collected the following fossils: "Scapula, ulna, partial radius, partial manus." The institution claims that the fossils were found in the "Summerville Formation," not the Morrison Formation. See David B. Weishampel, Peter Dodson, and Halszka Osmólska, eds. *The Dinosauria*, 2nd ed., (Berkeley: University of California Press, 2004), Table 13.1. (In layman's terms, the scapula represents the shoulder blade, the ulna and radius bones are found in the lower front leg, and the manus is in the hand. Martha C. Hayden, Utah Geological Survey, interview by author, September 4, 2007.)

82. Dimmock, Diary, August 30, 1859, VHS; Newberry, Abridged Diary, August 30, 1859, NA.

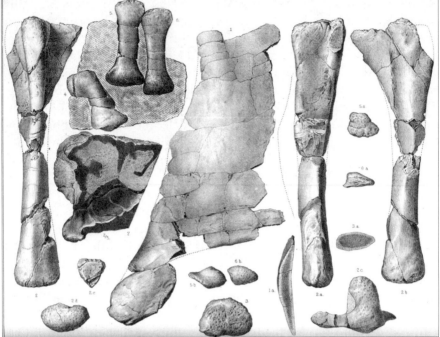

Lithograph of *Dystrophaeus viaemalae* dinosaur fossil bones. Illustrated in Edward D. Cope's report in part two of the Wheeler Survey paleontology report, 1877.

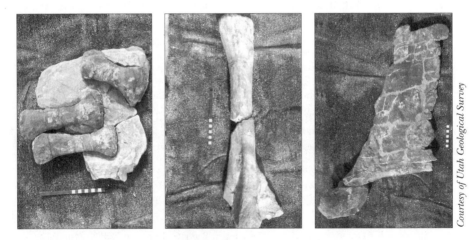

Sauropod dinosaur bone fossils discovered by Dr. John S. Newberry. *Dystrophaeus* metacarpals. *Dystrophaeus* right scapula. *Dystrophaeus* right ulna. One of the bones Newberry extracted measured 31 inches in length, he later recounted

Traversing the Great Sage Plain southward, the Macomb party skirted the eastern perimeter of the Abajo Mountains. Newberry did his scientific work "on three sides of this sierra." He discovered that its highest point rose "some 2,000 feet above the Sage-plain" and trended northwest to southeast. He noted "the sierra is composed geologically of an erupted nucleus" and has an "isolated character."[83]

Beyond the Abajo Mountains, south of today's Blanding, Utah, the expedition turned into the drainage of Recapture Creek and descended that stream as they approached toward the San Juan. Before reaching the creek, at the spring "Ojo del Alamo," the men discovered "fresh Indian tracks." They posted and placed a guard on alert. At Recapture Creek, Dimmock reported that he had become "quite sick." Newberry, the physician, apparently prescribed some unsavory medicine. But the "blue mass" Dimmock took that evening restored his health.[84]

At the San Juan River, some fifty miles east of its junction with the Colorado, Newberry scoped out the striking scenery to the west and south. Describing present Monument Valley, the scenic home to the Navajo straddling the Arizona-Utah border, he wrote, "[There] are many castle-like buttes and slender towers, none of which can be less than 1,000 feet in height, their sides absolutely perpendicular, their forms wonderful imitations of the structures of human art. Illuminated by the setting sun, the outlines of these singular objects came out sharp and distinct, with such exact similitude of art, and contrast with nature as usually displayed, that we could hardly resist the conviction that we beheld the walls and towers of some Cyclopean city hitherto undiscovered in this far-off region."[85]

Newberry reported that the process of erosion that carved out the valleys of the San Juan, Green, and Colorado rivers "left the most surprising monuments of its action." He wrote, "Domes, castles, walls, [and] spires" were among the structures "which by their vivid colors and fantastic outlines attract the attention and excite the wonder of every explorer who beholds them."

With the publication in 1877 of his splendid *Atlas of Colorado*, explorer Ferdinand V. Hayden named a tributary stream that originated in the Abajo Mountains and flowed into the San Juan "Macomb's Cr[eek]," in Macomb's honor. Sadly, the name no longer graces modern maps. Instead, the name Cottonwood Wash emerged and stuck. The present town of Bluff, Utah, now rests at its mouth.

83. Macomb, *Report*, 100.
84. Herbert E. Gregory, *The San Juan Country: A Geographic and Geologic Reconnaissance of Southeastern Utah*, U.S. Geological Survey Professional Paper 188, Washington, D.C.: Government Printing Office, 1938, 2; Dimmock, Diary, August 31, September 1, 1859, VHS.
85. Macomb, *Report*, 104.

Sketch of Church Rock, by Charles H. Dimmock.

Church Rock along U.S. Highway 191 south of Moab, Utah.

East of Bluff, the expedition turned up the north bank of the San Juan, which they ascended for about 120 miles. On September 5 at Camp No. 36, the Macomb party feasted on mutton for breakfast. "Our sheep a great institution," noted Dimmock.[86]

The following day, Dimmock witnessed the increased "turbidity" of the San Juan, swollen "by late rains." The rushing waters nearly swept away the mule train. He wrote, "[As the pack train passed] around the river bluff the mules fared badly. Several fell in the river & one we feared would be a loss[;] he, however, extricated himself. The mule with the Capt's box & my trunk fell from the path rolling over into the water's brink[;] here he was rescued." Dimmock noted that they had reentered New Mexico, en route to their camp, across from which they spotted "extensive ruins." (Newberry had observed, "From the time we struck the San Juan we were never out of sight of ruins.")[87]

At Camp No. 40, nearly seventy miles upriver from the point where Macomb reached the San Juan, Newberry noted the magnificent Ship Rock formation looming above the horizon. "On the south side of the river, now quite near to us, stand out in strong relief the picturesque basaltic pinnacles of 'The Needles. . . .' This is a mass of erupted rock, rising with perpendicular sides from the middle of the valley. From all points, where seen by us, it has the appearance of an immense cathedral, of rich umber-brown color, terminating in two spires. Its altitude is about 1,700 feet above its base."[88]

Dimmock waxed eloquent in his description of Ship Rock:

> Ejected from the long low mesa upon which it rests to a height of 1600 feet, standing alone, this mass of reddish brown trap, with its two spires & buttressed walls, requires no effort of the imagination . . . to distort it into a grander old cathedral than Christendom contains. Its finialed spires, lit by the evening sun, when the plain at the base is lost in the gloaming, seems bearing the mark of divine approbation—a shrine where assembled nations might bow, forgetful in emotions evoked by its presence, of the petty schisms dividing the world. Seen in the distance at midday, looming from its reflected image in the mirage, the fitness of its title is apparent—a phantom ship mirror'd upon a trembling sea.[89]

From this location, they followed the San Juan up to a ridge known as the Creston, a sandstone "upheaval" crossing the river at right angles.

86. Dimmock, Diary, September 5, 1859, VHS.
87. Macomb, *Report*, 109; Dimmock, Diary, September 6, 1859, VHS.
88. Macomb, *Report*, 107.
89. Dimmock, Topographical Memoir, 17, LOC.

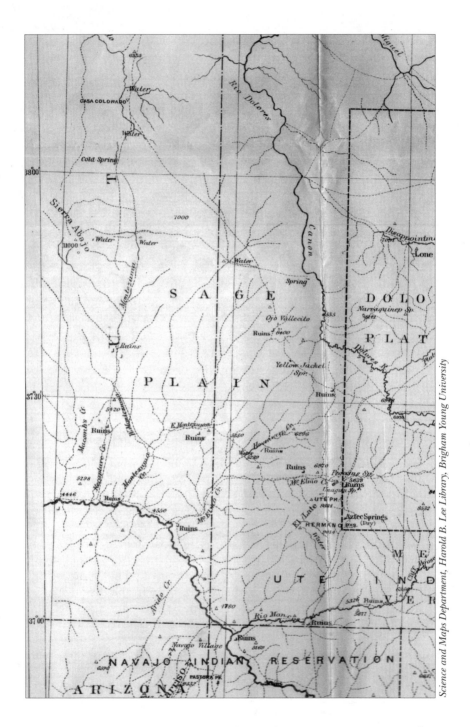

Section of "Drainage Map of Colorado," in F. V. Hayden's *Atlas of Colorado*, 1877, showing "Macomb's Cr[eek]."

(The Creston is the present-day Hogback monocline uplift eighteen miles west of Farmington, New Mexico. The steeply dipping strata define the western edge of the San Juan Basin.) In geologic time the river cut through the ridge to create "a narrow passage, through which we worked our way with extreme difficulty," wrote Newberry.[90]

From the Creston, their route took them through present-day Farmington, New Mexico. At the mouth of the Animas, within today's city limits, Dimmock took a bath in the muddy stream while the camp engaged in washing their clothes.

East of the Animas, the Macomb men found human bones in a Pueblo ruin. One of Newberry's assistants discovered "a well preserved skull." One of the Hispanic hands, "with his usual facility for names[,] calls this [pueblo] the 'Casa de Montezuma,'" wrote Dimmock.[91]

Several miles upstream from the ruin, the Macomb expedition reached the San Juan River ford, near today's town of Blanco, New Mexico. Opposite the mouth of Cañon Largo, the men crossed the San Juan in a "passage swift, deep and dangerous." The strong current swept down two of Lieutenant Cogswell's mules and one of his men, "who was saved, as usual, by Antonio," wrote Dimmock. The perilous crossing cost the expedition "the pack of one of the mules," containing "two sacks of bacon." Dimmock added, "The mules were with difficulty rescued." The group then began the ascent of Cañon Largo, "one of the longest dry washes in the world."[92]

At Camp No. 46 within the canyon, on the Old Spanish Trail's Southern Route, Dimmock gathered flower seeds and petrified wood, presumably for Newberry's collections. Dimmock reported finding the petrified wood "in cords." During the night, Navajos stole two horses belonging to the "Mex. packers." The deed was apparently done by "some of Kyatano's band in retaliation for those taken from him by the Utes with us, Aug. 4th," wrote Dimmock.[93]

At the next camp, the men awoke to icy conditions, "every thing out white with frost," noted Dimmock. "Ice in the basin," he added. At breakfast, the men crouched by the "cook's fire" while Macomb sat alone at the table. "In a spirit of self martyrization," he would not allow the men to build a fire as they dressed and struck camp. The following morning, at the next camp near the head of Cañon Largo, "Vail got one of the men to make us a fire so we breakfasted comfortably," wrote Dimmock.

90.   Macomb, *Report*, 107; Dimmock, Diary, September 9, 1859, VHS.
91.   Dimmock, Diary, September 13, 1859, VHS.
92.   Ibid., September 15, 1859, VHS; Anne Marie Matherne, "Effects of Roads and Well Pads on Erosion in the Largo Canyon Watershed, New Mexico, 2001–02," *U.S. Geological Survey Scientific Investigations Report 2006-5039*, http://pubs.usgs.gov/sir/2006/5039 (accessed May 5, 2007).
93.   Dimmock, Diary, September 16, 17, 1859, VHS.

Photo by author

The "Creston," or present Hogback monocline, in northern New Mexico.

Warmed by the fire, Dimmock recounted a local legend: "El alto del a Utah, across the valley, north-east from Camp 48, is a considerable hill, from whose rocky summit the Navajoes [*sic*] have hurled to sudden death their Ute captives."[94]

Proceeding southeast from Cañon Largo, the men left the Old Spanish Trail and ascended a narrow plain, gently sloping up to the Continental Divide along today's U.S. Highway 550. They crossed the divide at an elevation of approximately 7,380 feet and bore southeast toward the Sierra Nacimiento, or "'mountain of birth,' from whence flows the water into the Atlantic & Pacific." Newberry reported, "Just before reaching the base of the Nacimiento Mountain, we crossed the divide between the Pacific and Atlantic, and reached the highest point, geologically, attained on any part of our route." In the early morning of September 21, within three miles of the base of Nacimiento Mountain, Macomb observed "an eclipse of one of Jupiter's sattelites [*sic*]."[95]

In the valley west of Nacimiento Mountain, they reached the waters birthed by that mountain, the Rio Puerco. Dimmock observed, "Locality delightful &, for a treat, *clear, cool, water.*" Nearby, Newberry described

94.   Ibid., September 18, 19, 1859; Dimmock, Topographical Memoir, 20, LOC.
95.   Dimmock, Diary, September 20, 21, 1859, VHS; Macomb, *Report*, 112.

Rock profile in Cañon Largo, New Mexico.

Sketch of a rock profile in Cañon Largo, New Mexico, by Charles H. Dimmock.

Photo by author

Courtesy of Margaret Jones Perritt and the Virginia Historical Society

the view of the Cabezon (or Big Head), which he sketched for the Macomb report: "The most conspicuous" of the "many picturesque trap buttes . . . resembles in its outline a Spanish sombrero, but it is of gigantic dimensions, being at least 1,500 feet in height."[96] Dimmock took the cue and made his own pencil sketch of the formation.

The following morning, camped at the junction of two Rio Puerco tributaries, near present Cuba, New Mexico, Macomb sent out an exploratory party to find an alternate trail "through the vias," the Sierra de los Valles, to Santa Fé. He wished to bypass the route that ran through Jemez Pueblo and sent Armijo, Johnson, Campeau, and "2 *Mex[ican]s*" to explore a pathway. But their attempt failed, and they returned to camp. "Not finding a trail induces the Capt. to continue with Cogswell's command,"

96. Macomb, *Report*, 117; Dimmock, Diary, September 20, 1859, VHS.

wrote Dimmock. However, on the march south, crossing the headwaters of the Puerco, the guide, "Old Jaramillo, evidenced an entire ignorance of the country to day, carrying us over the worst places," wrote Dimmock. They "crossed by a steep and difficult pass" a southern spur of Nacimiento Mountain. (Dimmock noted that from the pass, the Nacimiento "still extends some 8 miles to South.")[97] Both Newberry and Dimmock observed white gypsum deposits on either side of the crest.

When Macomb's men reached old Jemez Pueblo, Dimmock gave a negative portrayal of the village and its inhabitants:

> The Padre [is] a rascally Mex. Priest who practices upon the liquor-drinking and credulity of those around him to no small advantage to himself. The Pueblo a squalid collection of adobe houses. Ovens, before the houses, conical in form, built of adobes. In some of these the fires for baking were seen, others were occupied by naked, filthy children while many seemed, for the time being, in quiet occupancy by the dogs. These dogs are disgusting objects, apparently a mingling of the meanest cur with the still more detestable Coyote. Three bears were killed by the Indians shortly after our arrival who were deprecating their corn fields. Over these the Indians had a grand dance.[98]

The bears were "grizzly bears," wrote Newberry. That evening, Dimmock reported that they "were visited by Hasta the chief of the Pueblo, an intelligent, shrewd fellow, very talkative."[99] He lamented that the expedition's Hispanic hands "were nearly all drunk," particularly the "old guide."

After spending the night in a "damp & uncomfortable" camp, full of sand burrs, the expedition parted company with the military escort, led by Lieutenant Cogswell, —who had transformed himself into a martinet of sorts. The departure of the escort "seemed a source of general satisfaction, as the Lieut. had, by his manner, afforded just cause for a distaste evidenced towards him by every member of the party, save the Capt.," reported Dimmock. He continued, "His command goes to Fort Fillmore." Cogswell had apparently stirred resentment throughout the march—ordering the bugler to sound reveille at an "absurd hour," as early as 4 AM.

---

97. Dimmock, Diary, September 22, 23, 1859, VHS; Newberry, Abridged Diary, September 25, 1859, NA; Dimmock, Topographical Memoir, 22, LOC.

98. Dimmock, Diary, September 25, 1859, VHS. Bishop Jean Baptiste Lamy on his arrival in New Mexico Territory in 1854 found ten Catholic priests, whom he recognized as "neglectful and extortionate, churches in ruins and no schools." See "New Mexico Magazine's timeline of important dates" at http://www.nmmagazine.com/NMGUIDE/memorias4.html (accessed June 8, 2007).

99. Newberry, Abridged Diary, September 25, 1859, NA; Dimmock, Diary, September 25, 1859, VHS.

Charles Dimmock Papers, Special Collections Research Center, College of William and Mary

Sketch of the Cabezon (Big Head), by Charles H. Dimmock.

Photo by author

The Cabezon in the valley of the Rio Puerco, New Mexico.

Earlier in the expedition, Dimmock complained about the unwelcome summons. He wrote, "All in ill humour at being waked so early" He continued, "To bed early as we are to start before sunrise tomorrow . . . This is a notion of Cogswell's, who feels the authority confided by the Capt."[100]

Since Macomb considered Cogswell a friend, this unhappy circumstance must have been embarrassingly difficult for him.

Leaving Jemez Pueblo, the expedition "jogged along" a road built for wagon traffic and crossed the divide between the Jemez River and the Rio Grande. At the summit, Dimmock waxed rapturous in his description of the countryside, "one of unusual beauty and grandeur."

> In front towered the Santa Fe Mts. whose tops were snow
> crowned. Conspicuous among the confreres of the chain, the
> Bald raised his superior front, con[s]cious of the awe & hom-
> age the lesser peaks seem crowded around to give as 'Mt. Blanc
> is the monarch of mountains, They crown'd him long ago, On
> a throne of Rocks, in a Robe of Clouds, with a diadem of snow,'
> so reigns he, supreme. To our right the Sandia swelled from the
> vale in huge proportions. A mountain mass of jagged pin[n]
> acles & fearful precipices raised high by the throes of mother
> earth above her surface.[101]

Beyond the divide, the expedition followed "along the table land approaching the Rio Grande" and reached the river just opposite the pueblo Santo Domingo. Dimmock described what happened next: "The Indians soon thronged around us, coming over the River with melons, corn & chilli to sell. One quite pretty girl sold her peppers for 37 ½¢ & offering her my ring (signet) for that amount she tried it on[,] looked admirably but refused the silver."[102]

Early the next day, the expedition crossed the Rio Grande with the help of the local tribe. Dimmock reported, "Much sho[u]ting for the Indians to come over with their boat. Soon made their appearance with the rudest but strongest square built affair by means of which the[y] carried us & our camp equipage across the Rio Grande in three loads. The Indians were up to their middles in water during half or three quarters of an hour talking vehemently all the time."[103] After crossing the river, Macomb's men went into the village and engaged in trading. Dimmock bought himself a blanket for twelve dollars. Newberry, Fisher, and Dorsey

---

100. Dimmock, Diary, September 26, 1859, VHS. See also Dimmock, Diary, August 9, 27, 1859, VHS.
101. Ibid., September 26, 1859, VHS. Dimmock quoted Lord Byron in his dramatic poem *Manfred* (act I, scene 1, line 62).
102. Dimmock, Diary, September 26, 1859, VHS.
103. Ibid., September 27, 1859, VHS.

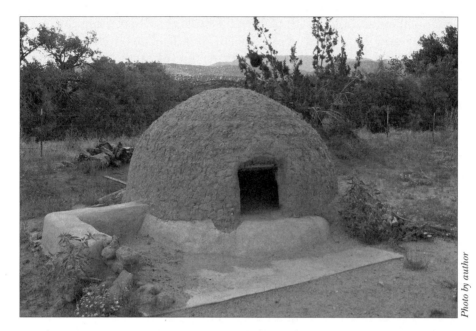

Photo by author

Jemez Pueblo oven.

"procured mocassins."[104] Today, Santo Domingo Pueblo lies between the I-25 corridor and the upper Rio Grande. In an obvious attempt to preserve its way of life and maintain the privacy of its people, the pueblo posts a warning to all visitors. The large sign, prominently placed in the center of the village, prohibits outsiders from recording their experiences in any format.

The homeward-bound expedition passed through Santo Domingo at midday and marched along the mesa top, with "no vegetation, nothing to mark the monotonous plain." They camped in cold and windy conditions along the Rio de Santa Fé, on a treeless, high plain, twelve and a half miles from Santa Fé. To build a fire, they found a corral nearby and dismantled it. "Hungry as wolves," they ate a late supper. The captain's mood reflected the dreary conditions. Dimmock recorded, "Capt. in bad humour & cross." The men "had to set him back to first principles."[105]

Macomb's command unraveled the following morning, on September 28. His civilian employees—Newberry, Dimmock, Dorsey, Fisher, and Vail—left his company and hurried on to Santa Fé. Macomb and the rest of his men marched with the mule train to Camp No. 57, at the Arroyo

104. Ibid.
105. Ibid.

Hondo, some six miles south of the city center. (Months earlier, Governor Rencher and his invited guests held a grand picnic at this location.) Macomb "expressed his resolve to establish himself" at the Arroyo Hondo, "until leaving for the States." Newberry rushed into the city, picked up the mail, and rode down to Arroyo Hondo to deliver the letters to the men in camp before returning to Santa Fé.

With trembling hands and moisture-filled eyes, Dimmock carefully opened the dozen letters from his wife and, adhering to their chronological order, read and reread them. Said he, "To me my darling little wife has endeared herself tenfold more, if possible, by her letters & conduct during my absence. A sense of utter unworthiness overcomes me when thinking of her gentle, loving goodness & kindness to all, contrasted with my habitual acerbity & asceticism."[106]

That evening, Macomb rode into the city and offered Newberry and Dimmock the "use of his room while we remain in this place." The following evening, Dimmock reported that the captain "concludes to remain in town himself."[107]

Finally, on October 1 Dimmock wrote, "Boys from Camp in. Hands, most of them, drunk." Two days later, Macomb, Fisher, and Vail rode out to Camp No. 57 to "take observations." On October 16 Dimmock recorded that "Fisher & Co[mpany]" arrived in Santa Fé from their camp at Arroyo Hondo, Fisher having made his final astronomical observations.[108]

106. Dimmock, Diary, September 28, 1859, VHS.
107. Ibid., September 28, 29, 1859, VHS.
108. Ibid., October 1, 3, 16, 1859, VHS; "San Juan River Survey: Astronomical and Barometrical Observation, 1859," October 8, 1859, NA.

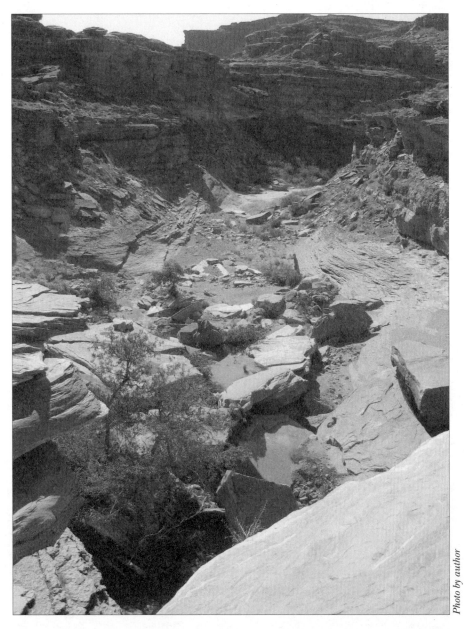

"Perpendicular fall" in Indian Creek Canyon that blocked the expedition's attempt to reach the confluence.

THE EXPEDITION'S
AFTERMATH

At journey's end, much work remained for the men of the Macomb expedition as they prepared for their homeward travel. The Army required Macomb to settle his accounts before he returned to Washington. In addition to selling off surplus provisions and equipment to balance the books, he needed to assemble a wagon train and arrange for a military escort to accompany him to Fort Leavenworth. He anticipated that all of his civil employees would accompany him on his homebound path, but two sought to convince the captain that they needed to travel a faster and, seemingly, less dangerous route home. Meanwhile, Macomb and his men faced the "hurry and wait" routine of military life.

Soon after his arrival in Santa Fé, Macomb expedited a letter to the War Department reporting "the safe return of my party to this place, from the Exploration of the Rio San Juan &c."[1] On September 30, he wrote his wife, "You will rejoice with me that I am once more safely on the East Side of the Rio Bravo Grande del Norte! I reached Santa Fé on the day before yesterday having been absent just eleven weeks."[2] Macomb continued, "I am now surrounded by the luggage & am more or less disturbed by the process of packing and unpacking & occasional calls upon me for money &c to say nothing of my anxiety to sell the animals & other property we have used on the expedition."[3]

In Santa Fé Dimmock drew his salary and promptly sent funds home to Emmy. He grew increasingly impatient for home: "Feel fidgety as possible.

1. Macomb to Humphreys, October 3, 1859, NA.
2. John Macomb to "Nannie" Macomb, September 30, 1859, LOC.
3. Ibid.

Can[']t remain ten minutes in one place. Fact is I want to go home & can[']t endure this delay."[4]

Perhaps to help pass the time, Dimmock retraced for Macomb "a wretched map of the surveys (land) executed in this Territory up to last January." (William Pelham, New Mexico's surveyor general, may have drawn the original map.) In addition, he spent time visiting local merchants James Johnson and Joseph "Joe" Mercure. From Johnson, Dimmock procured a set of earrings for his wife. Mercure and his brother, Henry, operated a store in town. In addition, Mercure had helped Newberry acquire several minerals and ores, including *chalchuitl*—"a variety of turquoise"—for the Ives expedition, which Newberry acknowledged in his final report.[5]

The War Department directed Macomb, on his "return to Santa Fé to reduce my party and come in to Washington to prepare my report."[6] Macomb began at once packing the expedition's instruments and specimens for shipment to Washington. His civil assistants engaged in packing trunks and repacking the geological specimens for the long haul.

Macomb lost no time in selling the expedition's mules and other property to balance their finances. To settle his accounts as fiscal agent, he sold at public auction and private sales "property belonging to the appropriations for 'Surveys for Military Defences &c.'" This included burros ($20 each), U.S. army trousers for mounted troops ($4.92 a pair), spurs ($1.10 a pair), lariats ($1 each), saddles ($6 each), rifles ($5 each), screwdriver (46 ¢), canteen (48 ¢), bootees or army footwear ($1.88 a pair), screw-top tin cans (50 ¢ each), and several apothecary items including mercurial ointment, Epsom salts, adhesive plaster, citric acid, iodine, camphor, arsenic, and opium. (Opium was used to treat diarrhea and dysentery.)[7]

The Army scrimped on virtually every expense, including salaries. Prior to the expedition, Judge Joab Houghton had been Captain Macomb's principal road construction assistant, receiving little remuneration for his yeoman efforts. Macomb petitioned the government to grant him better wages, to no avail. Judge Houghton left to strike it rich in the Pike's Peak gold rush. Following the expedition, Dimmock learned that Houghton had returned from the placer mines with "a little gold."[8]

Back in Santa Fé, far from the gold fields, Dimmock witnessed a wealth of degradation at the Fonda Hotel. Fighting, drinking, gambling and prostitution abounded within its walls. "To get drunk[,] gamble & fornicate

4. Dimmock, Diary, September 29, 1859, VHS.
5. Ibid., October 1, 1859, VHS.
6. Macomb, *Report*, 7.
7. "The United States in ac. with J. N. M. for San Juan Exploration," Letterbook, pages 74–75, [Macomb's accounts for 3rd quarter, 1859], NA.
8. Dimmock, Diary, October 6, 1859, VHS; Macomb to Col. J. J. Abert, September 29, 1858, Letters Received, Bureau of Topographical Engineers, War Department Records, NA.

seems absolutely the only duties of four-fifths of those who board here, at the Fonda." He was horrified by the "advances in the complicated forms of sinning as are here to be found. Plain sin is esteemed puerile & contemptible." Cogswell repeatedly overimbibed and called on Dimmock in his hotel room, much to his chagrin. Longing for home one night, Dimmock retired for bed "blue & miserable."[9]

Newberry seemingly felt the same way, although he continued to actively study the complicated geological structure of the area surrounding Santa Fé. He wrote, "The three months spent in the vicinity of Santa Fé during the past season by our party have . . . not been entirely without value."

Some highlights from Newberry's geological report reveal his efforts both before and after the expedition in confronting head-on the geology in the area of Santa Fé. Nevertheless, he confessed that "many questions are left unsettled." He reported, "Though I have examined outcrops of granite in many thousand different localities, I have never seen even a hand[-sized] specimen similar in character to the red granite of the Rocky Mountains." In the Santa Fe Mountains he found "bright brick-red" granite. He also found "light-colored, grey or white" granite in the same mountains. Furthermore, "veins of quartz and epidite are very common in the granite." In the region immediately about Santa Fé, Newberry also observed "repositories of . . . copper, lead, silver, and gold."

The Santa Fe Mountains, he observed, appeared "comparatively short" next to "most of the ranges" of the Rockies. The mountains extended possibly fifty or sixty miles to the north. On the south, the Santa Fe Range "falls off abruptly near Santa Fé" and is "represented at a distant point by some of the mountain chains which lie east of the Rio Grande." Among the mountain chains to the south stood the Sandia and Placer mountains.

The Los Cerrillos represented "a group of hills or small mountains between Santa Fé and the Placer Mountains, on the north side of Galisteo Creek," Newberry explained. The mountains appeared eruptive in nature. He discovered "many old mines worked by the Spaniards or Indians." The mines contained "gold, silver, lead, copper, iron, and turquoise or 'chalchuitl.'" The turquoise minerals "are rather abundant, but most of it is of inferior quality," he wrote. "I have seen ornaments of it worn by the Apache, Mohaves, the Navajoes [sic] and Pueblos, and so highly prized that a fragment of fine quality no larger than the nail of one's little finger and one-eighth of an inch in thickness was regarded as worth a mule or a good horse."

After much fieldwork, Newberry finally ended his geological studies of the Santa Fé district. Eager to get home, he and Dimmock pleaded

9.   Dimmock, Diary, October 6, 1859, VHS.

Photo by author

Santa Fé's present La Fonda bears no resemblance to the
original one-story Fonda, or Exchange Hotel.

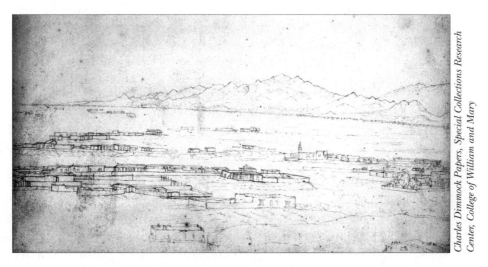

*Charles Dimmock Papers, Special Collections Research
Center, College of William and Mary*

A rare nineteenth century view of Santa Fé, New Mexico,
by Charles H. Dimmock.

102   Exploring Desert Stone

with Macomb to grant them an early departure by stagecoach, rather than traveling back east in a slow wagon caravan accompanied by troops. Macomb ultimately consented.

Before their departure, Dimmock met with Pfeiffer and Nepomuceno and a delegation of Ute leaders—from the Muache, Tabuache, and Capote Ute bands, which included "Tamuche (the rascal)." Quoting Pfeiffer, Dimmock buttressed his view of Temuché: "'Tamuche [sic] has a big conscience—a six horse team could turn in it.' By this he means an entire want of honesty—a pliable conscience." Following the parley, Dimmock presented gifts to both Pfeiffer and Nepomuceno.[10]

After bidding farewell to his associates, Dimmock embarked on his homeward journey, accompanying Newberry on the Eastern Mail Stage. Initially, they took the route up the Santa Fe Trail, but Indian hostilities beyond Pecos forced their return. Dimmock "learned that 20 miles on our road a band of robbers (one American & six Mexicans) have been committing general outrages."

Worried that the stage from the East had failed to make its required connection with the outbound stage, Dimmock wrote, "Nothing now remains but for us to return to Santa Fé & await further developments."

Four days later, Dimmock and Newberry boarded the Southern Mail Stage crowded with judges and lawyers bound for El Paso, via the historic "Jornada del Muerto" route. Included in the group was Judge John S. Watts's son, John, and Jimmy Edgar, John's new brother-in-law. (At a stage rest stop, Edgar offered fellow passengers some leftover cake from his sister's recent wedding to John's brother, Joshua Howe Watts.)[11]

Crowded together on the stage, it appears that Dimmock borrowed a book from young Watts, Pendennis, by William Makepeace Thackeray. Another book he read on his homeward journey was Life of Baron Trenck. He also "tried a specimen of yellow covered literature but abandoned it in disgust before reading 40 pages."[12]

Three hundred fifty-two miles from Santa Fé, the passengers reached El Paso. On his arrival, Dimmock decided to visit "Old El Paso, in Chihuahua, Mexico." He noted: "The town not much, but country around beautiful. Vineyards for miles around but hardly tended. Would make as fine a wine country as any in Europe." He subsequently bought four bottles of Vino di Carlow, which he shared with Newberry. (We learn from young John Watts that his father also procured two bottles of the local wine for a friend in Ohio.)[13]

10. Ibid., October 7, 1859, VHS.
11. Ibid., October 19, 1859, VHS; Remley, "Adios Nuevo Mexico," 201–203, 212, 215–16.
12. Dimmock, Diary, October 20, 28, 30, 1859, VHS; Remley, "Adios Nuevo Mexico," 7.
13. Dimmock, Diary, October 23, November 1, 1859, VHS; Remley, "Adios Nuevo Mexico," 216.

Photo by author

The Pecos mission church ruins in Pecos National
Historical Park, New Mexico.

Dropping to sleep one night on his "grid iron" bed, or "Guatamozin's
couch of agony," Dimmock overheard a girl singing outside. "[I] was
aroused by the sweetest voice, in a placito adjoining, gushing in strains
of the wildest melancholy—Softly trembling as with the last cadence of
a forsaken Dove or swelling with the power of pain pressed Philomela."

Sleepless nights seemed the least of Dimmock's concerns. Beyond El
Paso, potential dangers loomed on the horizon. Raiding parties threatened to disrupt their overland journey. Although the Army had built a
chain of military posts along the two routes leading east from El Paso to
safeguard overland traffic, frontier forces failed to discourage attacks on
travelers. Moreover, the frequent sensational stories from stage drivers
haunted the traveling public.

One driver from San Antonio arrived without passengers and claimed
that "1300 Indians on the Stake Plains . . . refuse to permit passage of
the overland Stage & . . . the passengers are all collected at one of the
Stations fearing to go on." Two days later, another driver told "of one
Station of mules having been run off by the Comanches since the passing
of the last mail."

On the next leg of their homeward journey, Dimmock and Newberry
chose to take the "lower road," a presumably safer way, on the San Antonio

to El Paso route. After spending 25¢ to ferry the Rio Grande, they each paid $100 to travel "to New Orleans from El Paso," via San Antonio. The first day proved wretched. Their stagecoach "was upset," and Dimmock found himself "undermost" the other passengers. "Fortunately no one injured," he added. At one of the stage stops, Dimmock wrote: "Meal oh! most miserable, but 50¢ for everything." That night the station failed to provide passengers with any beds, so Dimmock "spread [him]self on the counter of a [sixpenny] store & went to sleep."

On the rest of the trip of six hundred miles, they fared better. The road took them across the southern stretch of the Llano Estacado desert plateau and over the colorful Wild Rose Pass. They stopped at stage stations and at several U.S. Infantry posts—Fort Quitman, Fort Davis, Fort Lancaster, Fort Hudson, and Fort Clark.

Arriving at San Antonio, Dimmock described the city as "a strag[g]ling mixture of Stone[,] frame & adobe buildings. Some of the buildings constructed of a drab limestone are striking & architectural." In his diary, he made a random note of the frontier artist/photographer "W. H. Jackson, San Antonio, Texas."[14]

On the distant horizon beyond San Antonio, Dimmock and Newberry faced the possibility of more trouble. Juan Cortina (1824–1894) and his militant force had recently raided and captured Brownsville in retaliation for racist violence against local Texas Hispanics. Turmoil seemed likely to spread to other parts of Texas and engulf the region in bloodshed. (Cortina's war against Anglo racism ultimately launched his legendary fame.)[15]

Dimmock and Newberry chose an indirect course eastward from San Antonio by passing Cortina's uprising. They traveled by stage to Indianola, Texas, where they boarded the steamer *Matagorda*. (*Matagorda* later played a minor role in the Civil War, when it became a "blockade runner.") On board the paddle wheeler they wiled away the time playing cards as they navigated the Gulf Coast to Berwick's Bay via the wharf at Galveston. Both men avoided entering the city, which was in the grip of a yellow fever epidemic. Riding on the New Orleans and Appaloosas Railroad, they reached New Orleans, where they boarded and dined at the historic St. Charles Hotel.

From New Orleans, they resumed their eastward journey on the New Orleans and Jackson Railroad. Near Canton, Mississippi, they were forced

14. Dimmock, Diary, November Bills Payable and entries October 31–November 9, 1859, VHS.

15. Ibid., November 13 1859, VHS; "Juan Cortina (1824–1892)," PBS: The West, http://www.pbs. org/weta/thewest/people/a_c/cortina.html (accessed December 29 2007); Sonal Panse, "The Robinhood of the Rio Grande," http://www.buzzle.com/editorials/5-8-2004-53894.asp (accessed December 29, 2007).

Courtesy of Margaret Jones Perritt

Charles H. Dimmock in Richmond, Virginia, ca.
1861. Photo by C. R. Rees.

to take a stage to Duck Hill station on the Mississippi Central Railroad. From Duck Hill, they traveled to Grand Junction, Tennessee, where they parted company. Newberry took the Mobile and Ohio to Cairo, Illinois, and beyond, and Dimmock continued his zigzag course homeward.

Arriving at Stevenson, Alabama, Dimmock reached the terminus of the Mississippi Central and boarded "the Eastern going train," the Memphis and Charleston Railroad, which passed through Chattanooga toward Knoxville, Tennessee. Beyond Knoxville, he continued to Bristol, where he took the Virginia and Tennessee Railroad to Lynchburg. From Lynchburg, he took the "South Side cars" to the Danville Railroad Junction via Farmville, crossing the famous landmark, High Bridge, over the Appomattox River. At the railroad junction, he changed cars and moved on to Richmond, Virginia, where he stopped to visit his parents "at the Armory at tea" and to send a telegraph to his wife. Three days later, on November 22, he arrived home in Baltimore.[16]

16.   Dimmock, Diary, "Memoranda" and entry for November 19, 1859, VHS.

Not long after his arrival in Baltimore, it seems that his wife, Emmy, died in childbirth. However, the baby, christened Emily Moale Dimmock, survived. A widower and the father of two children, Dimmock decided to move to Richmond to be near his parents.[17]

In Richmond, Dimmock opened a law office and resumed his legal profession. Influenced in part by his father's military ties to Virginia, Dimmock over time became a Southern sympathizer. (Nevertheless, during his stay in Santa Fé with the Macomb expedition, he had refused to enter into a heated slavery debate among the civil engineers, stating: "[I] took no part [in the debate] as these contests engender ill feeling while the[y] change no one's opinion.")[18]

Newberry returned to his home in Cleveland on November 15 "after a long and wearisome journey from Santa Fé by way of El Paso, San Antonio, & New Orleans." He wrote his friend Baird at the Smithsonian, "We had a very pleasant & interesting expedition, and in geology particularly the results exceeded my expectations—In Zoology my efforts were rendered nearly fruitless by the barrenness of the field and the constant rains I fear you will be disappointed in my collections—but I assure you I did my *possible*— I hope to be with you within a month with Capt. Macomb & the collections—He is coming slowly across the plains to Ft. Leavenworth."[19]

Before setting off for his home in Washington, D.C., Macomb wrote his wife about his prospects for returning to New Mexico. Said he: "I trust I never shall." He also assured his wife, "We have *guns* and *pistols* enough to make it very uncomfortable for the indians in case they should determine to attack us."[20] The U.S. Army had ordered Macomb on his return trip "to stop at the southwest corner of the Territory of Kansas, to set up a new monument at a point some two and a quarter miles to the east of the one originally placed there."

Unaware of the full impact of his work, in mid-November 1859, with twelve men—including Louis Dorsey, Francis Fisher, and James Vail—and a military escort, Macomb veered from the Santa Fe Trail and "erected a rough stone monument" at the intersection of the 37th parallel and "the meridian of 103°." A regiment of thirty-five mounted riflemen and three non-commissioned officers, led by Lt. H. M. Enos, provided his "safe transit to Fort Leavenworth."[21] Ultimately, Macomb's monument played an important role in the establishment of the boundary between New Mexico and Colorado, later disputed in the U. S. Supreme Court.[22]

---

17. Dimmock, Papers, 1850–1873, Section 11, Obituaries, VHS.
18. Ibid:, Dimmock, Diary, June 22, 1859, VHS.
19. Newberry to Baird, November 25, 1859, SIA.
20. John Macomb to "Nannie" Macomb, September 30, October 23, 1859, LOC.
21. Macomb, *Report*, 7–8.
22. U.S. Supreme Court, *State of N. M. v. State of Colo.*, 267 U.S. 30 (1925).

Virginia Museum of Fine Arts, Richmond. The Virginiana Fund. Photo by Katherine Wetzel, © Virginia Museum of Fine Arts

High Bridge near Farmville, Virginia

Beyond the Colorado-New Mexico border the train returned to the Santa Fe Trail and made its way to Fort Leavenworth, where Macomb intended to sell his remaining outfit—"to come in out of debt." The Macomb train consisted of two wagons, a carriage, and an "old vehicle I have used here ever since I came with *power* in this country," he quipped. On December 8, 1859, Macomb stopped at the fort and sold twenty-three mules, one bell mare, and harnesses to "Falkerson & Elliott" for $1,185. Although the fort did not want the wagons he offered, the total sales of property "no longer required for the use of the Exp[editio]n" came to $3,684.39.[23]

Macomb arrived in Washington in mid-December, where he stayed for more than a year to prepare his report of the expedition. He submitted a preliminary report, published by the U.S. Senate, which announced "there is no practicable route from the settlements of New Mexico to those of Utah." Americans were also told that the expedition had made "valuable geographical and other scientific" contributions to mankind's body of knowledge. But unforeseen events would disrupt the writing and publication of the final report.[24]

23. John Macomb to "Nannie" Macomb, October 23, 1859, LOC; Macomb to "Quartermaster General, U.S. Army, Washington, D.C.," December 22, 1859, NA; "The United States in ac. with J. N. M. for San Juan Exploration," Letterbook, 74–75, [Macomb's accounts for 3rd quarter, 1859], NA.
24. See Capt. A. A. Humphreys, "Report of the Office of Explorations and Surveys," in *Report of the Secretary of War*, Senate Executive Document 1, vol. 2, 36th Cong., 2d sess., serial no. 1079 (Washington, D.C., 1860), 146–52.

THE BONES
AND THE MAP

Additional challenges awaited Macomb and Newberry following their safe return to their homes in the East. Macomb needed to oversee the completion of a final report of the expedition. A high-quality, large-scale map, based on information from Dimmock's exemplary fieldwork, that fully depicted the region explored by Macomb had to be created. But who would take on the task? Artifacts and other materials gathered by Macomb's men needed to be submitted to the Smithsonian Institution. In addition, experts in various scientific endeavors needed to study the specimens collected by Newberry and issue their own reports. With a looming Civil War, would Newberry be able to complete his assigned task? Moreover, would Macomb see the fruits of his labors?

In February 1860, Newberry sent Dr. Joseph Leidy, secretary of the Smithsonian Institution, "three boxes of bones from the Jurassic rocks of south[er]n Utah." In his letters to Dr. Leidy, Newberry begged him to write an article on the dinosaur fossils he had discovered for inclusion in the expedition's published report.[1] For unexplained reasons, Leidy failed to do so.

That year, Newberry also sent the Smithsonian several examples of ancient pottery he collected from New Mexico, Colorado, and Utah, including a stone hammer, arrowheads, and a flint saw from ruins on the San Juan River. This collection, however, was overlooked.[2] Furthermore,

---

1. Newberry to Dr. Joseph Leidy, January 17, February 8, 20, 1860, July 15, September 6, 1861, College of Physicians of Philadelphia.
2. "Ancient Pottery from New Mexico, Collected by Dr. J. S. Newberry," accession number 291, 1860, Record Unit 305, Office of Registrar, U.S. National Museum, SIA.

A. S. National Museum.

CARD CATALOGUE OF ACCESSIONS.

Macomb, Capt. J. N.

DATE.	Acc. No.	Cat. No.	NATURE OF OBJECT.	LOCALITY.
1860	27		Eleven boxes of Geol. & nat. Hist. Coll'n,	N Mexico
1860	35		Two spec'ms. Zoology.	San Juan
"	38		Skins of mammals.	N Mexico

Courtesy of the Smithsonian Institution Archives

U.S. National Museum Accession Record, 1860. John N. Macomb's contribution to the Smithsonian Institution.

by late November, the Smithsonian seemed to have lost the plants that Newberry had gathered on the expedition. He wrote a terse note to the staff: "McCombs [*sic*] plants you engaged to send to Dr [John] Torrey last spring did you not? I will write to Dr T. immediately about them and see if he can catalogue them for our report. If not, Dr. Engelmann will take them up at once." Newberry then hesitated: "They had perhaps better be left for the present."[3] (Later, Newberry visited Dr. Torrey "to look over the plants we collected." He noted that Torrey "will make a brief report" on the plants "without compensation." Torrey "would like some 5 or 6 plates to represent the new species if he can find any one to make the drawings. the cost would be about $50," added Newberry. But Torrey never issued his report.)[4]

The following year, Macomb asked the War Department for additional funds to make a chemical analysis of the mineral ores "now deposited at the Smithsonian Institution" and to make illustrations of specimens gathered on the expedition, which he hoped to include in his report. (In 1860, Macomb had submitted skins of mammals, eleven boxes of geological and natural history collections from New Mexico, and two zoological specimens from the San Juan River to the Smithsonian.)[5]

Accompanying his request, he reported the discovery of gold in the region, "A new interest has lately been given to the scene of our exploration from the fact that gold has been discovered, a short distance northward of it, in such quantities as to induce a considerable immigration thither,

3. Newberry to "Professor," Washington, D.C., November 27, 1860, SIA.
4. Newberry to Macomb, July 26, 1861, NA.
5. Macomb to Humphreys, February 15, 1861, NA; Capt. J. [N.] Macomb, accession number 027, 1860, Record Unit 305, Office of Registrar, U.S. National Museum, SIA.

and already we hear of the establishing of a settlement at the 'Pagosa' near our upper crossing of the San Juan."[6]

Nothing came of Macomb's petition. Moreover, following their return to Washington, the beginning of the Civil War diverted the explorers' energies and drew the attention away from the summations of the expedition. The three principal explorers would leave their homes to serve in the war.

However, as late as July 5,1861, Newberry was still revising the report. He complained to Macomb that his notes were "too long at one End and too short at the other—too much on the country East of Santa Fé—too little West—I have now omitted all East of Santa Fé and the Rio Grande. The Western notes I trust will be of some little help to you."[7]

In late July 1861, Newberry wrote Macomb to report his progress:

> I believe I said to you that I could hand in my report complete by the end of September and that I should like $100 for drawings. The M.S. [manuscript] is all written except the final chapter and the descriptions of some of the new species. These with the drawings which are giving me much trouble will I fear occupy all of the interval between the present time and the time specified—I am however doing my best to hurry on the work and it shall be done just as soon as possible, and have it well done. September I expect to spend in Washington and shall there be busy with our geological map & sections.—and in putting my report in perfect order for the printer.[8]

Newberry's geological map never made it into the final report.

When the government suspended the publication of the expedition's findings, Newberry lamented, "Much most valuable information in regard to the far West has been lost to the country and to the world."[9] (The Macomb report could not have been issued at the outset of the Civil War without the accompanying map, which was not completed until 1863 and made public the following year. Moreover, it's possible that the delay in

6.   Macomb to Humphreys, February 15, 1861, NA.
7.   Newberry to Macomb, July 5, 1861, NA.
8.   Ibid., July 26, 1861.
9.   Macomb, *Report*, 13. In his "Geological Report," Newberry recorded his extensive study of the Colorado Plateau. He noted that aside from some isolated mountains, the "rocks composing the plateau are sedimentary throughout." He divided the Colorado River drainage into two groups—mountain ranges and the great plateau. He explained that the mountain systems of the region would require "years of patient study" to fully comprehend; so he provided a "skeleton sketch of their extent, structure, and direction." He referred to the Rocky Mountain system as "the great backbone of our continent." The Rocky Mountain drainage furnished most of the water that flowed down the Colorado. The composition of the lower Colorado ranges, he reported, were markedly different from the Rocky Mountains and contained a "much greater degree of purely eruptive rocks."

finishing Newberry's illustrations for the Macomb report may have caused its late issuance. In 1875, Macomb apparently submitted Newberry's finished report, "with its twenty-two illustrations," to the Office of the Chief of Engineers for publication. That same year, Ferdinand B. Meek, updated his report on cretaceous fossils that he had prepared in 1860.)

Newberry's geological report comprises the bulk of the final work. He contributed more than one hundred pages to the report, while Macomb wrote less than ten. Moreover, Newberry submitted a thirteen-page report on the carboniferous and Triassic fossils he collected on the expedition. The final edition also contained a fourteen-page report by Ferdinand B. Meek on cretaceous fossils gathered by Newberry's team and a map of the region compiled by Prussian aristocrat Baron Frederick Wilhelm von Egloffstein.[10]

Before the printing of the expedition report, Egloffstein, who had been with Ives in the Grand Canyon, issued the official map of the expedition separately under his name in 1864 to capitalize on the mining activity in the San Juan Mountains of Colorado. (Thus, Egloffstein's map of the Macomb expedition was available for Powell to peruse five years before he launched his expedition down the Colorado. It seems highly unlikely, since Egloffstein's map had circulated among the military brass in Washington, D.C., and the Secretary of the Interior had studied it, that Powell possessed no knowledge of it.)

The Macomb expedition map plotted the easiest routes into the region and helped debunk the geographical myths of that time.[11] In addition, the *Preliminary Map of the Surveys in Colorado . . . 1873*, made under the command of Lieutenant E. H. Ruffner, stated that "use is made of . . . the topography given by . . . Macomb in 1859." When published, the final report of the expedition provided valuable information for prospectors traveling to Colorado's mineral-rich Rockies and for cattlemen who

10. F. B. Meek wrote his report in 1860, which he updated in November 1875, just before the publication of the full report. His material included "descriptions and illustrations of eleven new species of Cretaceous fossils." He described silicified trunks of trees, leaves, vegetable remains, mollusks, and oysters. Meek named one fossil, "Prionocyclus Macombi," in honor of Captain Macomb. Newberry wrote a separate report on carboniferous and Triassic fossils. Teeth, ferns, leaves, and fruit are among the fossils illustrated and described by Newberry. At the "Cobre," the old copper mine nine miles north of Abiquiu, Newberry discovered "great numbers of fossil plants," including trunks and branches of trees. Newberry also named a fossil, "Otozamites Macombii," after Macomb.

11. F. W. von Egloffstein, *Map of Explorations and Surveys, in New Mexico and Utah made under the direction of the Secretary of War by Capt. J. N. Macomb, Topographical Engineers, assisted by C. H. Dimmock, C. Engineer, 1860* (New York: Geographical Institute, Baron F. W. von Egloffstein, 1864). Egloffstein sent running proofs of his map to Macomb in Washington, D.C., and asked him to get critiques of his work from those who had been in the field, within the region covered by the map. He also displayed his map to a number of government officials for their input.

Courtesy of Kansas State Historical Society

Frederick Wilhelm von Egloffstein.

supplied the miners with beef, results that were not part of the original goals of the expedition.

In the realm of geography and cartography, Egloffstein was a pioneer.[12] He introduced Americans to a new way of visualizing geography. It was a radical departure from the two-dimensional, hachured maps of the past. Lieutenant Ives explained, "This method of representing topography is . . . truer to nature. It is an approximation to a bird's eye view, and is

---

12. Egloffstein's pioneering endeavor had begun earlier when he produced the maps for E. G. Beckwith (1854) and the Ives expedition (1857–1858). After he had seen the maps drawn for Ives, Macomb petitioned the government for additional funds so that he could contract with Egloffstein to produce a map for inclusion in his report. (The Macomb map, drawn by Egloffstein, was more finely ruled than his earlier maps.) See Macomb to Humphreys, October 1, 1860, February 15, 1861, March 16, 1861, NA; Humphreys to Macomb, October 8, 1860, March 18, 1861, NA; Wm. Pennington, Speaker of the House of Representatives, to C. Holt, Secretary of War, February 26, 1861, NA. Egloffstein is considered America's "Father of Half-Tone Engraving." "Frederick W. von Egloffstein," Catholic Encyclopedia on

intelligible to every eye."[13] According to historian William Goetzmann, Egloffstein's "process has been incorporated in every geography textbook from that time to the present."[14]

Egloffstein's complex mapmaking technique included the construction of plaster models of the terrain, experimentation with oblique lighting, the use of "daguerreotype technology" and a "half-tone process" that involved finely ruled lines and the use of acid to etch the steel plate.[15] His new process of mapmaking was also cost effective. Lieutenant Ives explained: "Nearly one-half of the most expensive part of map engraving—the hachures upon the mountain sides—is dispensed with."[16]

Historians consider Egloffstein's shaded relief map, issued in Macomb's report, his finest work. The map is "one of the most beautiful maps ever published by the Army," wrote Carl Wheat. A modern map seller has noted that the map "demonstrates the culmination in the process developed by Egloffstein to convey the idea of altitude." In addition, it represents "a remarkable 3–dimensional realism unmatched in the period."[17]

The Egloffstein map furnishes an added bonus for students of history. In addition to showing public surveys, key mining districts, and forts, it carefully retraces the routes of numerous other explorers who passed through the region: Lt. James H. Simpson in 1849, Maj. Oliver L. Shepherd in 1858, J. C. Brown's chain survey, Macomb's wagon road (from Fort Union

CD-ROM, http://www.newadvent.org/cathen/05327.htm (accessed June 20, 2007). In 1865, Egloffstein was awarded patent number 51,103 by the United States Patent Office for his "heliographic and photographic spectrum for producing line-engravings." In 1869, Egloffstein received a government pension for his Civil War service with the New York Infantry, Regiment 103. Ten years later, he petitioned the government for naturalization. "Frederick W. von Egloffstein," Civil War Pensions. Organization Index to Pension Files of Veterans who served between 1861 and 1900 (July 19, 1869). Publication no. T289. National Archives, Washington, D.C.; "Frederick W. von Egloffstein," Soundex Index to Petitions for Naturalizations filed in Federal, State, and Local Courts in New York City, 1792–1906, Publication no. M1674, National Archives, Washington, D.C. See http://www.footnote.com/searchdocuments.php ?query=Frederick+W.+von+Egloffstein&collection=1#7969122 (accessed April 21, 2008.) "In 1878 [Egloffstein] and his family moved back to Germany, residing near Dresden, where in lingering poor health he died in 1885." Richard G. Biedleman, *California's Frontier Naturalists* (Berkeley: University of California Press, 2006), 306.

13. Joseph C. Ives, *Report upon the Colorado River of the West* (repr., New York: Da Capo, 1969), appendix D.
14. William H. Goetzmann, *Army Exploration in the American West, 1803–1863*, (New Haven, Conn.: Yale University Press, 1959), 393.
15. J. B. Krygier, "Envisioning the American West: Maps, the Representational Barrage of 19th Century Expedition Reports, and the Production of Scientific Knowledge," *Cartography and GIS* 24, no. 1 (1997): 27–50, http://go.owu.edu/~jbkrygie/krygier_html/envision.html (accessed October 31, 2006).
16. Ives, *Report upon the Colorado River of the West*, appendix D.
17. Carl I. Wheat, *1540–1861, Mapping the Transmississippi West*, vol. 4 (San Francisco, Calif.: Institute of Historical Cartography, 1960), 142; Old World Auctions. "Lot #165—Map of Explorations and Surveys in New Mexico and Utah . . . ," http://www.oldworldauctions.com/auction106/detail.asp?owa_id=2145212957 (accessed April 13, 2005). See also Goetzmann, *Army Exploration in the American West*, 393.

to Santa Fé), Capt. H. B. Schroeder in 1859, Capt. Joseph R. Walker in 1859, Maj. Electus Backus 1859, Col. Wm. W. Loring in 1858 and 1859, Maj. John S. Simonson in 1859, Father Silvestre Velez-Escalante in 1776, Lt. E. G. Beckwith in 1853, Lt. Amiel W. Whipple in 1853, Lt. Joseph C. Ives in 1858, Lt. William H. Emory in 1846, Capt. Randolph B. Marcy in "mid winter" 1858, Capt. John W. Gunnison in 1853, and Capt. John C. Fremont in 1843, 1844, and 1845. Unfortunately, Egloffstein misplaced the Old Spanish Trail route above the Big Bend of the Dolores River, a fiction he copied from Lieutenant Beckwith's map of the Gunnision expedition.

Using precise reference points such as latitude, longitude, elevation, and lines of triangulation established by Macomb and other government expeditions, Egloffstein built a framework that enabled him to construct his large map of the region. He apparently used Dimmock's splendid field map and Macomb's manuscript map as base maps for the construction of his masterpiece. The extent of the region covered by the map reached some twelve thousand square miles.[18] (Near the center of this region rests the Four Corners of Arizona, Colorado, New Mexico, and Utah.)

Using data from surveys in addition to Macomb's, particularly the 1853 railroad expedition of Capt. John W. Gunnison, Egloffstein built a composite map. As noted earlier, Gunnison followed a route to the north of Macomb's path—along the North Branch of the Old Spanish Trail. Both surveys nearly intersected each other's path at the La Sal Mountains, above present-day Moab, Utah. Egloffstein took the information gathered by both parties to construct his large-scale map. He also took data from the 1854 Pacific railroad survey of Lt. A. W. Whipple. Whipple followed the 35th parallel from Fort Smith, Arkansas, to California via Albuquerque.

In addition to the data he collected from the Macomb, Whipple, and Gunnison surveys, Egloffstein combined the topographical features and geographical positions found on the Simpson, Emory, and Ives maps, taking "care to preserve the material of each party, exploring in their own fashion and mapping in their own language." He wrote, "Every map has its own character, difficult to read and impossible for one who has not been over the ground himself or close by. This new style of topography . . . reduces these different languages of mapping in *one*, plain and readable."[19] In addition, Egloffstein asked to borrow Macomb's copy of Josiah Gregg's map of New Mexico. He explained, "On those old maps many valuable features are delineated which disappear on the recent publications."[20]

18. Fremont proposed the same method for the construction of his 1843–1844 expedition map. Donald Jackson and Mary Lee Spence, eds., *The Expeditions of John Charles Fremont*, vol. 1 (Urbana, Ill., 1970–1984), 776. See also Macomb, *Report*, 7.

19. Egloffstein to Macomb, June 12, 1861, NA.

20. Ibid.; See Josiah Gregg, *A Map of the Indian Territory, Northern Texas and New Mexico, Showing the Great Western Prairies* (New York: Henry G. Langley, 1844).

CENTRAL GOLD REGION.

The Gold fields of four Territories, New Mexico, Colorado, Utah and Arizona unite in the centre of the Map, comprising the Southern portions of the various mountain ranges generally called the *Rocky Mountains*. Pike's Peak Denver City Colorado City the Pagosa mines, Animas mines Dolores mines of *Colorado Territory* the San Francisco mountain mines, the Coal beds of the Mesa La Vaca and the *Big Cañon* of the Colorado; a succession of deeply cut valleys, in places a mile in depth, in *Arizona Territory*, Santa Fe, Albuquerque and the old settlements of *New Mexico* the mineral districts of the valley of the Rio Grande del Norte and their fertile parks, are well known features. Distance from Pike's Peak to San Francisco Mountain, 550 miles.

The names of the explorers are stated upon the trails. The *Public Surveys* have been connected with the topographical explorations. The altitudes are expressed in English feet, above the sea level, varying from 3,000 to 13,000 feet. Average altitude of the plateaus 6,000 feet. All lower altitudes have been represented darker.

A delicate tint was ruled over the whole plate to give the effect of a plaster model of the country. Constructed and engraved by

BARON F. W. Von EGLOFFSTEIN

Topographer to the Surveys under the 35th and 38th parallels. Fremont's, Beckwith's and Ives' Expeditions.

Lower right corner of the Frederick W. von Egloffstein map.

In constructing the most accurate map of the region possible at the time, Egloffstein collected all available geographical information. He complained of the "endless labor" in searching for maps "scattered over so many Offices" in Washington, D.C. To help him in his search, he asked Macomb "to gather a few maps of the mining districts around Pike peak." He explained, "The work would gain much in value and secure a certain longevity."[21]

On his map, Egloffstein was careful to include the names of both the "Grand" and "Upper Colorado" rivers because "The blue river, or Na-un-ka-rea river has been called 'Upper Colorado' by the settlers of Colorado Territory giving rise to the name of that territory; I have therefore added both Grand river and Upper Colorado. This river rises at Long's peak and is fully as long as the Green river, deserving the main name Colorado as it drains the whole mountainous district between the del Norte and the Platte."[22]

Egloffstein admitted to Macomb that his depiction of the San Juan "mountain district" was "vague." He proposed that Macomb send a final proof of his map to Albert Pfeiffer in New Mexico "to get from him . . . the most reliable information of the San Juan Mountains [and] . . . the parks of the upper Animas, Dolores, and Uncompahgrea [sic] Rivers." He added, "There are many weak parts of the map, and as gold may be discovered in almost every section of that country, I fear the consequences; an early "exposition" of the errors embraced in the construction."[23]

Egloffstein felt that the map would "gain much in correctness and popularity" if preliminary copies of the map were also sent to Kit Carson, Antoine Leroux, Colorado Territory's governor, and the surveyor general

21. Egloffstein to Macomb, June 12, 1861, NA.
22. Ibid., June 2, 1861, NA
23. Ibid., June 12, 1861, NA.

for their review. Furthermore, he wanted to get input from "all parties who have travelled and explored" in the New Mexico region.[24]

Whether or not Egloffstein got what he wanted is unknown. Macomb was heavily engaged in Civil War duties at the time and, in 1862, Egloffstein too joined the war effort. He helped organize a regiment of New York volunteers and commissioned a colonel. Wounded in battle, he later retired from the Army and returned to his printing pursuits. Finally, in 1864 he published his great map of the San Juan Exploring Expedition. In all likelihood, his map made it possible for prospectors swarming Colorado's southern Rockies to take advantage of detailed landscape views.[25]

Egloffstein believed that the Macomb map was destined to become "a document of much value and an ornament to the bureau of topographical engineers." (The Egloffstein map is today a very rare and highly prized cartographic gem.) He praised Macomb for "the great amount of original work your map is furnishing, thus making a contribution to geography, which otherwise would have been burried [sic] perhaps forever in the reports and archives of the War Department." He predicted that Macomb's map of New Mexico, together with the Texas boundary map of that period, "will form a set of geographical maps much wanted in the scientific and travelling circles of Europe, and carry your name all over the world, where geography is cultivated." (On exhibiting his rendition of the Macomb map in Washington, D.C., Egloffstein had caught the attention of Secretary of the Interior Caleb B. Smith and the Prussian Ambassador, "Baron F. von Gerolt.")[26]

Sadly, that never happened for Macomb or Egloffstein. The Civil War arrested their dreams.

---

24. Ibid.

25. "Frederick W. von Egloffstein," Catholic Encyclopedia on CD-ROM, http://www.newadvent. org/cathen/05327.htm (accessed 20 June 2007). On 28 October 1862, Macomb reported, "But little progress has been made during the past year, upon the engraving of the steel plate of my map of the San Juan River, New Mexico and Colorado, for the reason that the person with whom the arrangement was made for the engraving, accepted the command of one of the regiments in the field (103d. N.Yk) and was severely wounded whilst rendering distinguished service against the enemy in North Carolina." Macomb to Colonel S. H. Long, Washington, D.C. Letters Received by the Topographical Bureau of the War Department. NA. Microcopy No. 506, Roll 53, M. In mid-1863, Egloffstein informed Macomb, "Your plate is doing well and you will receive a good impression of the same during the week." Egloffstein to Macomb, May 30, 1863, NA

26. Egloffstein to Macomb, [5], June 28, July 16, 1861, NA. John L. Hazzard "engraved the Lettering" and assisted Egloffstein with the topography of the "Map of New Mexico and Utah." See Hazzard to Macomb, July 16, 1862, NA. Samuel Sartain was responsible for the map's ruling and Frederick Langenheim was the photographer. See Egloffstein to Macomb, July [10], 1861, NA.

EPILOGUE

The Civil War broke out on April 12, 1861 and disrupted the plans for a timely report on the findings of the Macomb expedition. Futhermore, it changed the lives of the expedition's main participants. Ultimately, what happened to the men? What did they achieve? More importantly, what were the major contributions of their San Juan Exploring Expedition?

During the Civil War, Macomb and Dimmock broadened the skills they had developed in the expedition. Macomb served as aide-de-camp to Gen. George McClellan. As the war progressed, the Union Army placed him with a balloon reconnaissance unit and he produced detailed maps of battle zones. At war's end, he was brevetted a colonel for meritorious service.[1]

After the Civil War, Macomb remained a topographical engineer. For several years, he served as commander of the Philadelphia District of the U.S. Army Corps of Engineers. In 1874, in his honor, the government commissioned the *J. N. Macomb*, an iron snag boat employed on the Mississippi River. Continuing his military career, Macomb rose through

---

1. William H. Powell, comp., *List of Officers of the United States from 1779 to 1900. . .* , (New York: L. R. Hamersly, 1900), 448; Francis B. Heitman, *Historical Register and Dictionary of the United States Army from its organization, September 29, 1789, to March 2, 1903*, vol. 1 (repr., Urbana: University of Illinois Press, 1965), 680. U.S. Congressional documents show that Captain Macomb faced additional demands following his return home. In June 1860, the War Department charged him with the building of "light-houses." On April 1, 1861, Capt. Montgomery C. Meigs, Macomb's brother-in-law, arranged for him to take charge of the U.S. Capitol extension, the new dome, and the Post Office extension since the War Department had transferred Meigs to the Gulf of Mexico. Shortage of funds and the casualties of war—including the housing of soldiers in the Capitol—disrupted the work. Macomb made little progress. The following year, Congress gave supervision over Capitol construction to the Interior Department. During the war, Macomb fought at the Battle of Cedar Mountain and in other skirmishes.

Charles H. Dimmock in his Confederate
uniform, Petersburg, Virginia, November 5, 1863.

John N. Macomb, ca. 1862.

the ranks and created a large number of topographic maps; many are now considered rare antiques. In 1867, he achieved the rank of colonel in the U.S. Army. He retired in 1882, following fifty years of military service. Macomb died in Washington, D.C., on March 16,1889, and was buried in Arlington National Cemetery. His wife, Nannie, died in 1916 and was buried in the same grave.[2]

At the outset of the Civil War, Dimmock "promptly offered his services to Virginia." On May 6, 1861, the Provisional Army of Virginia commissioned him "Captain of Engineers." The army immediately ordered him to construct the defenses of Craney Island, near Norfolk. From Craney Island, the Confederate Army dispatched him to Gloucester Point for similar duty.[3]

In mid-war, on October 14, 1863, Dimmock married Elizabeth Lewis Selden in Gloucester, Virginia. (Five children resulted from their marriage—Mary Lewis, Robert Selden, Elizabeth Maxwell, and twins Blanche and Minna.)[4]

The army then reassigned Dimmock to Petersburg to supervise the construction of a line of breastworks. At Petersburg, he employed slaves and free black men to build the ten miles of earthen ramparts, dubbed the "Dimmock Line," zigzagging around the city. He requested two hundred men "to labor on the defense works" at a wage of $2 per day and "rations furnished by the government." Pleased with Dimmock's extraordinary work, the citizens of Petersburg presented him with a "magnificent stallion and equipment." (In the war, Petersburg experienced a nine-month siege from U. S. Grant's army—"the longest period that any Southern city held out against Federal capture.")

During the siege of Petersburg, Dimmock remained with the army, "engaged all the time in strengthening and building works, until General [Robert E.] Lee evacuated Petersburg and the quick following surrender at Appomattox court-house."

2.   "John Navarre Macomb, Jr., Colonel, United States Army," Arlington National Cemetery Web site, http://www.arlingtoncemetery.net/jnmacomb.htm (accessed August 14, 2003). There is an interesting story, c. 1834, about Macomb's association with Robert E. Lee, a fellow West Point graduate. Lee, who lived at Arlington, would ride into Washington to his office and return home each day. "One day as Lee was mounting his horse to start for Arlington, he saw Macomb approaching. He called, 'Come, get up with me.' Macomb leaped up behind him on the horse and the two galloped off down Pennsylvania Avenue. As they passed the White House they met Levi Woodbury, the Secretary of the Treasury, whom they greeted with a great assumption of dignity, much to that gentleman's bewilderment." Joseph Grégoire de Roulhac Hamilton and Mary Cornelia Thompson Hamilton, *The Life of Robert E. Lee for Boys and Girls* (Boston, Mass.: Houghton Mifflin, 1917), 42.

3.   Dimmock, Papers, 1850–1873, Section 11, Obituaries, VHS.

4.   "Charles Henry Dimmock + Elizabeth Lewis Selden," http://www.dimick.org/family. php?famid=F1805 (accessed December 28, 2007); Merrow Egerton Sorley, *Lewis of Warner Hall: The History of a Family*, repr. ed. (1937; repr., Baltimore, Md.: Genealogical Publishing), http://worldcat.org/wcpa/oclc/4953525 (accessed May 19, 2007).

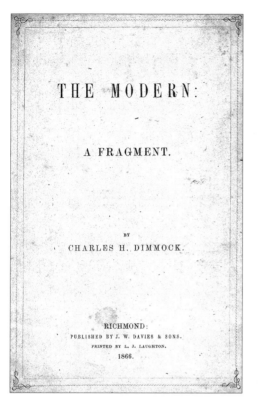

Cover to Charles H. Dimmock's
The Modern, a chapbook of poetry.

On April 10, 1865, following his surrender to the North, Dimmock was issued a "Pass for a Paroled Prisoner for the Army of Northern Virginia . . . by order of GEN. R. E. LEE." One month later Dimmock took the oath of allegiance to the United States.

Dimmock returned to his civil engineer profession and "added to it the kindred profession of architecture." Robert E. Lee later commended Dimmock for serving "the state of Virginia in peacetime." He helped organize the Ladies Hollywood Memorial Association, a group that initiated the removal, and reburial in Richmond, of fallen Confederates from the Gettysburg battlefield, and served as its engineer and business agent. Dimmock also designed a ninety-foot pyramid monument in Hollywood Cemetery to honor the Confederate dead.[5]

Soon after the war, Dimmock wrote a chapbook of classical poetry, published under the title *The Modern: A Fragment.* (Before the Civil War, he had hinted of his love of poetry when he drew a pencil sketch of Edgar A. Poe's headstone in Baltimore.) In his work, Dimmock denounced

---

5.   Dimmock, Papers, 1850–1873, Section 11, Obituaries, VHS.

Courtesy of the Ohio Department of Natural Resources, Division of Geological Survey

Dr. John S. Newberry in his later years.

modernity, longing for a return to an age of elegance and grace. He also showed his concern about the distant future and the contemporary human condition. Typical of Victorian-age literature, he appeared to imitate Alexander Pope, Shakespeare, Milton, and other classical writers. (Unfortunately, in his writings he overlooked the romance of his reconnaissance out West and the tragedy of his Civil War experiences.)[6]

In 1869, the citizens of Richmond elected Dimmock to the office of city engineer. He faithfully and efficiently discharged his duties. "The

---

6.   Charles H. Dimmock, *The Modern: A Fragment* (Richmond, Va.: J. W. Davies & Sons, 1866). The only known illustration of Edgar Allen Poe's headstone is a sketch drawn by Charles H. Dimmock c. 1860. See "Poe's Lost Headstone," E. A. Poe Society of Baltimore, http://www.eapoe.org/balt/poegravs.htm (accessed 17 May 2007).

improved and beautified condition of the streets of Richmond, made under his direction, [serve as] enduring memorials of his skill and taste," reported a local newspaper. Three years into his term of office he was stricken with cancer, but "he remained at his post often when he should have been in bed." "I must attend to my duty," he declared to his family and his physician.

On March 29, 1873, following an eight-month bout with stomach cancer, forty-one-year-old Charles H. Dimmock died at his father-in-law's home in Gloucester, Virginia. Richmond officials paid tribute to his memory and attended his funeral at the city's St. James' Church, followed by internment in Hollywood Cemetery. The city mourned Dimmock's death by passing resolutions "recognizing the calamity which the community has suffered by his death." Citizens praised "his virtues and noble qualities, . . . so well known and so highly esteemed." Petersburg subsequently honored his memory by naming a thoroughfare, Charles H. Dimmock Parkway, after him.[7]

In contrast to Dimmock, John S. Newberry stood firmly on the side of the North during the Civil War. In a letter to Macomb, Newberry expressed his outrage over the Confederate victory at Bull Run and predicted Union troops would sound the war cry, "*Revenge! Revenge for Bulls Run. And the murdered [&] wounded!*"[8] During the war, Newberry's medical skills aided him as a member of the United States Sanitary Commission, a private relief agency. He became the secretary of the commission's western department, directing the work in the Mississippi River Valley. He also wrote a number of reports outlining the contributions of the institution.

Following the war, Newberry became a professor of geology and paleontology at New York's Columbia School of Mines and continued his distinguished career in science. From 1869 to 1882, he served as Ohio's state geologist. During his forty-year career, Newberry wrote 212 scientific papers. One of the greatest geologists of the nineteenth century, his numerous achievements included corporate member of the National Academy of Sciences, president of the American Association for the

---

7.   Katherine Wilkins, Virginia Historical Society, Richmond, personal communication with author, November 14, 2006; Dimmock, Papers, 1850–1873, Section 11, Obituaries, VHS. Dimmock's father, Capt. Charles Dimmock, was a West Point graduate. Following Captain Dimmock's death in the Civil War a Southern composer dedicated a marching quick step in his honor. See Francis Buck, "Le Carnival de Venise, Quick Step: Composed and Arranged for Piano Forte and respectfully Dedicated to Captn. Charles Dimmock (of Richmond, Va.)," (Richmond, Va.: George Dunn, n.d.), http://scriptorium.lib.duke.edu/sheetmusic/conf/conf00/conf0011/ (accessed 17 May 2006). See also George W. Cullum, *Biographical Register of the Officers and Graduates of the U.S. Military Academy, from 1802 to 1867*, vol. 1 (rev., New York: James Miller, 1879), 212–13.

8.   Newberry to Macomb, July 26, 1861, NA. Today, Newberry's name adorns a number of American landmarks and fossils.

Advancement of Science, president of the Torrey Botanical Club in New York, president of the New York Academy of Sciences, vice-president and organizer of the Geological Society of North America, and organizer of the International Congress of Geologists. He died on December 7, 1892, in New Haven, Connecticut.[9]

Newberry's friend Charles A. White praised his great qualities, including honesty: "A crowning proof of his integrity of character is found in the full accounting which he rendered the Government for all the money and property, amounting to millions of dollars, that passed through his hands in the course of his official work."[10]

White also wrote about the loss Newberry experienced by the delay in publishing the Macomb report: "Dr. Newberry was deprived of the credit of priority, which was justly due him, in much of the important geological . . . work, which was afterward published by various authors from observations made in the region which he investigated when it was entirely new."[11]

Nevertheless, during his life Newberry made outstanding achievements in the development of science. Adding to his contributions to the school of fluvialism— the study of landform changes produced by the action of streams—and his studies of ancient ruins, Newberry laid the groundwork for more focused scientific studies of the individual mountain ranges in the Colorado Plateau province. Newberry's focused work, called "key studies," provided "a way to understand the basic principles of a region's creation."[12]

Newberry explained that the strata on the eastern edge of the Colorado Plateau, the western base of Nacimiento Mountain, "form the geological summit of the plateau." He wrote, "If properly studied, [Nacimiento Mountain] would serve to explain nearly all the difficulties of . . . the origin of mountain chains." Newberry believed that the mountain furnished "a key to the mode of formation of all the great ranges of the Rocky Mountain System." He also pointed to the need for further explorations west of the Colorado River to examine the geological structure of the "high table-lands."

Modern scientists have verified many of the conclusions that Newberry arrived at during the San Juan Exploring Expedition. He correctly observed that "the Rocky Mountains had undergone several periods of

---

9. Guide to the John Strong Newberry Papers, 1898, Provenance Note 2005, Special Collections, George Washington University, Washington, D.C., http://www.gwu.edu/gelman/spec/ead/ms0257.xml (accessed May 4 2007).

10. White, "Biographical Memoir of John Strong Newberry, 1822–1892," 9.

11. Ibid., 8.

12. Goetzmann, *Army Exploration in the American West*, 397; Schubert, *Vanguard of Expansion*, 90.

uplift and erosion, but the greatest period of uplift occurred between the close of the Cretaceous and the beginning of the Miocene," explained William Goetzmann.[13] Furthermore, Newberry accurately reported that "the pre-carboniferous rocks he had observed in the Grand Canyon were not present in the Nacimiento Mountains," wrote geologist Bill Chenoweth. Moreover, in his report, Newberry keenly observed that the volcanic rocks in New Mexico's Mt. Taylor had indeed, "been deposited at various times beginning in the Middle Tertiary and continuing into the present epoch," noted Chenoweth.[14]

Eventually, near the close of the Civil War's Reconstruction Period, the Secretary of War approved the printing of 1,500 copies of the expedition's report. Author Ann Zwinger has eloquently described the now-rare publication in its scarce morocco binding: "It is a handsome large-format volume an inch thick, corners and spine of leather, gold lettered, end-papers feather-patterned in maroon, dark blue, cream, beige, and gold; twenty-two plates, eleven of which are colored, of landscape vistas and fossils, meticulously rendered. A book of quality and substance."[15]

Out West, following Reconstruction, the heated atmosphere between federal troops and the Mormons had subsided. The government no longer needed to develop a military road to Utah's southern settlements. C. Gregory Crampton wrote, "After the Macomb survey men [and women] became concerned more with the canyon country itself than trying to find a way through it."[16]

For Old Spanish Trail researchers, the scientific observations and discoveries of the San Juan Exploring Expedition as well as its cartographic contributions provide new interpretations of the region surrounding the eastern leg of the Old Spanish Trail. Moreover, it sharpens our view of the trail itself and its grand legacy.

The expedition accomplished two important original goals: to explore the region traversed by the Old Spanish Trail and map the route of travel. Those goals left unrealized included finding the exact point where the Green and Colorado rivers merged and locating a suitable supply route through the region of the confluence to the southern settlements of Utah. It evolved from a political and military premise into a primarily scientific, geological study. It also made considerable contributions to the field of paleontology, and it set the stage for future archeological and geological

---

13. Goetzmann, *Army Exploration in the American West*, 397.
14. William L. Chenoweth, "John Strong Newberry: Pioneer Colorado Plateau Geologist," *Canyon Legacy*, no. 24 (Summer 1995), 3.
15. Ann Zwinger, ". . . a worthless and impracticable region. . . ," *Plateau* 52, no. 2 (June 1980): 25.
16. As quoted in Barnes, *Hiking the Historic Route of the 1859 Macomb Expedition*, 8; C. Gregory Crampton, *Standing Up Country: The Canyon Lands of Utah and Arizona* (New York: Knopf, 1964), 64.

Courtesy of the Rochester Historical Society

Entrance to Wild Rose Pass, painting by Capt. Arthur T. Lee, ca. 1855. Charles Dimmock passed through the pass on his return home from New Mexico.

studies of the region. Furthermore, according to Aton and McPherson, the survey "stimulated commercial activity and facilitated settlement."[17] Ultimately, the San Juan Exploring Expedition laid the foundation on which later explorers and scientists could examine up close its contributions to a "region unexplored scientifically" and thereby enlighten and enrich the collective human mind.

---

17.   Aton and McPherson, *River Flowing from the Sunrise*, 50.

PART II

Selected Documents of the San Juan Exploring Expedition

Sketch of the Pecos mission church ruins, by Charles H. Dimmock.

The Great Sage Plain stretching southeast of the Abajo Mountains was named and crossed by the Macomb party.

The Camps of the San Juan Exploring Expedition

T he following information comes from primary documents of the expedition and from Macomb's published report:

Camp No. 1	Near Pojoaque (Valley of the Nambé)	13–14 July
Camp No. 2	Near Pueblo of San Juan	14–15 July
Camp No. 3	About one mile below Abiquiu (or five miles above the Cuchillo) on the north side of the Rio Chama Labeled: "Don Francisco Antonio Salazar y Romero"	15–16 July
Camp No. 4	In the Bosque near the Pueblo of Abiquiu Labeled: "Donna Francisquita Valasquez"	16–19 July
Camp No. 5	Arroyo Seco	19–20 July
Camp No. 6	Ojo del Navajo (Mouth of Canjilon Creek)	20–21 July
Camp No. 7	Rio Nutria	21–22 July
Camp No. 8	Vado del Chama	22–25 July
Camp No. 9	Laguna de los Caballos (Horse Lake)	25–26 July
Camp No. 10	Rio del Navajo	26–27 July
Camp No. 11	Rito Blanco (Little White River)	27–28 July
Camp No. 12	On grassy bottom of San Juan River (Near Pagosa Hot Spring)	28–30 July
Camp No. 13	Nutrita del Francais (or "Nutrita Frances")	30–31 July

Camp No. 14	Rio Piedra	31 July-2 August
Camp No. 15	Rio de los Pinos	2–3 August
Camp No. 16	Rio Florida (or Rio Florido)	3–6 August
Camp No. 17	Rio las Animas	6–7 August
Camp No. 18	Rio de la Plata	7–8 August
Camp No. 19	Rio de los Mancos	8–9 August
Camp No. 20	Nutria del Dolores (or Nutritas Dolores)	9–10 August
Camp No. 21	Rio Dolores	10–13 August
Camp No. 22	Surouaro (or Sarouaro Spring)	13–14 August
Camp No. 23	Tierra Blanca (or "Tierra Blanco," or "spring in an arid canon")	14–15 August
Camp No. 24	Guajelotes (Water Lizards or Salamanders) (or Juajoloté, or Quajalote, or Guajolotes)	15–16 August
Camp No. 25	Ojo del Cueva (or El Ojo de La Cueba, or Ojo del Cuerbo)	16–17 August
Camp No. 26	Cañon Pintado (or Cañon de las Pañitas)	17–18 August
Camp No. 27	La Tinaja (or La Tenejal, or El Tenajal, or Ar te najal, or La Tenajales…)	18–20 August
Camp No. 28	Ojo Verde (or El Ojo Verde)	20–22 August
Camp No. 29	In the Cañon of the Rito Colorado (or Cañon Colorado, or Labyrinth Cañon)	22–24 August
Camp No. 28	Ojo Verde (or El Ojo Verde)	24–27 August
Camp No. 27	La Tinaja (or La Tenejal, or El Tenajal, or Ar te najal, or La Tenajales…)	27–28 August
Camp No. 30	Cold Spring	28–29 August
Camp No. 31	Cherry Creek	29–30 August
Camp No. 32	Mormon Spring (or Silver Spring)	30–31 August
Camp No. 33	Ojo del Alamo(or El Ojo del Alamo)	31August-1 September
Camp No. 34	"Ritito de Sierra Abajo" (or Ritito del Sierra Abajo, or Rito del Sierra Abajo, or El Ritito de Sierra Abajo)	1–2 September
Camp No. 35	Rio San Juan	2–4 September
Camp No. 36	On the Rio San Juan	4–5 September
Camp No. 37	On the Rio San Juan	5–6 September
Camp No. 38	On the Rio San Juan	6–7 September
Camp No. 39	On the Rio San Juan	7–8 September
Camp No. 40	On the Rio San Juan	8–9 September
Camp No. 41	On the Rio San Juan	9–10 September
Camp No. 42	On the Rio San Juan (or mouth of Rio de las Animas)	10–13 September
Camp No. 43	On the Rio San Juan	13–14 September
Camp No. 44	Near mouth of the Cañon Largo	14–15 September

Camp No. 45	In Cañon Largo (at mouth of Cañon Blanco)	15–16 September
Camp No. 46	In Cañon Largo	16–17 September
Camp No. 47	In Cañon Largo	17–18 September
Camp No. 48	"El Alto de la Utah" (or El Alto del Utah) (Near head of Cañon Largo)	18–19 September
Camp No. 49	Cañada de los Alamos (or Cañada de las Alimas, or "La Canada de los Alamos")	19–20 September
Camp No. 50	Ojo de San Jose (or within three miles of base of "La Sierra Nascimiento")	20–21 September
Camp No. 51	Junction of tributaries of Rio Puerco	21–23 September
Camp No. 52	El Rio Puerco (On branch of Puerco)	23–24 September
Camp No. 53	Rio de Chacoli (Near the southwest end of Nacimiento Mountain)	24–25 September
Camp No. 54	Near the village of Jemez	25–26 September
Camp No. 55	Opposite Santo Domingo (Right bank of Rio Bravo del Norte, or on west bank of Rio Grande)	26–27 September
Camp No. 56	On the Rio de Santa Fé	27–28 September
Camp No. 57	Arroyo Hondo (About six miles south of Santa Fé)	28 September—16 October

DIARY OF CHARLES H. DIMMOCK
MAY 4 TO
NOVEMBER 19, 1859

Before his adventure began, Dimmock procured a pocket diary, published by Denton & Wood of Cambridgeport, Massachusetts. The book's limited space for daily entries seemed well suited to his tiny handwriting. He also carried along a fine lead pencil and a pen to make notations and a sketchbook for making drawings. (In addition he created a portfolio of other drawings made on the journey. Over time, the acidic content of the paper nearly destroyed his work.) Dimmock wrote his experiences in this printed pocket diary, which included an almanac, printed postage rates, "a blank space for every day in the year," and space for memoranda and for a register of financial accounts. It was titled "A Pocket Diary for 1859; containing a Blank Space for Every Day in the Year for the Record of Interesting Events, a Cash Account for each Month, Bills Payable and Receivable, &c., &c., &c. Published annually by Denton & Wood, Cambridgeport, Mass., 1859."

The one centimeter thick pocket diary measured 7.5 by 17.5 centimeters. The publication consisted of 163 *unnumbered* pages. However, only about 80 pages contained handwritten notes/sketches by Dimmock. Dimmock's diary constitutes a record of 199 daily entries over a period extending from May 4 to November 19, 1859. In addition, he scribbled several random notes and sketches on the endpapers and blank leaves of the publication, as well as in the portion assigned to financial records.

From the Virginia Historical Society, Richmond.

The space alloted for each day's entry was limited, and often Dimmock continued daily entries begun under the correct date in the available February to May spaces earlier in the book and informed the reader of that date where the resumed narrative would be found. He also continued his entries at the top of the page or in the margins, where he wrote them vertically. (However, this publication does not follow the same arrangement. The extended text flows seamlessly down the page.) Between lines he often wrote the number of that day's camp in a slanted hand, which I have represented here by italics and enclosed in brackets. Under the "December Bills Payable" section of the book, Dimmock provided a detailed log of distances along the Santa Fe Trail from Independence, Missouri, to Santa Fé, New Mexico. The total distance, as he calculated it, was 773.5 miles.

The diary's provenance follows: Margaret Jones Perritt in 1983 deposited the Charles Henry Dimmock Papers, 1850–1873, including Dimmock's diary, in the Virginia Historical Society. Ms. Perritt's great great grandfather was Robert Colgate Selden. Robert's daughter, Elizabeth Lewis Selden, nicknamed "Lizzie," married Charles Henry Dimmock on October 14, 1863 in Glouster, Virginia. (Dimmock's first wife, Emily Moale had died c. December 1859.) Elizabeth and Charles bore five children, including twin daughters, Blanche and Minna. Blanche married Burr Powell Noland and their daughter, Elizabeth Lewis Noland, became Ms. Perritt's godmother. Elizabeth Lewis Noland inherited the Dimmock Papers, which were subsequently given to Ms. Perritt. In turn, she placed the collection with the historical society in Richmond.

A perusal of historian David Remley's work *"Adios Nuevo Mexico"* and other significant documents enabled me to identify several people named in Dimmock's diary and to lightly edit the work, which I transcribed.

Chas. H. Dimmock
Baltimore,
Md.

Apus = The footless
Life size
Aquatic. A Crustacian.
& allied to the horse shoe crab
Found near the Arkansas River, Kansas [T]er. [Dimmock drawing not shown]

Santa Fé to El Paso 5 ½ days
El Paso to St. Louis 12 days

pinnacle
pinnacle

Horn of Antelope
Found at Whetstone Spring, New Mexico
12 in. [long by] 4 in [wide]
Front [Dimmock drawing not shown]

Stamps from Dr. Newberry May 29 = 5.1.1
///

{Me trae V. mi pañuelo?
{Do you bring me my handkerchief?

{ Ha traido V. mi rope? }
{ Have you brought my linen? }

{ Dame mi peine}   { quieu Sabé
{ Give me my comb}   { who knows

Dr. N. gave Ute pair of pants. His acknowledgements were a "how you do?"
"Recile a leetle forwards" = Capt. Thistle
Kicking the penitent soldier
Judge Benedict having a writ served on Indians
                              { [Ce[c]ia [or Sarcilla]_largo Navajoe
                              { Long ear[r]ring
{ Mangus Colora
{

Red sleeve

Firing the wagon at Comanches Apache
"[Thou?] a cow on a common or a goose on a green."
"Your horse, my lord, was very backward in coming forward; he was be-
hind before, but he's first at last."
To Hammersmith [British rail station] the way to Turnham Green

{ —Reply to enquiring Mexican—"Jones? Jones? This is not my day for
    keeping him."
El Paso Oct. 25th 1859.
Drunken man in mud fanning himself with an adobe. El Paso. Oct. 28/59.

	Santa Fé,	June 6th 1859	13th	[20th	27th	[Tl]	[Ju]
√	Shirts White _	2	2	1	2	2	
√	" Coloured _	3	0	1	0	0	
√	" Under __	2	0	1	0	1	
√	Collars White __	3	2	1	3	2	
√	" Coloured __	3	0	0	0	0	
√	Draws ___	2	1	1	1	1	
√	Socks ___	4	1	2	2	1	
√	Handkerchiefs	2	1	7	1	1	
		15 Pieces	5	7 Pieces $1.69⁶ 6			
				37¢			

Camisa = Shirt
Escarpines = Socks
Paño = handkerchief

July 11th
Shirt	1
Collar	1
Socks	2
Draws	1
Handk	1
	5

"Ay, but a man's first book is sometimes like his first babe, healthier &
stronger than those which follow." Robert Burns

Sketch of the Cathedral of Tecoloté, New Mexico, on the
Santa Fé Trail, by Charles H. Dimmock.

{[Tizwinnie?] & the old Mexican}
{woman's idea of straining}
El Paso

Cathedral of Tecoloté—
Built of Adobes
New Mexico

Send [Joseph] Mercure Music
2 Mercure

Church at the Pueblo at Pécos.
more than 200 years old.

Sketch titled "Peralta" by Charles
H. Dimmock, drawn in the vicin-
ity of the stage station at Peralta,
New Mexico.

Peralta Oct. 18th 1859.

11 ¾ miles

5280
132

Crossed Chama 2 miles Back
N 65 W   from Camp 5 = 4 m
" 50 "   for   1 m

" 40 "	"	½ m
" 30 "	"	¼ m
" 15 "	"	¼ m
N 20 E	"	1 m
N 20 W	"	1 m
N	"	1 Leave Arro. to R
"	"	¼ { Summit Stream enters R
"	"	½ In Arro.
N 10 E.	"	¾ 0 ¾ = 1 ½
N	"	½ { O. del N. [Ojo del Navajo] begins Here we find C. 6. 7:30 A.M.
N 80 W	"	¼
N 10 E	"	½
N 20 W	"	1500 ft or ¼
N 20 E	"	2000. or ½
N 50 W	"	1 ¼ miles
N 40 W	"	½ "
N 75 W	"	1500 ft or ¼
N 50 W	"	½ mile
S 85 W or 95	"	1200 or ¼
W		2 mile
S 70 W		2 ¼
W		1
N 70 W		¾ onions C [Onion Creek]
N 50 W		1 ¼ mile
" " "		1 ¼ "
N 40 W		¼
N 60 W		¼
N 40 W		½ mile
N 60 W		1 ¼ "
N 50 W		1 mile Camp 7 in valley of Nutria

Aug 10th	Shirts	1.	Draws	1.	U Shirts	1.	Socks	4.	Coat	1.
" 21st	"	2	"	1	"	1	"	2		0
Sept 12th	"	3	"	2	"	1	"	3		0
		6		4		3		9		1 }23

Santa Fé Oct 4th

Shirts W.	Shirts C.	Undr Shts.	Draws	Socks
2	3	1	1	4

MAY WEDNESDAY 4 1859
Left in the 5:05 P.M. train for New York. Fare $6.00
Hack [carriage] hire $1.00.

THURSDAY 5
Hack to St. Nicholas [historic New York City district]—.50¢
Bill at St. Nicholas—2.00
Hack for Self & Fisher to Depot—1.00
Fare to Balto. Self & Fisher—12.00
Supper at Phila. for do.—1.00

FRIDAY 6
Hack hire home for Self—$1.00
Bagage [sic] for Self—0.25

MAY SATURDAY 7 1859
Hack for Self to Cars—$1.00
Fisher's Bill in Balto. [terminus on the Baltimore and Ohio]—5.00
" Riding & Baggage to Depot—1.00
Self & Fisher's fare to St. Louis 52.00
" " Supper at Martinsburg [in present West Virginia]—1.00

SUNDAY 8
Breakfast Self at Grafton $0.50

MONDAY 9
Bill Self & Fisher Bellaire $3.00
Breakfast " " Zanesville 1.00
Bill Self & Fisher at Cincinnati 1.50

MAY TUESDAY 10 1859
Breakfast Self & Fisher at Vincennes $1.00
Reached St. Louis to day 3 P.M.

WEDNESDAY 11
[Blank]

TUESDAY 12
Left St. Louis this evening at 4. Fare to Independence $10.00 Reached
the Steamer "South Wester" at Jefferson City tonight at 10:15 P.M.

MAY FRIDAY 13 1859
On board South Wester [riverboat operated by Captain David DeHaven]
Rather a fine boat. All hands at paint washing in saloon. We are treated to
the drippings. Card playing the order of the day, as on all these western
river boats. Meals rather fare [sic].

SATURDAY 14

On board South Wester Passengers restless at the number of landings, at which we spend about an hour each time. Poor [J. T.] Watkins, en route for St. Joseph, has walked him-self down by his very restlessness—& bitterly laments having taken this route. All hands grow weary of the River. Missouri wretchedly muddy.

SUNDAY 15

Reached Independence to day at 1 P.M. Ind. 3 miles from River. Road hilly & deep. Stopped at Jones' Hotel. Population of Ind. about 3,000. Locality unusually pleasing, while country adjacent is the fairest part of Missouri.

MAY MONDAY 16 1859

Left Independence, for Santa Fé, to day at 12 [N]. Fare $115 & 40 lbs. baggage allowed. Travelled 20 miles to day. Stopping at Alexander's. Mules wretched, & roads fearful. Stalled frequently. Had good supper & nice beds. Mrs. A. from Washington D.C. & quite the intellectual superior of Mr. A. Locality—"Shawnee Reserve" [in Kansas Territory]

20 MILES

TUESDAY 17

This morning the sun rose most gloriously. Air bracing & fresh. One of the mules, in Baggage Wagon, hard to get in ranks; kicking out of traces [unhitching itself]. Dined 20 miles from Alexanders & 40 from Ind. Changed ~~horses~~ mules at same place. Stopped at Barreclaugh's [Barraclough's] 55 miles from Ind. Supper rather heavy. Teamsters slept in our room, on floor, were awaked, at midnight, by horrid yells. Discovered to be Conner (Driver) with nightmare.

35 M.

WEDNESDAY 18

Raining this morning—commenced during the night. Breakfast is last night. Old B. garrulous about the Kansas war. As for the last two day[s], in the Shawnee Reserve. Saw 2 Indians, yesterday—Squalid & wretched. Came 20 miles before stopping to feed mules & dine. Walters kindly gave us fried middling [pork or bacon] & coffee @ 50¢ per head. Reached [M.] Gilkey's this evening, 45 m. from Barreclaugh's [out?] 100 m. from Ind. Gave us a first rate supper. Contradicts old B's statement of the extent of the Kansas troubles.

100 TO IND. 45 M.

MAY THURSDAY 19 1859

Met 1st Mail.

Morning bright & beautiful. Air cool, fresh & bracing. Had a admirable "shake-down [makeshift bunk]," and slept like two tops. Given us a good breakfast, at 5 A.M. All wrote home last night. Best location we have seen.

Belongs to Stage Co. & is a 640 acre Section. Nooned mules to day with-out dining ourselves. Met Kaw Indian chief with Squaw & son. Fine look-ing, gave him 25¢ a piece—was indignant because he received so little. Have seen a number of Kaws & one or two Ki[o]was [in the area of the Kaw Indian Reserve]. Road quite good. Reached "Council Grove" this evening. Distance from Gilkey's 40 miles. Stopped with Robinson who gave us a fare supper but a feather bed.

FRIDAY 20

Slept well however & woke this morning to find it raining heavily. Coach leaks, so we'll have a moist time. In Kaw Reserve. Cleared off! Dined at Diamond Spring, 155 miles from Ind. Here we take the team that is to carry 520 miles us to Fort Union. Came 15 miles from Diamond Spring this evening, travelling late. Slept in Coach, others on the ground. Had no supper. Cold & very windy, passed a wretched night.

SATURDAY 21

Clear & chilly. Up before sunrise & travelled 10 miles to breakfast, at Little Muddy. Branch justified its title. A mud puddle! Such a breakfast! Cooked by teamsters with unwashed hands. Bill of fare—Fried Bacon, Crackers & Coffee, muddier than Little Muddy. Enjoyed it however, as the cold & morning drive gave an appetite, cannabol [sic] like. We are now to sleep under the sky for some time to come. Saw 4 antelope & several grey wolves. Supped 30 miles from last night's camp. Killed 2 Plovers at one shot. Saw 4 antelopes & many gray wolves. Stopped for the night 43 miles from morning. Night pleasant. Dew heavy.

MAY SUNDAY 22

A Pike Peaker's experience—"Could make 10¢ a day & d—d hard work at that! Good chance to starve unless you steal & if you steal you're certain to be hung."
Met Mail 2

Heavy dew last night wetting our blankets. Up by day & came 10 miles to breakfast. Morning lonely. Buffalo in all directions. About 20 crossing the road ahead of us[.] I shot at them. Struck one but not in a vital part so he escaped. All sorts of game about us. While breakfast was preparing of Buffalo meat we went in pursuit of Buffalo—saw an immense herd & fired 2 shots at [them]. They were too distant for effect. Nooned one mile beyond the Little Arkansas. Buffalos innumerable.
Supped 28 miles from morning's staring point. Crossed Cow Creek about sundown & stopped for night about 40 miles from Camp 2nd.

MONDAY 23

Night windy but pleasant—not much dew. Up by light & off. Windy still.

Many buffalo. One herd crossed the road in advance of us at which I took a shot without apparent effect. Came about 11 miles to breakfast. Nooned at Allison's Ranch [at Walnut Creek Crossing on the Arkansas River], 20 miles from morning. Saw Indians, many Kiawas, Comanche, &c. Fi[n]e, matronly, looking Squaw

^Blowing great guns—all day!^

with two very pretty girls, amuses herself <u>eating</u> the lice from the head of the younger. Supped 10 miles from Allison's. Prairie dogs in myriads. Camped 40 miles from C. no. 3, & 6 miles East Pawnee Fork Arkansas. Night—cool & windy.

293 IND. 40 M.

Tuesday 24

Daylight found us stirring. But little dew. Crossed Pawnee Fork & breakfasted 4 m. beyond (10 P.M.). Morning pleasant—Smart breeze from west. Country of Kiawas & Comanches, they having expelled the Pawnees. Dr. S. bug-bottling. Nooned 20 miles (about) from C. 4. Day pleasant. Supped 30 miles from C. 4. No more Buffalo. Prairie dogs innumerable. Pike Peaker's returning in a continuous train, foot sore & disgusted. Camped for night 40 miles from C. 4.

333 IND. 40 M.

May Wednesday 25 1859

Met Mail 3

Change during the night, wind shifting to N. East. Cold as winter this morning, with a wind that pierces to the marrow. Rode 10 miles to breakfast. Oyster can, at fire, bursted, filling Dorsey & self with fragments. Nooned 20 miles from C. 5 on the Arkansas, at the end of "the Dry Road." Windy, with mist. Supped upon the Arkansas 30 mile from C. 5. Still windy, cold & misty. Neither Indians nor game seen to day. Camped 42 miles from morning. Night very cold & heavy mist that wet our blankets. Mules getting away from their pickets [unhitching themselves from stakes] crowded around the wagons for protection from wind. One dropped its manure upon Dorsey's bed.

375 IND. 42 M.

Thursday 26

Morning very cold. Rain ceased. With a late start travelled 4 miles to breakfast at crossing of the Arkansas. Nooned on west side of Arkansas R. Dr. Newberry shot wild Goose. Came 20 miles to Supper. Dr. Newberry killed 4 snipe. Self 2 wild ducks. Moderated, still windy. In country of Comanches & Kiawas. High, sandy prairie. Came 33 miles to camp. Night clear pleasant & starry. Wolves seen & shot at this morning. Camp 6.

408 TO IND. 33 M.

Friday 27

Up by day & travelled 15 miles to breakfast. Saw many ducks. Dr. N. shot one. Morning cool but promising. Came 28 miles before nooning.

Supped at the Cimarron Spring, distance not known, as teamsters are Sulkey & cant tell how far. Supposed to be about 35 miles. Evening pleasant. Camped 44 miles from C. 6. Night unexceptionable. But little dew. Still on the Cimarron. Camp 7.

May Saturday 28 1859
Met

Morning bright & pleasant. Up before the sun & travelled 10 miles to breakfast. Country of the Cimarron continues—dry & impregnated with alkaline. Meet with little of interest. Teamsters amiable this morning. Clouded since breakfast & promises rain. Battle of bugs on the increase. Nooned about 20 miles from C. 7 on the Cimarron. Supped 30 miles from C. 7. Have seen many antelopes. Rained a little during supper. Camped about 44 miles from C. 7.

Sunday 29
Met 3rd 4 Mail

Night pleasant, but heavy dew. Up early. Morning cloudy & air heavy with mist. Came 12 miles to breakfast. Still on the Cimarron & breakfasted with wretched water 4 miles east of the crossing. Shot at an Antelope—distance too great. Met 3rd Mail about 11 A.M. All sent letters. Nooned 22 miles from C. 8. Supped 30 miles from C. 8, at "the Enchanted Spring." Saw many Antelopes. Topography of country very Striking. Supped 6 miles from New Mexico line. In the Indian Territory—Road passes about 35 miles through I. T. [Indian Territory]. Came 43 miles to Camp. C. 9.

Monday 30

Rained during the night. The Dr. & myself hustled for the wagons, soon ceased. Morning pleasant. Came 10 miles, to Cedar Spring, to breakfast. Now in New Mexico. Nooned at McNeese's Creek—20 miles from Camp 9. Day pleasant. Supped at Cottonwood Spring 31 miles from C. 9. Passed train of Burrows (Donkeys), ladened for the Indian trade. Windy this evening. Wrote Emmy. Night pleasant, with but little dew. Camped 41 miles from C. 9.

May Tuesday 31 1859

Morning fresh & pleasant. Came 10 miles to breakfast (2 miles East of Round Mound). Saw Antelope following a wolf who had eaten her fawn. Nooned at Rock Creek 23 miles from Camp 10. Wrote Emmy to day. Supped at Whetstone Spring 31 miles from Camp 10. Character of country volcanic. Fossils of plants found in the sandstone around spring. Stone fused in many places by volcanic action. Came 2 miles west of Willow Creek & camped. Distance since morning 41 miles.

June Wednesday 1

Met Mail 5

Slept delightfully. Night bright & balmy. Team, going after Buffalo, approached us as we were hitching up & one of the Teamsters (Mexican) shot two Antelopes near us, in pursuit of which Vale [Vail] had gone. Bough[t] the hind quarters. Doe with two young in her womb. First view of Rocky Mountains—Snow capped.

Came 8 miles to breakfast near breaks of Red River. Nooned at the crossing of Red Fork of the Canadian (Red River) 20 miles from Camp 11. Passed many such herds of Antelopes. Supped at the Ocaté 30 miles from C. 11. Red River & Ocaté valleys much occupied by sheep.

Thursday 2

Camped at Dragoon Spring, 40 miles from C. 11. Night cool & clear, no dew. Morning bracing & cool, with wind north. Country parched & dusty, volcanic. Travelled 12 miles to breakfast, at Burgwynn's Spring. Mountain scenery unusually striking. Reached Fort Union at noon 24 miles from C. 12. Queer looking cluster of cabins, built of round pine logs & "adobes." Saw several officers & were invited to drink the meanest possible whiskey, as we found it. Country around a Sodom—No rain having fallen for more than six months. Hot! Very hot! Left for Santa Fé at 3 P.M. Little rain this evening. Reached Las Vegas [in New Mexico] 27 miles from Ft. Union about 9 P. M. Dirty little Mexican town where we have to sleep on a filthy floor.

June Friday 3 1859

Slept wretchedly last night. Las Vegas a fair specimen of Mexican benightedness. Up this morning & off by sunrise. Day bright & pleasant. Country broken, arid, poor & badly wooded with pine & scattered cedars. Travelled 12 miles (to Tecolaté) to breakfast. Filth. Adobe huts, cow-hide, with man for team, dragged on ground in lieu of cart, naked children & worse than filthy men and women, make up the place—a counterpart of Las Vegas. Came to San José (St. Joseph) to dinner, 28 miles from Las Vegas. San José but a duplication of Tecolaté. Came to Arroyo de Pecos for the night, 23 miles.

Saturday 4: 25 Miles; 788 to Ind.

Our host a Pole (Kousloski) gave us a first rate supper & admirable beds. Slept well & not called at so unpleasant an hour this morning. Good breakfast & off for Santa Fé. Road rough & dusty. Country almost barren. Reached Santa Fé at 15 minutes past 12 N. Stopping at the Fonda, the American hotel of the city. Gave us a good dinner & in comfortable rooms we feel like taking "mine ease in mine Inn." Distance from Pecos to Santa Fé 25 miles.

661 to Ind. 40 M.

712 to Ind. 51 Miles

763 to Ind. 51 Miles

788 to Ind. 25 Miles

SUNDAY 5

Attended Catholic Church. Strolled about town & wrote Emmy 9 pages. Saw Capt. Macomb & had quite a pleasant chat. He is an unostentatious, cultivated gentleman, & I like him much. The Exchange [or Fonda, Hotel] we find quite an exchange from the experiences of some days back. It is comfortable! Eminently so. Drew Salary up to June 30th: $232.25 which I enclosed to Emmy.

JUNE MONDAY 6 1859

Slept well. Morning delightful. Assisted Capt. Macomb in Sextant observations & adjusting Barometers. Walked with Capt., after dinner, about the city. Visited a worker in gold, whose work is Aztec [ancient American Indian]. Supped with the Capt., at his mess & was introduced to Lieut. [Milton M.] Cogswell, Mrs. Smith, [Preston] Beck &c—

TUESDAY 7

At Pecos there was a young man shot "with a colt's pistol, old style, brass mounted & of such are the kingdom of Heaven."
Slept soundly. Not yet experienced the Mexican Bed bug, which has a decided reputation. Assisted, again this morning in Sextant observations. Evening's result not satisfactory on account of clouds. A little rain. No time fixed as to the starting for the field. Had music at [Joseph] Mercure's [store].

WEDNESDAY 8

Not feeling well this morning, quite bilious. Temperature luxurious. After breakfast called on the Capt. No observations taken to day. Ridiculous demonstration on hearing the nomination of [Miguel A.] Otero for Congress. Band preceeded [sic] by a flag, the bearer of which danced to the music most grotesquely. Getting very home sick. Cloudy this evening with rain. Sharp lightening to night.

JUNE THURSDAY 9 1859

Pleasant & cloudy this morning. Breakfast at 7. Called on the Capt. The Catholic Bishop [Jean Baptiste Lamy] soon came in & chatted quite agreeably, insisted upon our visiting his flower garden & gave us a boquet [sic] of very delicate construction. Given up smoking again & feel the better for it. Attended the concert this evening, given by the regimental band. A "Bailé" also to night attended by Dorsey & Vail. Cloudy with showers.

FRIDAY 10

Morning cool & clear. Capt. Macomb left at 8 A.M. for Albuquerque, where he goes to accomplish his out-fit. Dr. N. geologizing among the hills near here. Vail sleeping off last night, & Dorsey, with the Dr. specimen hunting. Took Barometrical observations to day at noon, 2 P.M. & 6 P.M., Capt. to do the same at Albuquerque or its vicinity. Wrote six pages to Emmy. Cloudy all day & cool. Visited Lieut. [John D.] Wilkin's office & saw maps of the Navajoe country. Lieut. Cogswell sat with us awhile as did Major [Albert J.] Smith.

SATURDAY 11
Day pleasant. Spent in Barometrical observations, writing & loafing. Mail in about 5 P.M. Fisher all safe & with him the missing trunk. Received one letter from Emmy & one from Stewart, besides a travelling cap. Got a short note from Capt. Macomb, from Algadones. Evening warm. Visited D^{na}. Carmalita Abila's Bailé. Saw enough in ten minutes to satisfy me.

JUNE SUNDAY 12 1859
Feel unusually well this morning. Day bright & beautiful, as usual. Morning occupied in writing. Closed letter of 16 pages to Emmy. Wrote mother & Stewart. Did not attend the Cathedral to day. Band performed this evening on the Plaza. Most excellent music. Had a visit from Capt. [John] Pope & Lieut. [C. H.] McNally.

MONDAY 13
Morning perfect. After breakfast made Barometrical observations. Opened Barometers brought by Fisher. Also trunk. Made observations to day & instructed Fisher in reading vernier. Evening cool & pleasant. Had a visit from Major Smith & went with him to the Panoramma [saloon]. Soon expelled by the fearful fog of smoke from vile cigaritas. Took a walk & went to bed.

TUESDAY 14
Lovely morning, but promises to be hot. Great ringing of bells since day-light. The Virgin carried from the Cathedral, Sunday 5th, is to be returned amid music, banners & a motley crowd. She is bourne down the street & into the Church. Dr. N. & Fisher gone to Pécos. Visited Major Smith after dinner—had a chat & a glass of native wine. Little rain this evening.

JUNE WEDNESDAY 15 1859
Morning sultry. Cool & satisfactory by 9 A.M. Took Barometrical observa-tions. Sketched the house of the "Padres" of Santa Fé. Dr. N. & Fisher still absent. The usual visit from my Mexican Flower boy, with "Rosa Castilla." Quite a nuisance whose odour counteracts those of his roses. Capt. Macomb returned this evening. Nothing decided yet as to the time of our departure. Band played this eve.

THURSDAY 16
Morning hot. Assisted the Capt. in time observations, also calculated the

Barometrical elevations of Santa Fé & Algadones. Occupied all day with the Capt. & walked with him this evening. He introduced me to ~~Major~~ Col. [J. B.] Gra[y]son & old West Point chum of Fathers. ("I would as soon have taken a porcupine for a pillow!") Cronometer 10'.13".7 East. Rate of increase per day 15".

FRIDAY 17
Quite hot this morning. Engaged to day in Barometrical calculations. Results very satisfactory. Observations this evening to determine the difference in elevation between the Court House at Santa Fé & old Fort Marcy [on a hill above the city].
Mail in the evening & no letters for self. Band performing, sweetly. Evening hot & dry.

JUNE SATURDAY 18 1859
Morning hot. Called on the Capt. Calculated the Barometrical observation of yesterday. Correspondence with line of levels within 13 feet. Mail from Albuquerque brought me a letter from Emmy. Received invitation to Bailé [dance]. Did not attend.

SUNDAY 19
Unusually hot to day. Ther. 95° in Shade. Morning occupied in letter writing. Determined not to go to church this morning, for reasons just & conclusive. Major Smith passed some hour with us this morning. Circus company out to day in full blast. Band of Regt. performing this evening. But little air this morning & too night a continuation of same.

MONDAY 20
Cronometer 10'.58".7 Fast
Hot this morning as can be. Not feeling well to day. Reading nearly all the morning. Called on Major Smith who insisted upon my taking a glass of Champagne with him. A horse race some three miles out of town. I did not attend. Much drinking upon the return of the parties & a couple of fights as sequence. Pleasant breeze to night.

JUNE TUESDAY 21 1859
Hot this morning. Little to do, save to beguile the [day] by reading. Borrowed the "Scarlet Letter" from Major Smith & read it with much interest. Took a walk this evening with Capt. M. & Major S. Fine breeze from the East. Sunset more glorious than imagination could paint. Fine night for sleeping.

WEDNESDAY 22
Morning pleasant. Took observations this morning with Capt. M. & spent most of the morning with him in chat. After dinner assisted the Capt.

in placing the Transit table. Quite a fine shower this evening—the thermometer falling from 82° in shade to 64°. Returning to room found the Dr., Fisher, Vail & Dorsey in a slavery discussion. took no part as these contests engender ill feeling while the[y] change no one's opinion.

THURSDAY 23
To day is a great one with Catholics—Corpus Christie.
Last night glorious for sleeping & this morning cool & delightful. Assisted in time observations. Was introduced and had a conversation with Kit Carson. He has a broad, german head, do. face, hair long & in elf locks, eyes small & restless, colour gray. Mouth broad & decided, filled with strong, irregular teeth. Body heavy & shoulders broad. Lower limbs comparatively slight & a little bowed. Height about 5 ft. 9 in. Age 48 years.

JUNE FRIDAY 24 1859
Warmer this morning. St. Juan's day & observed by the masons. A procession & oration. This evening a Mexican Cock chase. On yesterday evening Hon. Mr. [John S.] Phelps, of Mo. reached here—was met by an escort & band, received by the [New Mexico] Gov[ernor Abraham Rencher]. Many Speeches. He is the friend of this route for the Pacific R.R. This evening rain. Bailé to night. Phelps present & dancing. Self did not go. Mail in late this evening. No letters for us to night.

SATURDAY 25
Up rather late. Temperature pleasant. P.M. opened mail for Ft. Defiance & got letters for the Dr., Fisher & Dorsey. Hope for some by the Southern mail this evening. Kit Carson left this morning. Southern mail in & letter from Emmy. Leveled from Courthouse to Ft. Marcy, elevation 155.20. This agreed with a former line run by the Capt. 0.04. Very pleasant this evening.

SUNDAY 26
Cronometer fast 12'.43".7. Rate in. [increase] per day 15" Morning warm but pleasant breeze stirring. Corpus Christie Sunday. Observed by the Catholics with much form. Morning the Host carried from Shrine to Shrine by the Bishop & his assistants, followed by the girls from the Convent in white & men in the rear shooting blank cartridges to scare the Devil. This evening a heavy storm of hail & rain, deluging everything. Soon cleared off when the Dr.[,] Major S. & myself took a walk to the Almada & tracked pretty…

JUNE MONDAY 27 1859
Cronometer fast—12'.31". Increase 13" per day. Ratherish warm this morning. Breakfasted & took a short walk. Assisted the Capt., with Fisher,

in a time observation. Visited [Fort Marcy] Post library & got a Book. Took a walk this evening with Capt.[,] Lieut. C., Dr. N & Fisher to a hill near, where the Dr. took a sketch of the Placier [Placer] Mountain &c. A grand Bailé here to night. Hon. Phelps footing it quite extensively. Looked in a few minutes, but soon got enough.

TUESDAY 28
Awakened this morning by a <u>woman</u> in our room, who quietly had gotten in bed with the Dr. She proved to be crazy & we hustled her out—Locking the door. Started at 8 ½ A.M. for Galisteo with the Dr. & Fisher. Reached that place at about noon. Capt. Pope & Lieut. Macnally gave us a cordial welcome & a good dinner. Rode this evening ten miles to the Artesian boring. Got back to Galisteo about 9 P.M. After a pleasant evening retired.

WEDNESDAY 29
Slept most delightfully. Our mules late appearing. Morning pleasantly passed in anecdote telling. Left Galisteo at half past ten A.M. reached the old Placer about half past one—12 miles from Galisteo–. Left the Placer after looking in vain for gold, about 4 P.M. & reached Santa Fé (25 miles) after dark, encountering a rain. Found upon ar[r]iving that to day had been devoted in a dinner, to Mr. Phelps, who leaves tomorrow. With difficulty got a cup of tea & went tired to bed.

JUNE THURSDAY 30 1859
Morning warm. Visited the Capt. who had nothing for us to do save a scuffle [foot dragging] through the day. Cut up some drawing paper to proper size & with Fisher & the Dr., went on the hill back of the town to sketch the Placer & Sandia Mountains. Thus spent the day with reading. Evening charming went to see Major Smith for a while & found him in his portal &c. Feeling quite unwell retired early.

JULY FRIDAY 1
Got up this morning feeling most wretchedly[;] took a glass of water which nauseated me until I threw up considerable bile. Ate but little for breakfast. Sketched a little this morning. Felt better after dinner. Southern mail in, but no letters for any of us. Assisted the Capt. this evening & calculated the diff. in height. Barometrically, between this place & Galisteo = 700 ft. Retired early & went to sleep at once.

SATURDAY 2
Slept well & feel quite myself this warm morning. Called on the Capt. & found little to do. Read & sketched during the morning. Last evening's Southern mail brought nothing for us—Rather a disappointment. Eastern mail in & from package for Ft. Defiance, we all were made happy

by letters. This evening spent in reading the Capt's papers. To night in assisting in Astronomical observations. Went to bed early.

JULY SUNDAY 3 1859

Up late this morning. Excessively warm. Kept quietly at home all ~~day~~ morning, writing Emmy & mother. Went to see the Capt. & Major Smith. Assisted with the Dr. in receiving our supplies from Albuquerque. Find the hams bad so will probably have to go without them. Fisher, Vale & Dorsey moved to the Store-house alias Castle.

MONDAY 4

Morning lovely. Awakened at day by the Band of the Reg. discoursing most delicately all the national airs. The Gov's Picnic party leave here after breakfast—will not go. Col. Bonneville has arrived so we will leave here tomorrow week, perhaps. Circus in full blast on the Plaza & the crowd in attendance dense. Day closes with a grand Bailé. Col. B. dancing.

TUESDAY 5

Hot to day. Had [U. S. Army] soldier pants examined & are to be made over. Hams the Capt. thinks past redemption. Long visit from Major Smith. Col. Bonneville will not afford us a larger command than 40 men, a force entirely inadequate for our trip. The Capt. in great disgust. So much for having an old woman (Col. B.) in a position of importance. We will be much circumscribed it is feared in our operations.

JULY WEDNESDAY 6 1859

Pleasant this morning. Nothing of interest going on. Visited the Capt. and had a pleasant chat. After dinner fired our pistols & cleaned them. Copied an account for the Capt. Strolled around until tea. After tea the Capt. invited us to observe the moon through his telescope. View so fine he went for the Gov. & Mrs. Rensher & Squire [James L.] Collins & his grand-daughters ["Hattie" and "Bec" Edgar]. They all came & looked & chatted glibly.

THURSDAY 7

Slept soundly & late this morning. Quite warm. Hunted around, unsuccessfully, for wooden stirrups. Visited Capt. M. found him amiable & pleasant this morning. Read a little & loafed a little, until dinner. After dinner Fisher & self went on the hill adjacent to continue our sketch of Santa Fé. To night we had another moon gazing & were beset by the city gamblers, desiring a look. They all saw in the moon something of their avocation—one silver, another a woman's dress &c.

FRIDAY 8

Passed much as usual, with but little to interest or employ. Southern mail in but with it nothing for any of us.

July Saturday 9 1859

The time hangs heavy enough. Weather pleasant. Eastern mail comes with letters for all. Two to me from Emmy. Nothing of interest occurring. Day generally spent in reading.

Sunday 10

Hot this morning. Occupied ourselves in writing home. Wrote 12 pages to Emmy & 4 to Mother. Expect to take up our march on Tuesday. All our preparations about completed. Band playing this evening. This is a treat we enjoy two or three times a week. The usual Sunday observances— Church, Manté [Monté card game], Faro & Circus.

Monday 11

Morning pleasant. Capt. brought me an invitation from Mr. [James M.] & Mrs. [Eliza Collins] Edgar to meet Maj. Phelps this evening. Laid in a supply of tobacco &c. Assisted the Capt. in his [financial] accounts. The Dr. & myself attended the party where we met all the officers & their ladies as well as those of both sexes fancy free—all American. Two Miss Edgars very pleasant & the younger dances beautifully. Self danced & frolicked until 3 o'clk. Dr. came home early.

July Tuesday 12 1859

Morning delightful—Slight rain of yesterday cooled the air. Feel rather blue this morning, as I slept but 3 hours last night. Major Smith & [Major James L.] Donaldson off for the States this morning. Aided the Capt. in packing &c –. Will probably start tomorrow. Much depends on the docility of the mules. Home sick to night, horribly!

Wednesday 13

Morning cool & pleasant. Roused early as baggage is wanted to be packed. Mules all packed by 10 A.M. & off. Some of them however exhibit decided indications of dislike for the packs. Visited Gov. Rensher & lady, took a glass of wine & bade them good bye. The Capt. dined at the Fonda with us. Off directly after dinner & travelled 18 miles to the valley of the Nambé [to Pojoaque Pueblo], to Camp 1.

18 MILES

Thursday 14

Up before sunrise. Breakfasted at 5. Mules quiet & easily packed. Off by 7. Travelled well; came 12 miles, to crossing of the Rio Grande, by 10:30 A.M. Excessively hot &, as grass cannot be had on the other side of the river within easy reach, we camp here for the day. Camp No. 2. While unpacking a wild mule with Cook's tripods & axes kicked herself free of her load, cutting her legs severely. Camp near the San Juan village. [Camp 2]

12 MILES TOTL. 30 M.

JULY FRIDAY 15 1859

Slept last night like a top. Waked at 5 A.M. Morning clear & warm. Mules quiet under the packing. Off before 7. Crossed the Rio Grande without difficulty & travelled up the valley of the Chama for 10 miles, through the [*Camp 3*] most wretched region imaginable. Sand very deep. Stopped for camp at 11 A.M. Some rain this evening. Tents ditched [trenching to drain rain water] &c—. Slept unusually well last night. Camp 3. "Don Francisco Antonio Salazar y Romero."

SATURDAY 16

Visit yesterday evening from [Albert H.] P[f]eiffer. Up this morning at 5:30 A.M. Mules behave admirably. Goat's milk for breakfast. Little after 7 we got off. Morning delightfully cool. Made the remainder [*Camp 4*] of the distance (12 miles) to Abiquiu by 11:30 A.M. Met by P[f]eiffer & escorted to his home where we were chocolated & dined. After which visited the Castle cañon; had glorious view from summit of cañon. Came tired home after seeing the Ute chief Temuché. Camp 4 "Donna Francisquita Valasquez"

SUNDAY 17

Morning very warm. Up quite reasonably late. Breakfasted at 7 A.M. We delay here with camp until the escort comes up from Santa Fé. P[f]eiffer over early this morning to escort us to the old [military] mines. After riding ten miles through a most beautiful series of views though an exceedingly rough & sterile country, we came to the region where the early Spanish residents had penetrated the side of the mountains in several places, one to the distance of 150 ft. Colouring of hills most exquisite, distinct stratas (sandstone) red, white, bright yellow, green & gray. Got to camp at 6 P.M.

JULY MONDAY 18 1859

Slept most wretchedly last night; beset by mosquitoes until we were all nearly crazed. Up at 6 A.M. & breakfasted under an excessively hot sun. Lieut. Cogswell came up shortly after, with P[f]eiffer & Temuché. The Lieut. was so mindful of us as to forget our letters, for which we had to send to his camp, 3 miles off. Campo just arrived with letters. The Capt.[,] Dr. N & myself fortunate in getting letters. Mine from Emmy of the 19th June. All hands wrote home.

TUESDAY 19

Morning hot; up at 5 A.M. The Capt.[,] Dr., Fisher, P[f]eiffer & myself off this morning for Abiquiu peak & the ruins adjacent. Pack off by 7:30 A.M. After crossing several high masas [*sic*] & descending into deep ravines we came to a cañon, 10 miles from Abiquiu, travelling up this cañon some

2 miles, we ascended a path, evidently the result of art we came upon a high masa [*sic*] whose top was covered with the ruins of an old Pueblo raised [*sic*] to its foundation. The material from which it was constructed, a pumice stone. Ruins very extensive. Stopped in the evening & night at [Nepomuceno Valdez] Pomosima's.

WEDNESDAY 20

Up at 5:30 & off for Abiquiu Peak reached the summit of the Peak, after most desperate climbing, at 10 A.M. Reading of Barometer, on Peak, 21.316, about 9,000 feet above level of Sea. View of the grandest & most extensive character. Returned to Pomosima's at 5 P.M., where we got dinner & started for camp which had been moved, first, to the Arroyo Seco some 15 miles & then on to the Ojo del Navajo about 12 miles making Camp 6. Still on the Chama. We came on to the deserted Camp 5 where we stopped for the night,as the Camp is too far ahead for to nights ride.

JULY THURSDAY 21 1859

Slept well, with head upon my saddle, & was interrupted only by Pomosima's firing his rifle at an "ignis fatuus [illusion]," which roused us thinking we were in difficulty. This & the mosquitoes our only trouble. Up at 3:30 A.M. & [*Camp 7*] off for camp—after only a cup of coffee, came to the "Ojo [Spring] de Navajo"—Camp 6—& found, the Packs gone. Started on in pursuit & over took them at the "Cebolla" (9 miles) finding no water came on to the Nutria where we camped at noon[;] distance travelled to day by packs 15 ½ miles; by us 28 miles. Camp 7

FRIDAY 22

Rain last night. Slept well after the fatigue of the day & after being up later finishing my Topography. Up at 5 A.M., Camp wet. We wait for the sun to dry the tents a little before starting. Off at 9:30 A.M. Camp 7 = 93 ½ miles from Santa Fé. Started late as we have short march. [*Camp 8*] Passed through a country filled with wild Sage, & came down to the valley of the Brazos del Chama & travelled up same one mile to Camp 8. Distance accomplished 7 miles. Reached camp, passing through a heavy shower about noon. Camp in a beautiful locality, at the "vao" of the Charmer [Chama River ford], about 100 miles from Santa Fé.

SATURDAY 23

Rain all the evening & night. Rose late this morning as everything is wet & must dry before packing. Breakfasted at 7. gathered at least 20 different varieties of most delicately beautiful flowers. Rain again set in, preventing us from moving camp. Occupied ourselves in mending rents & adding patches. The Capt. enabled to take a time observation through breaks in the clouds. Lieut. Cogswell dined with us & amused all by his punning proclivity. Have a chance to write home by a Mexican from Abiquiu, who followed us seeking employment. He returns tomorrow with letters from us all.

JULY SUNDAY 24 1859

Spent some hours around the Camp fires last night. Up at 6 A.M., breakfasted during an interval of showers, but the watery descent began immediately thereafter. Took down one of the tents & began preparations for a start, as the rain for a time had ceased, when again it began to fall so rapidly as to force us to delay for fear of getting our flour & sugar wet. All day the rain continued with scarcely an intermission. Dr. N. left early this morning with Pfeiffer & Temuché for the "Lagoon des Chavias."

MONDAY 25

Rain all night. The Dr. safely housed, we hope, in Pfeiffer's lodge. Up this morning at 5:30. A little blue in the sky & the rain intermitted but every indication of its continuance. Off at 8:20 A.[M.], as go we must. Cloudy & little rain. Trail very heavy. Passed [*Camp 9*] through some fine country, well timbered. Reached the "Laguna de los Caballos" [Horse Lake], 12 miles, at 12:30 P.M. [Lieut. Cogswell's] Command in ahead of us. Scarcely in camp before a heavy thunderstorm came up driving us & dinner tables into tents. Lightening struck the cliff just above us. Clear during the evening. Took from the bluff, a sketch of the Laguna. Camp 9 Excessively damp.

TUESDAY 26

Morning beautifully bright. Up at 5 A.M. Escort started in advance of us. Killed yesterday a half dozen Rattle Snakes around camp. Packs moved at 10:40 A.M. Passed through much Pine timber & good grass. Country genarally[*sic*] picturesque & attractive. Day exceedingly hot. Just 5 hours on the road, reached the Rio del Navajoe at 4:40 P.M., pretty well used up. The R. del N. quite a stream, some 3 ft. deep & 40 ft. wide. Fish for supper (the Gila Trout). Mexicans discontented & threaten to leave. Capt. astronomizing with success. [*On the Pacific Slope*] Self quite unwell. To bed early. Rain to night. [*Camp 10*]

JULY WEDNESDAY 27 1859

Up rather late. Breakfasted at 7 A.M. Morning heavy & cloudy. Started with the escort at 8:30. Packs moved some time later. The trail to day has passed through an extremely striking country, for New Mex. Fine pine timber & well grassed [*Camp 11*] valleys. Mule travelled well. Came 13 ½ miles by 1:30 P.M. Camped on the Rito Blanco, or Little White River. Visited by a detachment of Utes who received tobacco & were off. Much of verdure & beauty around. Rained during the night. Slept well

THURSDAY 28

Made an early start, & passing down well grassed valleys & through much good timber, came to the San Juan River at 10 A.M. Water very high. Escort in crossing had much difficulty, one man Swept down & but for a Mexican [*Camp 12*] would have been drowned. Camped upon the grassy bottom of the river. Recrossed to visit the Pagosa or boiling spring, which much interested us. The spring is some 40 x 50 ft & of indefinite depth. Temperature 150°. Water strongly impregnated with sulphur, magnesia &c. Rain this evening. Had a nervous chill to night from my bath.

FRIDAY 29

Camp called late, as we are not to move to day. Rain all night; ceased long enough for breakfast, when set in again. A lull & little sunshine induced the Capt. to propose that I should take a walk up the River to mark the course above. Dr. N, Fisher & Dorsey accompany me some 2 miles from Camp when rain again began turning us hastily homeward, rather wet. Cleared off this evening. A Ute brought in Ferry's lost bag an evidence of honesty so rare among Indians as to induce approbation, likewise Tobacco &c. Night doubtful for astronomical[in?].

JULY SATURDAY 30 1859

Capt. Successful last night with his observations, having been aroused by the Sentry when the sky cleared at midnight. An early call this morning. Heavy mist which soon swept from the view & all clear. Packs moved at 7:10 A.M. came, with an easy [*Camp 13*] travel, 12 miles by 11 A.M. & camped upon the "Nutrita del Francais." Visited by some 30 Utes. Shot their arrows for a Coat & drove them deeply into an oak block. Gave them all tobacco &c—& bade them adieu. Souvetah [Sowiette], the chief of this detachment, will accompany us to Rio las Animas. Rain this evening making camp excessively uncomfortable.

SUNDAY 31

Rained much during the night. Up early. Clouds threatening. Breakfasted, when the rain began to descend. an intermission induced the [striking] of camp, & a general move. After travelling about seven miles the clouds began to give us a perfect deluge, & continued so to do for an hour, wetting everything. In the midst of [*Camp 14*] it reached the Rio Piedra (12 ¾ miles) where we camp. A beautiful locality, but seen under unfavorable auspices. The sun soon out & we dined most pleasantly. Again this evening the rain troubles us. Passed to day the "Piedra Parada", a singular pinnacle.

AUGUST MONDAY 1

Morning damp & cloudy. No astronomizing last night; this with the promise of rain induces the Capt. to stop here to day. A delegation of Utes, from one of the tribes ahead of us, came in to day, headed by Delgarito their great man. Had a long talk professing most friendly relations to the whites. Delgarito dressed beyond measure, a proud supercilious but dashing fellow. Employed the day in clothes washing, which used me up completely. Rain this evening, a little. Clear sky to night. Tamuché, Souvetah[,] P[f]eiffer, Tomasonia, & all the party around a cheery fire to night, also Manolita [Manuelito].

AUGUST TUESDAY 2 1859
An early call, as we have a long march before us. Camp struck & off at 6:40 A.M. Passed up the Nutrita Piedra & at its head we found the lodges of Delgarito's tribe. Cogswell, P[f]eiffer, Dr. N &—delayed & took a pipe with Degarito who they found shorn of all his yesterday's finery. Climbed [*Camp 15*] mountain & passed over the slope of the "Rio los Pinos" which we crossed & camped upon at 1 P.M. By far the finest stream we've passed & full of Trout. Delgrarito's & Cabazon's tribes in to day, by delegates & all received either Blankets[,] Shirts or Cotton. All much pleased. Good night for astronomizing.

WEDNESDAY 3
Morning cloudy & pleasant. Started at 7:25 A.M. for the "Rio Florida." The view of the Sierra la Platta [*sic*], in the distance very striking. Passed through not so good a country as for some ten days previous. At 10:25 A.M. reached the Florida, a beautifully clear [*Camp 16.*] stream though smaller than the Pinos. All hands successful in Trouting, some of the fish of 2 lbs. Mexican Indian traders passed on way to Abiquiu. Evening cool & fires essential as for the last 10 nights. Clear sky to night for the Camp. Distance to day 9 miles.

THURSDAY 4
Breakfasted at 7:30. Morning too cool to be pleasant, sun soon out intensely hot. Dr. N., Fisher, P[f]eiffer, Dorsey &c. Start this morning for the Pueblo on the "Las Animus" [*sic*], some 15 miles distant, noted for the state of preservation in which it exists. Capt. Vail & Self forego the hot ride for letter writing. Clothes mending & Chronometer rating. Will remain here to day & tomorrow. Day very hot. Letter writing to Emmy &c. Mexican trader passed this evening with a story that came from the Indians to the effect that our troops had bombarded Salt Lake City. This we are inclined to believe. Fine sky to night.

AUGUST FRIDAY 5 1859
Up at quite a reasonable hour & breakfasted at our leisure. Aided the Capt. in time observations; during this the Pueblo visiting party came up having found the distance to the Pueblo 40 rather than 15 miles. All

rather disgusted with the trip. Temuché, Rio Vajo, Nutria & another Ute sent to Kyatano, the renegade Navajoe, desiring him to come in. Last night the rascal Nutria assisted by the other Utes ran off all of Kyatano's horses. This news Temuché & Rio Vajo brings as well as that they passed 4 Mexicans in a starving condition who had lost their way coming from Salt Lake City. At 10 P.M. the Capt sent a party & provisions for their relief.

SATURDAY 6
Morning bight & hot. Started with escort at 8:30 & travelled 7 ¼ miles by 10:55 A.M. to the Las Animas. Pfeiffer, Pomosamia, Temuche, Souvetah &c. left us this morning for Abiquiu. [*Camp 17*] The 4 Mexicans came in to day, most pitiable objects. They had lost their way & had been wandering about this wretched country with nothing to eat until on the eve of starvation. Temuché yesterday extorted from one of them his coat & $16 (all he had) for a piece of dried meat as large as one hand. Just the scoundrel we should have believed & doubtless is an aider [*sic*] in the horse stealing.

SUNDAY 7
Camp moved at 7:10 A.M. 2 of the estray Mexicans retained as hands, the other two, with two of our worthless ones loaned a pair of Buros & provisions for the ten days & sent to Abiquiu. Morning delightful, country sterile but picturesque. Came to the "Rio la Plata" (12 ¾ miles) by 11:55 A.M. The La Plata a small but beautifully clear, rocky [*Camp 18*] stream in which a bath was a great luxury. Fine grama grass & a waste of flowers upon which we bedded. Fisher & self, after dinner climbed the bluff a cross the River from which we had a most extended & magnificent view. Took a sketch of the La Plata Mts. Saw an Indian encampment at foot of Mt. on the River.

AUGUST MONDAY 8 1859
Cool during the night. Slept well. Thermometer this morning at 44°, a fire an essential. Camp moved at 6:50 A.M. Passed up the valley of the Rio la Plata, leaving the Mts.on the Right, crossing 1 mile above camp. Our trail lay along a series of fine valleys & crossing the [*Camp 19.*] divide, (11 miles) came to the Rio los Mancos (14 miles) at 12:10 P.M. The Mancos a small, ~~muddy~~ clear stream. Camp ground shady & pleasant. Good grass. Stream upon close observation proves to be clear & full of Trout. All hands caught quite a number. Fine Sulphur Spring near which we partook of freely.

TUESDAY 9
Last night cold. Bugle sounded at 4:30 A.M. Up shivering. Thermometer at 34° at 6 A.M. Breakfasted at 5 A.M. Packs moved by 6:10. All in ill

humour at being waked so early. Passed over broken country, desolately [*Camp 20.*] sterile & parched. Day hot. Came to the Nutria del Dolores to camp; distance 14 miles. Reached the Nutria at 11:25 A.M. Small stream & no fish. Evening pleasant. Clouds interrupt entirely the observance of an occultation. To bed early as we are to start before sunrise tomorrow for the Dolores, distance 5 miles. This a notion of Cogswell's, who feels the authority confided by the Capt.

WEDNESDAY 10

Morning pleasant. Not so much so to be roused at 4:30 A.M., the time the Bugle sounded. Off at 6:25 A.M. Came to the Rio Dolores (5 miles) by 8:15 A.M. Rio Solado [*sic*] 20 miles above camp. A locality as beautiful as possible. Flowers everywhere. Gathered a variety of seed. Fine fishing in which all indulged. Pleasant [*Camp 21.*] Shower about dinner time. Will remain here tomorrow, resting & preparing for the "jornadas" ahead. Evening pleasant, with a little rain. The occultation obscured & the Capt. much disappointed. Slept well, though rather unwell the result I fancy of the Mancos Sulphur Spring.

AUGUST THURSDAY 11 1859

Morning delightful, though quite cool in early dawn. All hands engaged in washing &c. Aided the Capt. in time observations. Self very unwell, bowels much disturbed. Dr. N. & Fisher off to visit an old Pueblo some two miles up the river. Darned draws, socks &c. quite successfully. Finished sketch of the La Plata Mts. Evening cool & cloudy. But sparce observations made to night. Some rain & much wind. Capt. resolved to remain over tomorrow for an occultation that may determine his Longitude.

FRIDAY 12

Disturbed much last night. Up late, breakfasting at 7 A.M. All went to the top of the masa [*sic*] adjacent to see an old Pueblo & enjoy the view. Found ruins indicative of greater antiquity than any we have seen. Mingled with the stone is much pottery, broken & of a ruder stamp than that previously collected. View unusually fine; the Dr.[,] Fisher & self took sketches. Whiled away the evening in chat & anecdotes. Sky most beautiful to night. Occultation did not occur, from some probable mistake in the almanac.

SATURDAY 13

By some stupid blunder camp called this morning at 3 A.M. Breakfasted at about 4, by candle-light. Found that our bell-mare has had a colt during the night. This induces hesitation as to moving to day. Capt. finally resolves to kill the young one & move on. The Ute with us prevents this [*Camp 22*] cruel necessity by making his squaw take it, with her, on her horse. Country wretched to day naught but sage & stunted cedars & piñons. Contour of country flat, extending to the Mts. Came 10 ¼ miles by 11:30 A.M. to the Sarouaro Spring; an extensive old Pueblo ruin.

AUGUST SUNDAY 14 1859
Called at 4 A.M. Morning cool & delightful. Mules brought up, when the colt is found missing, the mules having pitched into him & bitten him to death. Packs moved at 6:40 A.M. Country passed [*Camp 23.*] through much as yesterday, a long, dry sage plain. Fatigued more by to days march than any since leaving Santa Fé. Reached the "Tierra Blanco" at 12:05 P.M. distance from last camp 16 miles. Fine spring in an arid canon. Quite unwell to night.

MONDAY 15
Morning cloudy & pleasant. Up & off at 7:20. Sky overcast. Country still as for two or three days past; an unbounded Sage Plain, whose scrubby growth tugs at one's feet continually. Nothing to note in this dreary waste. The only [*Camp 24.*] live thing seen on the march a pair of sage grouse. Came to the "Juajolote" (17 1/8 miles) by 1:15 P.M. A long unpleasant drive. The Juajoloté (water lizards) not a desirable locality as the water is infested by water puppies, Apus' &c. Refreshing rain this evening. Not much done in astronomics.

TUESDAY 16
Up early this morning. Still cloudy for which we are all duly grateful in this hot land. Breakfasted at 6 A.M. Camp moved at 7:20 A.M. Day pleasant during the march. Same unending sage plain, the Sierra la Sal on our [*Camp 25*] right & the Abajo on left. Travelled 9 ½ miles to the Ojo de Cueva [Cave Spring] by 10:30 A.M. Much such a locality as the Juajoloté [salamander], perhaps more so. A refreshing shower after reaching Camp, which allayed in some degree the dust which appeared alive. Mexs. caught Scorpion & R. Snake. To our surprise Souvetah (the dispatch from Santa Fé & Pfeiffer) came in. Brought nothing for me.

AUGUST WEDNESDAY 17 1859
Slept well last night owing to my abstemiousness for some day or two. Morning pleasant & cloudy. Breakfasted at 5:30 A.M. Train moved at 7:50 A.M. Souvetah given presents, with which he seemed much pleased, [*Camp 26*] & bidding us adieu took the back trail. Day pleasant & breezy. Struck a side cañon [South Canyon] to the Cañon de las Pañitas (cañon of large Rocks little cliffs) after marching 5 miles; descending this we Camped in the Cañon. Having come 12 miles by 11:50 A.M. Shower this noon.

THURSDAY 18

Last evening most delightful. The Capt's astronomics kept us all silent to our disgust. Morning the perfection of early fall. Dr. N. up in the wall of the cañon excavating a fossil Icthyosaurus, whose gigantic [*Camp 27.*] bones are our wonder. Our start somewhat retarded by this. Train moved at 9:15 A.M. Still in the Cañon de las Pañitas; at the mouth of a tributary ravine we find water holes, (La Tenejal) 7 miles from starting & Camp at 11:40 A.M. Fine rain this evening, which has rendered our water chocolate in colour & consistency. Walked to the top of an adjacent sandstone hill where we had an extensive but sterile view.

FRIDAY 19

Two parties sent out this morning, one the Indian & guide to see the practicability of the trail to the junction of the Grand & Green Rivers, the other, under guidance of Juan [Martin], to discover, if possible, a return road by way of the San Juan. All hands growly from waiting for breakfast & having to use such muddy water. This can be prevented as clear water is to be found in sandstone holes, within half mile. Kegs sent for it after the muddy has done its duty. The Sargent & Stephen returning from 10 miles towards Grand River report a favourable camp ground at that distance. Orders for moving tomorrow. Gathered quite a number of Flower seed. To bed early[.]

AUGUST SATURDAY 20 1859

Camp called quite early. Packs moved by 7:30 A.M. No return yet of our explorers. Trail to day through a country which we doubt to have been God forsaken as its wretchedness is suggestive of its belonging to the Arch enemy from the beginning. "Nothing to right of <u>us</u>, nothing [*Camp 28.*] to the left of <u>us</u>," but deep mouthed cañons. But little vegetation save the salt weed. Travelled 10 ½ miles by 11:15 A.M. Reached camp—El Ojo Verde [Green Spring]—in the midst of one of the hardest rains made in the region. The Ute Indian [scout] in to night. Reports that the remainder of the Grand River party will be here tomorrow.

SUNDAY 21

Evening (last) most charming. Up at quite a city hour & breakfasted at 7. The Grand [Colorado] River explorers in about 10 A.M. & represent the trail as utterly impracticable for our packs. Distance about 55 miles to the junction, which they did not reach. They report fresh Indian signs. It is now determined that the Capt, Cogswell, Dr. N, Self & five others, cooks &c—shall start tomorrow for the junction of the Grand & Green Rivers, an expedition fraught no small degree of danger. All our arrangements perfected for an early start, so we are to bed early in view of the fatigues ahead.

MONDAY 22

Morning pleasant. Up early & breakfasted about 5:30. Party started for Grand River at 7:15 A.M. Party [included] Capt. M, C., Dr. & Self. Campo [Campeau], Hathaway, Jaramillo, & two Mexicans. With the wistful looks of all following we mounted the side of the cañon of Camp 28, passing over a broken sage plain came to the head of one of the cañons tributary to the Cañon Colorado [Hart's Draw], leading to the [*Camp 29.*] Grand River. For 27 miles, down this, we passed between walls varying in height from 800 to 1200 ft. aroded [*sic*] into all imaginable curves, shapes & fancies. The ride, hot & fatiguing. Reached a point where water was found in holes at 4:15 P.M. where we conclude to stop for the night. Aided the Capt. in observations by light of a newspaper lantern.

AUGUST TUESDAY 23 1859

One of the mules vamo[o]sed for Camp 28 immediately after stopping last evening, disgusted doubtless with the trip. Off for the Grand River at 6:25 A.M. Plodding down through the mazes of the Cañon Colorado, through which passes, at times, a rapid, muddy stream, we find our journey most arduous from the steepness of the bank & frequency of crossing the stream. The banks of the stream vary from ten to fifteen feet in height & are so perpendicular that when our mules slide down we cling by the cantle of the saddle to avoid going over their heads. ☞ See April 10th. [April 10] This stream, going & coming, we crossed 270 times & as the banks average 10 ft. in height we must have passed over about 5400 ft. of perpendicular (nearly) distance—little over a mile (?). To accomplish 9 ¼ miles occupied us until 10:30 A.M. At this time & point we could advance no farther with one mule. Dismounting Dr. N., Cogswell & self resolved to climb one of the mesas if possible, & see the Grand River, its junction with the Green &c. The Capt attempted to follow but failed. Towering 12 or 15 hundred feet above us, to all appearances absolutely inaccessible, the tops of these wall-like structures—trembling in the heat & glare of a noon day sun, whose radiations raised the thermometer to 92° in the shade, seemed to defy our approach. Starting with our usual clothing the intolerable heat & difficulties of ascent soon forced us to shed by degrees article after article, until at last the summit was reached & exultingly stood upon, by three men stripped to shirts, draws & boots. All our labour found its reward[,] when on looking around there met our eyes such a view as is not to be seen elsewhere on earth. But few, if any other whites, were ever the beholders of so magical a variety of towering sierra-like masas [*sic*], deep cut by canons, penetrating in all directions, into whose depths the rays of the sun at mid day can only fall. In the distance—to the south—the masas [*sic*], broken into isolated pinnacles &

clustered, castled, summits gave the effect of a grander city than dream land contains. The colours varying from the darkest brown of the old Red sandstone pass through the changes of richest tone to chocolate light.
From Santa Fé to Abiquiu 52 m.
From Abiquiu to Grand River 322 m
Red & _, capped, in many instances, by a sandstone of lightest drab. Enjoying this until our time, given by the Capt., had more than elapsed we were forced to descend, after the Dr. had taken a hasty sketch of our surroundings & self the courses to various points. The time occupied in our ascent & descent was about two hours. This time in occupation, climbing about 1200 ft. will give one ~~some~~ an idea of the difficulties to be surmounted. After resting for some short time, for the heat & labour made both Cogswell & the Dr. sick, we turned our mules +1 heads east-ward, making the first steps on our homeward march. To me this was the greatest pleasure of our expedition. At 6 P.M. we had retraced our steps to where we slept the night before & where the pack mules (2) had been left in charge of Hathaway & the 2 Mexicans. Clouds in the distance, hanging over the Sierra Abajo, gave us, just at night fall, a slight shower. To night I stood my first guard, in an Indian country, from 12 to 2.
During these two lonely hours every incident of my life came clearly before me & the future with wife & baby boy was peered into until my mind grew weary as my body in scheming & suggesting. After my watch sleep came with double sweetness. At the time I first took my watch the discharge of water upon the Abajo came thundering along giving for a time much uneasiness as we were in a position where the water might have reached & troubled us; these fears soon subsided with the torrent, whose rise was in one big wave which fell, with a cessation of the supply, as promptly.

WEDNESDAY 24
Started at 7 A.M. for Camp 28, having still to pass for several miles up the Cañon whose stream, banks & quick sands had so troubled us. Once my mule fell & failed in her efforts to climb the bank. During her struggles I felt it safest to scramble off. Again as with the others my mule sank deeply into quick sand from which with mighty struggles she could barely extri-cate herself. Tired & heated we reached Camp 28, glad as possible to get safely back, having happ[i]ly met with no Indians. All at camp greeted with cheerful smiles & congratulations whose influences tended very ma-terially to aid digestion at supper.

THURSDAY 25
At bed time, last night, the sentinel stopped, at the mouth of the cañon, a party of 18 Utes, headed by the father of the Indian who had acted as

guide to the Grand river. It was thought advisable to make the Indians camp at the mouth of the cañon & allow them to come in this morning. To do this & have a fair understanding with these red fellows we cannot move camp to day. Juan Martin & party came in, from the San Juan, the evening of the day we left for the Grand River. He reports the return route by that trail practicable. Presents made the Utes which they think to be hardly their due. Orders to start in the morning.

August Friday 26 1859
Rain nearly all night—ceasing before breakfast. we had our tables placed out doors, when just as our seats were taken the big drops began to rattle a roll-call on our tin plates & cups. Thanks, however, to India rubber coats we got quite comfortably through, though an infusion of rain water does not improve tea nor wetting add to the edibility of biscuit. Most persistently the rain continued until 1 P.M. too late thereafter to pack the mules & move. Our next Camp, on way to the San Juan, & home, will be at the point of our former Camp 27. Horse racing this evening. Sky clear.

Saturday 27
Camp called at the absurd hour of 4 A.M. Breakfasted at 4:30. Sun soon out hot. Packs moved at 7:30. The first comfortable ride I've had for a month, as in returning [Camp 27] to to [sic] El Tenajal [sic] there is no necessity for again taking the topography which is secured in passing to the Ojo Verde. Train moved slowly, reaching Camp at 11:30 A.M. Rain having allayed the dust we find the camp ground improved. Completed this evening the topog. of trail to Grd. River.

Sunday 28
Morning cloudy & pleasant. Dr. N, Fisher, Dorsey, Steve, Delis [Dély] & a Mex. off immediately after breakfast for Camp 26, to take another pick at the old petrified monster in the masa's [sic] bluff. Packs [Camp 30.] moved at 6:50 A.M. Trail passed up a valley course nearly South, towards the Sierra Abajo. Valley smooth & good travelling until reaching a point, 12 miles, where masa's [sic] side gave hard climbing. Came 14 ½ miles to the Cold Spring by 11:45 A.M. This locality perhaps the most favourable we've had. Waited dinner till 5 P.M. for the Dr's party. They not in at 10 P.M. which gives us great uneasiness. (The Aurora Borealis to night superb) At 10:30 the Party are here much to our relief. Assisted in astronomics to night.

August Monday 29 1859
The temperature of autumn this morning. As the remnants of the Saurian have to be packed this morning camp is delayed in moving until 8 A.M. Short march, passing over the high land near the foot of the Sierra Abajo.

Came 8 ½ [*Camp 31.*] miles by 10:50 A.M. & camped at cherry Creek. In evening a heavy rain, driving us from the supper table; this continued nearly all night. An immense quantity of wild cherries found here which have sent us all to bed bellyachey [*sic*].

TUESDAY 30
Morning cloudy & cool, up rather late. The Abajo shrouded in mist. Breakfast in the gloom not comfortable. Packs moved at 7:45 A.M. Day chill and dark passed along the base & within 6 miles of the Abajo, through a sage [*Camp 32.*] plain intersected by slight cañons in one of which we camped, during a heavy rain, at 10:40 A.M. Distance travelled 8 ½ miles. Camp at the Mormon or Silver Spring. The last name given from Dr. N. having found a 25¢ & 5¢ pieces near the spring, proving the white man to have been here before us.

WEDNESDAY 31
Rain yesterday gave us all much discomfort & made self quite sick. Morning cloudy & cool. Up & off at 6:50 A.M. Trail to day passes over a gently broken country, cut by occasional cañons; these difficult of passage. Heavy hail-storm passes to our right & over the [*Camp 33*] Sierra Abajo, giving it for the time a snow-capped point. Country covered by sage & uninteresting generally. Reached the "Ojo del Alamo" at 11:40 A.M. & camped among rocks. Rain this evening. Indian tracks (fresh) seen this evening. Guard on the alert. Night cool & cloudy.

SEPT THURSDAY 1 1859
Exceedingly damp & cool this morning with every indication of rain. Camp called quite early. Packs moved at 7 A.M. Trail traversed a broken country for seven miles when falling into a cañon. Continued in same [*Camp 34.*] to its junction with that of the "Ritito de Sierra Abajo" [Recapture Creek] (14 ½ miles) which reached & camped upon at 11:50 A.M. Water much the colour & consistency of a mixture of chalk, clay & water. Makes wretched tea &c—Self still quite sick. Took blue mass to night. Nothing to interest particularly.

FRIDAY 2
Slept unusually well last night. Morning bright & bracing; quite the temperature of fall. Mule knocked over the tripod with both barometers, fortunately without injury to either. Moved at 7:15 A.M. Passing down the Cañon of the [*Camp 35*] Ritito del Sierra Abajo came to the San Juan (11 miles) at 11 A.M. The Cañon of the Ritito not offering anything of especial interest. Walls about 200 ft high. The San Juan muddy, with a low sandstone wall for its south bank & a broad flat on the north. Will remain here tomorrow.

SATURDAY 3

Morning delightful. Breakfasted comfortably at a reasonable hour. Dr.,
Fisher & Dorsey off for the masa [*sic*] near. Self engaged in finishing
sketch of the Rio Dolores. Assisted the Capt. in time observations. Day
continues pleasantly cool. The masa [*sic*] party back by two &, after snack-
ing, smoked all around. Rain, accompanied by much wind, this evening,
& in departing gave us the most brilliant bow the eye ever beheld. The
bow, was strongly reflected in its secondary & had beside a triplication of
itself. Evening chilly, to bed early.

SEPT SUNDAY 4 1859

Cooks called at 3:30 A.M. Breakfasted at 4:30. Had the Lieut. [Cogswell]
to breakfast as at tea last night. Morning glorious. Packs moved at
6:50 A.M. Route up & along the San Juan whose valley averages a mile
in width. Appears [*Camp 36*] to have once been thickly settled: casas
[houses] in the face of every bluff & Pueblos at short intervals. All now
is sandy sterility. Passed around two bluffs where we had to make the
roughest sort of path. Camped at 11:35 A.M. having come 13 miles. Rain
this evening. Cool.

MONDAY 5

Morning cool & cloudy, quite Septemberish. Breakfasted at 6 A.M., which
all enjoyed—our sheep a great institution. Camp up & off at 6:50 A.M. Our
trail to day less obstructed than during yesterday. The San Juan [*Camp 37*]
very crooked & as muddy as possible, yet this our only drinking water.
Ruins of Pueblo's still friquent [*sic*]. Came 13 ½ miles by 11:25 A.M. &
camped. We are now 145 ½ miles from Grand River. Day cool & windy.
Night heavy & damp. Moon encircled. Very cool.

TUESDAY 6

This morning as yesterday quite cool but very bright. Breakfasted early.
Train moved at 6:40 A.M. March still up the San Juan whose turbidity has
been increased by late rains. Trail pretty good until reaching [*Camp 38.*]
12 ½ miles where passing around the river bluff [again in New Mexico]
the mules fared badly. Several fell in the river & one we feared would be a
loss, he, however, extricated himself. The mule with the Capt's box & my
trunk fell from the path rolling over into the water's brink, here he was
rescued. Reached camp 13 miles at 11:40 A.M. Change of temperature &
rain this evening. Very cool. Across the River, from Camp, extensive ruins.
this evening very cold

SEPT WEDNESDAY 7 1859

Morning very cool. Had to resort to a heavier coat. Breakfasted & off
at 6:45 A.M. Trail leaves the River, crossing the Mancos 3 ½ miles from

Camp 38. At intervals the trail approaches the [*Camp 39*] River & diverges immediately therefrom keeping upon the 2nd bottom, or masa [*sic*] of river. Pueblos seen every short distance indicating the once presence of a numerous people. Camped at 11:40 A.M. Distance travelled 14 ¾ miles. Night pleasant. Fine air. Old Fortification near, on the high masa [*sic*] back of camp.

THURSDAY 8
Up quite early. Morning as beautiful as possible. Packs moved at 6:45 A.M. Trail, as yesterday, passes along the River upon the surface of the high-[*Camp 40*] land. Pueblos still friquent [*sic*]. Day pleasantly cool. Came 14 miles by 11:25 A.M. & camped on River. All day in sight of "the Cathedral"—a magnificent trap pile 1600 ft high standing isolated & at this distance, 11.6 miles, much as possible like a grand old church with towers and pinnacles. Night cool.

FRIDAY 9
Thermometer at 43° this morning. Ate our breakfast with a shivering accompaniment. At sunrise Packs ready to start. Moved at 6:35 A.M. Report of Navajoes in the vicinity, not believed. Still we continue our trail [*Camp 41.*] up the San Juan. Day delightful but the country exceedingly dry & dusty. Left the Cathedral behind us. Passed a remarkable line of volcanic upheaval, The Creston [Hogback ridge]. Pueblos still seen at short intervals. Came 12 ½ miles by 10:55 A.M. & camped. A large ruined Pueblo near camp. Evening cool but pleasant. 200 miles from Grand River.

SEPT SATURDAY 10 1859
Cloud this morning. Camp called as usual. Packs moved at 6:45 A.M. Trail, as for some days past, follows the River, departing therefrom at intervals but again returning. Road dusty & uninteresting save in the presence of [*Camp 42*] Pueblo ruins the number of which are so great that since striking the San Juan we have never been out sight of one. Crossed the La Plata at 14 m. from Camp 41 & reached the Las Animas at 12:10 P.M. a long ride & all much fatigued. Dis. 17 miles. Rain this evening. Fine camp ground. Mex. found corn-field on the Animas above. Will remain here tomorrow.

SUNDAY 11
Rain during the entire night. Up late. Self with wretched pain in my back. Breakfasted at 8 A.M. Rain again which continues, without a hours cessation, during the day. No chance for washing or a general cleaning up. Lolled away the day most unfavourably, in tents & feeling glum enough. Pueblos all around us. Dr. N. & Fisher found a number of small beads, ornaments of the Puebloites. Heavy clouds this evening & soon in [*sic*]

increase of rain which falls as if the windows of heaven were opened. Can do nothing so all turned in at 8 for the night.

MONDAY 12
One of the longest & most uneasy nights I ever tossed through. Up late as we cannot move to day. Still cloudy & chill. At half past nine a ray of sunshine struggles through to comfort us. Washing going on tho' the Animas is sadly muddy. Self took a bath which refreshed in spite of the undue admixture of mud. Walked with the Dr. to the Pueblos near & collected sundry bright flints &c. Evening unusually clear. Dined very lightly & feel the better. Washing in to night looking wonderfully white. Capt. astronomizing with entire success. Went to bed at 10 P.M. Slept unusually well.

SEPT TUESDAY 13 1859
Passed to day the Arroyo Chaco & reached camp at 11:35 A.M. Morning cloudy. Off at 7 A.M. Train crossed the Animas (half as large as the San Juan & fully as muddy) without difficulty. River 300 ft wide & averaging 3 ½ ft. in depth. Sky clear by 9 A.M. & day delightful. Travelled [Camp 43] quietly up the San Juan (passing the most perfect ruin of a Pueblo yet seen. Much of the walls are still standing & many bones (human) remaining. Vail found a well preserved skull. Mex. with his usual facility for names calls this the "Casa de Montezuma." Distance to day 12 m. Night cloudless!

WEDNESDAY 14
Got up quite unwell this morning. Cool & cloudy. Train moved at 6:45 A.M. Trail along the San Juan about 1 mile from river. Valley of River broader & bluffs less high than those of a week past. Day clear & at midday hot. Came twelve miles to the mouth of the "Cañon Largo" but finding no ford camped [Camp 44] that the river may be explored. Armajillo found a ford below camp which we will try tomorrow. Night clear & cool. Have refrained from smoking this evening & feel the better for it.

THURSDAY 15
Up some time before sunrise. Morning cool. Thermometer at 46°. Camp moved at 6:40 A.M. Came one mile down the River to where there was a possibility of fording. Passage swift, deep and dangerous. Water to our knees on the mules. Two [Camp 45] of the Lieut's mules washed down & one of his men, who was saved, as usual, by Antonio. Also the pack of one of the mules (two sacks of bacon) was lost. The mules were with difficulty rescued. Came up the Cañon Largo & with much satisfaction left the San Juan behind us. Travelled 9 miles to the Cañon Blanco by 10:45 A.M. Bur[r]os ate soldiers Bread!

SEPT FRIDAY 16 1859

Camp called quite early. Morning bright but cool. Thermometer at 45°. Our last view of the La Plata Mts. yesterday presented them covered by snow. Packs moved at 6:45 A.M. Crossed the Cañon Blanco & continued up Cañon Largo. The Cañon filled [*Camp 46.*] with flowers & fine grama grass, but the water is dilute mud, with an admixture of salt. Walls of Cañon 600 ft high—width of Cañon 1 ½ miles. Came 12 miles by 10:50 A.M., & camped. Day delightful. Gathered Flower seed & silicified [petrified] wood—The last found in cords. Evening clear &, as we have moved considerably south, warm. 263 miles from Grand River.

SATURDAY 17

Morning bright but cool. Ther. At 43°. Two of the horses of our Mex. packers stolen last night by Navajoes. Supposed to have been some of Kyatano's band in retaliation for those taken from him by the Utes with us, Aug. 4th. Train moved at 6:45 A.M. Still in Cañon [*Camp 47*] Largo which seems resolved to string out till crack of dawn. Day delightful. Came 15 miles, & to where we could see the head of the Cañon, by 11:40 A.M. & camped. Gathered flower seed, & one of the Astor variety named after my own—("Astor Emelia.") Evening clear & pleasant. Night cool.

SUNDAY 18

Awoke this morning two hours before day by the cold. Up before sunrise & found everything out white with frost. Ice in the basin. Thermometer at 30°. Dressed without fire, which the Capt. in a spirit of self martyrization seems disinclined to [*Camp 48*] have. Ate our breakfasts from our knees at the cook's fire. The Capt. alone at the Table. Packs moved at 6:45 A.M. Passed up the Cañon Largo, which gives promise of termination. 2 miles from Camp 47 passed fine spring. Flowers in profusion. Day hot. Came 12 ½ miles by 10:55 A.M. & camped at the "El alto de la Utah," near head of Cañon Largo. Thermometer descends 20° during the first hour after sunset = 70° to 50°.

SEPT MONDAY 19 1859

Up rather too early for comfort. Ther. before sunrise, at 34°. Vail got one of the men to make us a fire so we breakfasted comfortably. Morning bright & clear. As yesterday quite a frost. Train moved at 6:40 A.M. Variation of Ther. during the last 24 hours 80°. Still following the water tributary [*Camp 49 "La Cañada de los Alamos"*] to Cañon Largo & flowing down the Pacific slope. General course to day, as for three days past, about 15° South of East. Trail through wide open valley. Many flowers. Day bright & pleasant. Camp 15 miles by 11:40 A.M. & camped. Night clear. Ther. 38°.

TUESDAY 20

Slept unusually well last night, which I attribute to a new arrangement of Buffalo Robe. Up early. Ther. 36°. Sun rose in an unclouded sky. Packs moved at 6:40 A.M. Day delightful. Course, as for some days, a little South of East towards "La Sierra Nascimiento" [*Camp 50.*] (The mountain of birth) from whence flows the water into the Atlantic & Pacific [at the Continental Divide]. Camped within 3 miles of its Base, at 10 A.M. Dis., accomplished 10 miles. Locality delightful &, for a treat, clear, cool, water. Remnants of previous occupation seen in broken pottery &c. Evening cool. Ther. 60° at sundown.

WEDNESDAY 21

Morning pleasant. Up a little earlier than usual. Capt. last night at 2 observing an eclipse of one of Jupiter's sattelites [*sic*]. Train moved at 6:35 A.M. Trail passing down a tributary of the Rio Puerco. Country opening more & timber [*Camp 51.*] of quite respectable size. Within 3 miles of the base of the Nascimiento Mt. during the day. General course south. Crossed one of the tributaries of the Puerco & following down another to its junction with the 1st, camped at 10:45 A.M. Dis. travelled 12 ½ miles. Dis from Grand River 327 ¼ miles. Locality favourable.

SEPT THURSDAY 22 1859

Resolved to remain here to day that the route through the vias [Valles Calderas] may be explored; the Capt. wishing, if practicable, to reach Santa Fé by that route rather than by Jamez [*sic*]. Jaramillo, Johnston, [John Campeau] Campo & 2 Mexs. sent on this expedition. Dr. N., Fisher, Vail & Dorsey off this morning for the Nascimiento Mt. (4 miles to base). The Dr. to explore geologically, the others as amateurs (?). Self engaged during the early day in securing flower seed. Rain about noon & fall of Ther. 18° in an hour. Rain continues & the wind with it very chill. ☞ See April 16th [April 16] Thermometer 48° at 1 P.M. Mountain Party rather unfortunate. They returned about 2 P.M. pretty well moistened. Cessation of rain during the dinner hour & the fall but fitful thereafter. Jaramillo & Johnston return at 5 P.M. They report no trail found through the vias though Johnson thinks he can find the way through. Not finding a trail induces the Capt. to continue with Cogswell's command & pass through Jamez [*sic*]. In this there is a general acquiescence as all long to reach Santa Fé without further delay. Cloudy tonight & rain impending. Turn in early.

FRIDAY 23

Slept miserably last night—dream following dream, of such wretched characters, as to keep me in a semi wakeful condition all night. Morning cloudy. Ther. 46° at Sunrise: Train moved at 7:20 A.M. Trail passes along

& within 3 [*Camp 52 Saw antelope & coyotes.*] miles of the Nascimiento Mt. crossing the head branches of the Puerco. Passed to day 3 old houses built by the Mexicans many years ago & which for some reasons they were compelled to forsake. Old Jaramillo evidenced an entire ignorance of the country to day, carrying us over the worst places. Came 13 ¾ by 11:55 A.M. Camp on branch of [Rio] Puerco. Rain this evening.

SATURDAY 24

A scotch mist this morning. Temperature pleasant. Camp 52—341 miles from Grand River. Sun soon out bright. Train moved at 7:00 A.M. Still the trail passes along the foot of Mt. Nascimiento about 3 miles from its base. Passed much fine grass & [*Camp 53.*] some new flowers. Country opening. A fine view of the Cabazon [*sic*] (or big head) Mt. as well as Mt. Mateo. Came 12 miles by 11 A.M. & camped near the end of the Nascimiento. Triangulated distance—Capt. operating—to Cabazon. Found it 13 miles from camp & 1311 ft. above it. Rain after dinner flooded our tent. Cloudy night.

SEPT SUNDAY 25 1859

Rain nearly all night. Morning cloudy & damp. Up quite early & off at 7 A.M. For several miles trail continues along the foot of the Nascimiento & then turning into an opening ascends the same. Ridges [*Camp 54.*] of purest Gipsum [*sic*] (almost alabaster) cross our path in the ascent. Around us a maze of high towering rocks & deep ravines. From the summit the descent was not so great to the valley of the Jamez [*sic*] River, which we reached at 1 P.M. & camped near the village of Jamez [*sic*]. ☞ See April 18ᵗʰ. [April 18] Distance traveled 18 miles. The Rio Jamez [*sic*] a small stream (30 ft. wide) & the town one partly of Pueblo Indians & Mexicans. Visited the Pueblo after dinner & saw the Padre, a rascally Mex. Priest who practices upon the liquor-drinking & credulity of those around him to no small advantage to himself. Vail bought from him a Navajoe blanket for $6, Dorsey a Tilma [cloak] for $5. The Pueblo a squalid collection of adobe houses. Ovens, before the houses, conical in form, built of adobes. In some of these the fires for baking were seen, others were occupied by naked, filthy children while many seemed, for the time being[,] in quiet occupancy by the dogs. These dogs are disgusting objects, apparently a mingling of the meanest cur with the still more detestable Coyote. Three Bears were killed by the Indians shortly after our arrival who were depredating their corn fields. Over these the Indians had a grand dance. To night we were visited by Hasta the chief of the Pueblo, an intelligent, shrewd fellow, very talkative. He represents the desertion of the many Pueblos we have seen, & which are scattered everywhere through this country, to have been occasioned by their going into lower Mexico to aid Montezuma against the Spaniards &c. This may or may not be true. Rain ever since we pitched tent. Now 75 days out from Santa Fé & in that time we certainly have not had 20 days of fair weather. Mexicans nearly all drunk. Old guide lamentably so. Tomorrow we part from our escort & strike for the Rio Bravo Grande del Norte.

MONDAY 26

Rain during the night, damp & uncomfortable. Sand burrs in quantity. Up this morning at 4, long before day as we have a 24 miles-jaunt to the Rio Grande. Packs moved at 6:25. Parting company with the escort seemed a source of general satisfaction, as the Lieut. had, by his manner, afforded [*Camp 55*] just cause for a distaste evidenced towards him by every member of the party, save the Capt. His command goes to Fort Fillmore. From Jamez we have quite a good wagon road & jogged along without trouble. From the Summit between the waters of Jamez River & the Rio Grande ☞ See Apl. 22nd. [April 22] the view was one of unusual beauty & grandeur. In front towered the Santa Fe Mts. whose tops were snow crowned. Conspicuous among the confreres of the chain, the Bald raised his superior front, con[s]cious of the awe & homage the lesser peaks seem crowded around to give as "Mt. Blanc is the monarch of mountains, They crown'd him long ago, On a throne of Rocks, in a Robe of Clouds, with a diadem of snow," so reigns he, supreme. To our right the Sandia swelled from the vale in huge proportions. A mountain mass of jagged pin[n]acles & fearful precipices raised high by the throes of mother earth above her surface. A little to the left & behind, stretched out the long chain of the Placiers whose outline is the perfection of a mountain chain. For a long distance our road lay along the table land approaching the Rio Grande. Descending a canon we reached the valley of the Rio & camped on the verge at 2:55 P.M. Quantities of obsidian strewn along our descent to the River. Distance traveled 24 miles. Camp opposite Santo Domingo. The Indians soon thronged around us, coming over the River with melons, corn & chilli to sell. One quite pretty girl sold her peppers for 37½¢ & offering her my ring (signet) for that amount she tried it on[,] looked admiringly but refused the silver. Capt. Macomb astonished the weak faculties of the natives by means of his telescope. Tried to buy an Indian bow but failed.

Evening delightful. Capt. astronomizing.

Dr. Antonio   } by Ruffini
Lorenzo Benoni ∫
Get & read
Ruxton's Rocky Mts.
"Life in Mex.

TUESDAY 27

Up & breakfasted before sunrise. Much sho[u]ting for the Indians to come over with their boat. Soon made their appearance with the rudest but strongest square built affair by means of which the[y] carried us & our camp equipage across the Rio Grande in three loads. The Indians [Camp 56] were up to their middles in water during half or three quarters of an hour talking vehemently all the time. After crossing we went to the Pueblo of Santo Domingo to secure, if possible, Navajoe Blankets, Tilmas &c. Found the natives as cute as Yankees in a trade. Self bought a blanket. ☞ See April 26th. [April 26] for which I was compelled to pay $12. Dr. N, Fisher & Dorsey procured mocassins. Train passes through the village at 11 A.M. when we all moved off for Santa Fé. The road lay along a dreary masa's [sic] top, no vegetation, nothing to mark the monotonous plain. Dr. N. soon quickened his pace for Santa Fé at 4 P.M. where we camped. Distance 16 miles. No wood to be had for cooking, but fortunately a corral near could be procured which the Mexicans soon dismantled. Supper late & party hungry as wolves. Night cold & windy. Capt. in bad humour & cross. Had to set him back to first principles.

SEPT WEDNESDAY 28 1859

Morning bright & cold. Up & breakfasted before sunrise. Self with Fisher, Vail & Dorsey started at 6:55 for Santa Fé. Capt. & men for the Arroyo Honda where he expressed his resolve to establish himself until leaving for the States. Dr. N & Self will stay in Santa Fé at our own expense. Travelled the 12 ½ miles to town as briskly as possible, taking courses & topography. Found Dr. N had gone to Camp with our letters, so did not get mine until after dinner. See April 28th. ☜ [April 28] Taking them (12 of them) I ran for my room where "trembling and with heart in mouth I broke that of the latest date; to find—thank God! All are well, to that time, with those I hold most dear on earth. Beginning then at the oldest date I read up, enjoying the richest pleasure I ever tasted. My eyes I found too often filled with moisture to allow much progress, so nearly all the evening was spent before the letter of latest date was reread. To me my darling little wife has endeared herself tenfold more, if possible, by her letters & conduct during my absence. A sense of utter unworthiness overcomes me when thinking of her gentle, loving goodness & kindness to all, contrasted with my habitual acerbity & asceticism. May heaven send me the boon of a confiding faith in man's honesty & disinterestedness! Dr. N. & Self pitched into the grapes & peaches from which I have suffered. Capt. Macomb came in after dinner & offered us use of his room while we remain in this place. Put on some clean clothes this evening & feel an approach to gentility. Distance from Grand River to Santa Fé 423 miles.

THURSDAY 29

Morning cool but clear. Took a round of the town in pursuit of Aztec earrings for Emmy & a Navajoe tilma for Charly. Unsuccessful in both instances, but do no despair. Capt. in from camp late. Concludes to remain in town himself. Luggage brought in from camp this morning. Feel fidgety as possible. Can[']t remain ten minutes in one place. Fact is I want to go home & can[']t endure this delay.

FRIDAY 30

Quite wintery last night. Ice at camp ¼ in. thick. Dr. & self both disturbed by grapes during the night. Up quite early. Went to see Johnson who is to get the earrings made for me. Col. Grayson, the Capt. & O. Bannon [L. W. O'Bannon] came in, talking so to make Major Smith's ears burn. Changed all the wrappings of my specimens & arranged my flowers. Dined sparingly. Capt. unusually kind. Attended concert to night (Negro Minstrels), quite amusing. Night pleasant.

OCTOBER SATURDAY 1 1859

Morning delightful. Long to be off across the Plains. The delay here is irksome beyond measure. We loaf about restlessly. Boys from Camp in. Hands, most of them, drunk. Tracing a wretched map of the surveys (land) executed in this Territory up to last January. Looked around for a Navajoe Tilma for [son] Charly but without success. Disturbed by the noise of drunken men next room. Still not free from the effects of the Grapes. Mail in (Southern) & letter from Emmy.

SUNDAY 2

Up this glorious morning & breakfasted at city hour. After breakfast wrote Emmy until church time. Attended church (Baptist) & heard a pretty fare sermon but such singing as would delight an ear attuned to board sawing. Saw my little Texas lady [Harriett Edgar], who has been married during my absence. After church continued my letter to Emmy, finished at 17 Pages. Wrote Mother 9 pages & after a walk turned in for the night. Enclosed Emmy a Draft for $200.

MONDAY 3

What a misfortune that these superb mornings are not spent upon the Plains! Nothing can be added to the glories of such a morn. After breakfast finished tracing map. Dr. & Dorsey repacking geological specimens. Fisher & Vail at Camp. The first placid the second grumbly. Capt. poddering [sic] around. No offer for the mules, nor any prospect for their early sale. Saw Johnson this morning & the Mex. who he secured to make earings [sic] for Emmy. Johnson kindly let me have native gold for

their construction. Lieut. Cogswell in town & tight as bricks [drunk].
Night cool.

OCTOBER TUESDAY 4 1859
Retired last night quite unwell. Slept well however & feel prepared for
breakfast. Capt. out at Camp. Went out last evening to take observations.
Self wandering about like a lost spirit. Two weeks of such life will drive
me desperate. Dr. finished rock packing to day. Cogswell sober, sorry &
apologetic, insisting upon my taking from him a Bear Skin. Drunk again
to night. Dr. & self debate going in by stage & resolve to propose the same
to the Capt. tomorrow.

WEDNESDAY 5
Woke with the memory of last nights conversation. After breakfast endea-
voured to find a pair of Mex. Spurs, unsuccessful. Called on the Capt.
who consents to the Dr. & myself going in by next stage. We are joyful at
the prospect of thus getting in one month ahead of the Party. Secured
a pair of Spurs. Packed trunks &c. Band this evening. Cogswell tight &
giving numerous presents. Capt., cool in conduct, passing our room but
never, as formally [sic] entering. Negro minstrels to night. Dr. & Self attend. Funny.

THURSDAY 6
Morning cloudy & cool. Dr. off for the coal mine at the Placiers. Went
to the Capt's room & "set a while." Johnson tells me the earrings will not
be done in time for me to take them in with me Monday, but that he will
bring them with him. No mail yet from the East. Due on Tuesday noon.
High water on the Arkansas River supposed to delay it. Judge [Joab]
Houghton home from Pike's Peak, brings a little gold. Capt. darning
his socks comfortably. Day pleasant, but Oh! it drags miserably. Lieut.
Cogswell visited me to night, with the usual ☞ See May 1ˢᵗ. [May 1] brick
in his hat [drunken condition] while he is chatting me with the thickest
tongue upon subjects dire & dreadful, the sash in the door adjoining
me, (entering from the street into a room separated from mine by a thin
partition and a curtain is being smashed in by one or two drunken gamblers, lately arrived to swell a number whose name is now legion. As the
glass was broken by naked fists it is gratifying to know that the theory of
difficult hardness & density of material finds a glowing demonstration in
the streams from cut hands. The horrors of this drunken orgie drive me
from my room & I go to sit with Mercure for a while. Dr. not back to night.
Cloudy & cool. To get drunk gamble & fornicate seems absolutely the only
duties of four-fifths of those who board here, at the Fonda). It is doubtful to my mind if the people of Sodom had made such advances in the

complicated forms of sinning as are here to be seen. Plain sin is esteemed puerile & contemptible & none follow it save in its highest branches. Rain to night. No mail at bed time. All alone I sit here & long for home, until I go to bed as blue & miserable as all the rest of my hotel "compadres".

OCTOBER FRIDAY 7 1859

Slept well in my lone room. Up rather late. At Breakfast met Pfeiffer who came down last night. Seemed delighted to see me. He brings the Dr. an Arrapahoe scalp lately taken by the Utes. With Pfeiffer is Tomosamia, Tamuche a chief of the Capotes, Nantos wounded & Sicicavané chiefs of the Tabawatches [Tabequache], & Kaniatché [Ka-ni-ache] a Mauwache [Muache] chief, who carries a bullet wound from the late fight. After breakfast went up to the Capt's. Copied for him notices of Sale. ☞ See Feb. 15th. [February 15] Started with him to take a walk when we were met by Pfeiffer & his delegation of Utes & had to return. All the Indians embraced us & Tamuche (the rascal) appeared delighted to see us. The Capt. gave them all a drink & astonished them with ~~some~~ pictures of some [of] the principal buildings of the world. They soon took their departure. Dr. N. in after dinner from the Placiers with specimens of Silver ore & Cichuiti [chalchihuitl] (Turquois). Mercure & Pfeiffer in after supper & talked us sleepy. "Yes," says Pfeiffer, "Tamuche has a big conscience—a six horse team could turn in it." By this he means an entire want of honesty— a pliable conscience. Sleep overtook me comfortably though a little uneasy for the mail from the East now 3 days over due.

SATURDAY 8

Morning bright & pleasant. Pfeiffer and Pomosamia in our room before I was up. After breakfast bought a Pipe for the first & a silk handkerchief for the second. Dr. divided the Bear Skins, sent by Pfeiffer, giving the choice to the Capt. As he give me one I will give mine (the one the Lieut. gave me) to Fisher. Southern Mail in. Letters for all. One for me from Emmy. Nothing yet from the Eastern mail. Dr. & Self entered ourselves for next mail going East. Pfeiffer & Co left.

SUNDAY 9

Rose at a reasonable hour. After breakfast went down to Johnson's & saw the earrings made for Emmy. Am much pleased with them & find the price most reasonable ($13.00) Took walk with J. [Johnson] up Taos road. Returning pitched into Newcomes as I could not again place my ears in such peril from the discordant singing. Dr. N. went to church as I fancy, doing a melancholy duty. Went round to Mercures & sat a while. After dinner called around on the Capt. who endeavors to be very pleasant. Nothing tonight from the Mails.

OCTOBER MONDAY 10 1859

News this morning from Fort Union of the arrival of Major Donaldson's party. They represent the Indians, about Walnut Creek, to have given indications of bad feeling at the time of their passing & that no mail passed them. This looks squally. No mail will leave here to day to give opportunity for a second mail picking up the first, if loss of mules is the only trouble, & reaching this place. Dorsey gave me a specimen of "Peloncia" & a Mex. Bit. Evening cool.

TUESDAY 11

Nothing yet from mails. Capt. Macomb left this morning for Alburquerque [*sic*]. Mail will not leave here for the east before noon. Dr. & self resolved to go on, at least as far as Fort Union. The troubles may have passed ere we reach that point. Payed [*sic*] bills & ready for a start. Storm & cold set in after dinner. Mts. covered with snow. Hail & rain with us below. The mail from the East still wanting. Resolved by Post Master to wait until tomorrow morning. Johnson insists upon my taking from him 2 bottles of whiskey.

WEDNESDAY 12

Slept most brokenly. Disturbed frequently during the night from some unknown reason. Stage at the door of the Fonda at 8 A.M. Bidding all good bye & with the most heartfelt pleasure Santa Fé is put behind us. Still I have misgivings as to whether we will get through. We have for passengers, a Santa Fé gambler & Mr. [R. P.] Kelley [New Mexico's deputy surveyor], who is seeking his wife & two children. They started for the States in the last mail & he dreads their meeting with Indians. Day delicious. Sunny & cool. Came to the Pecos to dinner. Passed between Santa Fé & Pecos Col. Bonneville & lady. Found Major [James L.] Donaldson & train at Pecos. The Major rather unwell & tells us his entire ☞ See Feb. 17th [February 17] command & escort have suffered exceedingly from Ague & fever contracted in Kansas. At the time he passed Walnut Creek the Comanches, Kiawas, & other Indians gave evidence of hostile feelings. Capt. Dessasure [William D. DeSaussure] with 300 men was at that point on his return from a summer's camp on the Arkansas. On his arrival the Indians asked if he had come to fight them & if so they were ready for it, withholding the usual government bounties from them, on account of their hostilities in Texas, has much irritated the miscreants. An Indian while drunk, attempted to kill [George H.] Peacock & it was this among other reasons that induced Donaldson to write Dessasure, who with his command had passed Walnut Creek, such a letter as must have made the necessity for his return apparent. The Indian who attacked Peacock he saw in time to avoid his knife & springing behind the counter seized a pistol & knocked the savage down with its butt. Muttering curses & the vengeance of his tribe the Indian went off. There must doubtless have been a conflict on this & the delay of the mails occasioned thereby.

Got a rather poor dinner from our friend the Pole, as the Major's party has monopolized supplies. Mules had to find & start from Pecos delayed until 4 P.M. (2 hours). Learn that 20 miles on our road a band of robbers (one American & six Mexicans) have been committing general outrages. Hardly think they will attack us. Evening closed pleasantly & the night superb—Moon full & not a trace upon the sky to dim its unusual brilliancy. Reached San Jose at 8:30 P.M. & ordered supper. Scarcely seated at table when the Stage which left Santa Fé for the States Oct 3rd drove up. In it Mrs. Kelley & children. Kelley of course delighted. From Fort Union the Stage had gone to Cold Spring (153 miles) & not meeting with those from the East—turned back, most properly. There were Indians seen immediately after their resolve was placed in execution. Nothing now remains but for us all to return to Santa Fé & await further developments. Supper quite fare & beds comfortable. Rather more comfortable than traveling, as we expected, all night.

OCTOBER THURSDAY 13 1859

Morning cool & bright. Aroused by the sound of the Mexican gong, (a hog chased through & around the placita by dogs.) Passed the night in most undisturbed & luxurious sleep. Breakfasted and off for Santa Fé. Day indescribably lovely. Our one team of mules has the entire distance (48 miles) to travel. Reached Pecos at noon & there dined, resting the mules for a hour or two. Off again reaching Santa Fé about 8 P.M. having enjoyed a most delightful drive.

FRIDAY 14

Slept comfortably in the old room. Up late & got butter for breakfast which the Doctor <u>earlier</u>, did not. Have to give up our room to Mrs. Kelley &c so conclude to take up our quarter at the Capt's who is still at Alburquerque. Day very pleasant. A delegation of Navajoes in from whom I bought two Navajoe's Tilmas for Charly &c. So restless & miserable to get home that I roam around like one bewildered. Tomorrow the P Master will ask an escort.

SATURDAY 15

We learn this morning that Col. Bonneville has afforded the Eastern Stage an escort of 35 men. A force entirely inadequate to the emergency, as in all probability, the Indians are arrayed against the whites in large numbers. The Col. Much inveighed against. Spent the day reading up the Virginians—so happily different from Thackery's usual satirical style. Met [David V.] Whiting at Mercure's & had a long pleasant chat. W. has kindly had my Tilmas washed for me. Capt. home tonight from Alburquerque & thinks he ma be compelled to take the southern route. Night dark & chill.

OCTOBER SUNDAY 16 1859

Morning cold & damp. Capt. pleasant & kind. Dr. & self determined to take the Southern route rather than risk the inadequacy of the eastern escort. Did not attend church. Fisher & Co. in from Camp. Day very chill. Snowing upon the Mts. Saw Henderson (Stage Agent) who kindly returned to me the fare paid him by the Dr. & myself. This we hardly expected & will make H. some presents in evidence of our appreciation. Sat a while with Mercure. Slept at the Fonda to night. Capt. gave us a ham.

MONDAY 17

Awaked last night by Col. Clemens telling Kelley, in next room, of the return of the Stage which preceeded [sic] the one in which his wife had gone. The Stage had gone beyond the Arkansas & met with the remains of a murdered family, scalped. Fearing to advance farther the mail returned. Sleep slow in again closing my eyes, as the Stage still in advance has Otero his wife (in an interesting condition) & one or two children, with [F. J.?] Porter & [A. L. H.] Crenshaw. All of whom probably have fallen beneath the cruelties of the Comanches. We (Dr.& Self) are off this morning for home by southern route. ☞ (See Feb. 21) [February 21] Mail delayed by [David V.] Whiting who demands an escort for the Eastern Mail of 75 men. While this is before Col. B. he hesitates as to which way he will send the mail. Off about 9 A.M. Stage rather crowded. Judge Tallieferro [J. W. Taliaferro], Messrs. [Merrill] Ashurst, [James C.] Edgar, [John] Watts[,] Dr. & Self passengers. Day rather cool. Road good. Come 15 miles to dinner at Nicholas Peno [Pino] where we had given us a most insignificant dinner charging 75¢. Come to Algadones, 45 miles from Santa Fé, to Supper & bed. The greatly vaunted valley of the Rio Grande as desolate as "a garden of cucumbers." Our host (Townsend) gives us quite good accommodations. Turned in early as we are to be called at 1 A.M.

TUESDAY 18

Slept well & not called until 4 A.M. Soon dressed & off. Morning cool & clear. Passed Bernalillo at day-break, 7 miles from Algadones. 3 miles beyond came upon Indian battleground. At Alamada (8 miles from Albuquerque [sic]) got breakfast. Pretty good fare. Came to Albuquerque about 11 A.M. A. much in appearance like Santa Fé & is the headquarters of supplies for the Department. 18 miles from Albuquerque, & 93 from Santa Fé, we dine at Peralta. Here resides Otero. Had given us a good dinner for a Mex. village. At sundown off for Tome which we reached some time after dark. Here we sleep until the moon rises. From Santa Fé 103 miles.

OCTOBER WEDNESDAY 19 1859

Called at 3 A.M. & soon on the road. Throat very sore this morning. 30 miles to ride to breakfast. Morning delightful. Reached La Joya at 10 A.M. All hungry as hawks. The valley of the Rio Grande covered with salt ef[f]lorescence [alkali]. Barren & miserable. Travelled to opposite Socorro (28 miles from La Joya) where mules w[e]re rested. Mail carried over the River. Jimmy Edgar treated us here to wedding cake. Geared up at sunset & came 10 miles to the house of a Mex.—for supper. Lay down with clothes for an hour or two.

THURSDAY 20

Called at 4 A.M. Up & off. Not so cold as yesterday. Throat worse & serious in chest. About 13 miles from starting we stop for breakfast. Driver officiating as cook. Self brewed a cup of tea. Enjoyed this off hand meal. Many sheep passing down the River. Saw 2 herds of 10,000 each. Day hot & dusty. But for "Pendennis" the time would hang most pressingly. Reached Fray Cristobol at 2:15 P.M. The last & most miserable little town before taking the "Jornada." Dinner given us here pretty good. Driver pretending sick sends the man at the station on with us. Shrewdly suspect his sickness a sham. at Fray Cristobal saw curry comb placed with down, in the coffee mill

FRIDAY 21

The "Jornada del Muerto" diverging from the River does not approach it again for 90 miles. Road smooth as a beach. Find sleeping in full stage not satisfactory. Stopped for breakfast at 6 A.M. which we cook for ourselves. Day hot & road dusty. Saw an antelope & packs of coyotes. Nothing to eat all day. At dark[,] D[r]iver missing the road bogged us all deeply. This some 4 miles from Doñna Anna. Sent for aid. In the mean time with the trouble of unloading & the unpleasantness of getting full of mud we extricated the Stage in a hour or two, just as help arrived. Reached Doñna [Doña] Anna at 10:30 P.M. Distance from Santa Fé 302 miles. Got supper & started for an all nights drive.

OCTOBER SATURDAY 22 1859

Passed Las Cruces (6 miles) & Ft. Fillmore (13 miles) from Doñna Anna, early in the night. At the first Dr. Newberry secured an unusually pretty pair of Aztec earrings for his wife. Sleeping in Stage out of the question. Lost Judge Talliaferro at Fillmore, which none of us regret. Morning came tediously but bright. Came to the Cottonwoods, 28 miles from Doñna Anna, to breakfast. Now 600 yds in Texas. Learn here that the Comanches have commenced depredations on the overland line & that last week two of the station keepers were found murdered by them. This may force us to take the San Antonio & New Orleans route home. Country thoroughly Mexican in appearance. Cactus. Mescal. Yucca. &c. (See Feb. 23rd) [February 23] To our right (all day) we see Chihuahua, in old Mexico, Road exceedingly dusty & day a parallel in heat. Reached El Paso at 5 P.M. A small dirty, dusty, little cluster of houses built by Americans. On the Mexican side of the river is the old town of El Paso. Our stopping place in a state of transition from unendurable to uncomfortable so all is dust, mud & adobes. Hutled [*sic*] in a cage of a room smelling of wet [yeaso?]. Supper scarcely eadible [*sic*] & Beds a Guatamozier grid iron. We will however sleep well as there has been but little afforded us since leaving Santa Fé. Distance from Santa Fé 352.

SUNDAY 23

Up at 7. Slept well despite the bed, & a glass of beer taken at [Céran] St. Vrain's last night. Breakfast execrable. Tea astringent as gargle & no hot water to dilute it. Day as summerry [*sic*] as July. Sat the morning away at St. Vrain's. Major Rett & Lieut. Jackson in from Ft. Bliss. Was introduced. After dinner went over the River to Old El Paso, in Chihuahua, Mexico. The town not much, but country around beautiful. Vineyards for miles around but hardly tended. Would make as fine a wine country as any in Europe. Tried to find a bright Mex. Blanket, not successful. Night cool. Retired at about 10. Fandango in town.

MONDAY 24

Up at 7 A.M. No mail in yet from the East. Had to delay my breakfast to get tea made. Feel badly to day & entirely disheartened finding the mail (Eastern) not in at 10 A.M. It [H?] last night. Much fear that the Indians have detained it as those upon the Santa Fé Road. Day glorious. Mail in from East tonight, detained by heavy roads on the Llano Estacado. Papers to the 10th from St. Louis with information of an attack upon the mail party coming west, on the 24th Sept., at Pawnee Fork by the Kiawas, killing the conductor & his brother & wounding the only passenger, who jumped from the coach & firing his pistol, killed an Indian. Secreting himself then in the tall grass (See Feb 24th) [February 24] he eluded the search of the Indians & next morning went into the Camp of a Pike Peakers who escorted him back to Independence. As Otero's party was but a short distance from the one attacked it is feared they have "gone up." A party of dragoons were at once sent, from Ft. Riley in pursuit of the offending Indians. Mail from St. Francisco going East due tomorrow early. Wrote Emmy by it.

OCTOBER TUESDAY 25 1859

Slept badly. Up at 7:15 A.M. No mail yet from the west. Stage left at 9 on return to Santa Fé, bearing sad news for Otero's friends. At St. Vrain's

store met the clerk of the Overland mail company who quietly let fall
the news of Otero &c's safe arrival in Independence. He has a paper
of two days later date, in which the former killing is sustained but that
the mail with Otero meeting a Mex. was told of the trouble & fell back
on a wagon train thus strengthening themselves so as to prevent an attack (See Feb. 25ᵗʰ) [February 25] While with this train they passed by
the bodies of four murdered Pike's Peake[r]s (stopping however to bury
them). Evidences are strong of many murders committed by the Indians
& that the troops are now down upon them. Mail for East not yet (11
A.M.) in. Dr. & Self resolved to go on to day if Stage does not come up too
full. An Express sent to overtake the Santa Fé mail & relieve the Driver of
his sad tail. Turned in at 8:30 P.M., while dropping to sleep was aroused
by the sweetest voice, in a placito adjoining, gushing in strains of the wildest melancholy—Softly trembling as with the last cadence of a forsaken
Dove or swelling with the power of pain pressed Philomela. I listened
unable to sleep for two hours to this strain, [anon] varied by others less
beautiful until the sound of the approaching horn told of the Eastern
coming stage. At 10:30 P.M. the Stage drove up but, with the two added
from here, so full as to exclude Dr. & Self. Turned over & went to sleep.
San Antonio Stage in without passengers. Driver tells of 1300 Indians on
the Stake Plains who refuse to permit the passage of the overland Stage
& that the passengers are all collected at one of the Stations fearing to go
on. This doubted as the drivers of rival routes are much given to stories
prejudicial to each other.

WEDNESDAY 26

Aroused this morning by Parsons (our landlord) at 7:30 A.M. who tells
us that our neighbouring roomsmen when leaving last night stole the
blankets from their beds—American & Mexican. After breakfast saw the
Agent of the San Antonio Stage in hopes we could induce him to send us
immediately on rather than delay until this day week. This he declares to
be out of his power, so we will see what we will see. Loafed away the day
most unprofitably. Nothing to be done, nothing to see. To bed early.

El Paso THURSDAY 27 *October*

Morning cloudy & a little rain during the night. I went up to St. Vrain's after
breakfast. Soon the wind & rain sent all shivering within. Mail from the East
in at 10 A.M. But one passenger. The conductor tells of one Station of mules
having been run off by the Comanches since the passing of the last mail.
Still if the Stage going East has room for us we will go that way. Went over
the River this evening with St. Vrain's clerk, who carried me the rounds—to
"Robber's roost" &c. Had some good music from a Senorita on the Guitar—
voice quite sweet. Bought a Mexican Blanket for $10. Wrote Emmy.

OCTOBER FRIDAY 28 1859

Dark, chill & gloomy this morning. Rain[,] hail & snow by turns. No mail yet from the West. Wind cold as winter. Mountains around white with snow. Weather unusual. Dr. & Self again visited the Agent of the San Antonio line. After a long talk have come to the conclusion that we will take the Overland Mail, unless crowded, otherwise the San Antonio route. Day intensely disagreeable—a regular Norther. No mail yet in from the west. Got hold of the Life of Baron Trenck which I read with interest. A most remarkable man.

SATURDAY 29

Up as usual. Sky still cloudy & day cold. Mail from west still behind. Home & Emmy each day seem farther off. Well night desperate. Mail from west in & so full as exclude us. This being the case we have taken Seats to go on Wednesday next by San Antonio. Our route fixed we feel more at rest. Day continues uncomfortable as possible. Indulged in a Segar (?) this evening. Amusing description by Roman of having been stung by a Stingaree [*sic*]. Moderated a little.

SUNDAY 30

Morning clear & charming. Breakfasted at the usual hour. Loafed away the morning at St. Vrain's. Finished reading the life of Baron Trenck. Tried a specimen of yellow covered literature but abandoned it in disgust before reading 40 pages. Day glorious beyond compare. Mexicans enjoying themselves in the sunshine, as thoroughly animals as their ef[f]eminate little dogs. Too lazy to do aught else than follow their mere animal movings. By strong inducements they work one day & idle six, living upon what an American would starve & yet when fortunate in a sufficiency wasteful to an excess see with no other people.

OCTOBER MONDAY 31 1859

Again the morning presents itself lovely & bright. Slept badly. Bed as hard as a board & arranged upon the plan of Guatamozin's couch of agony. Mail to day in from Santa Fé. Judge [John S.] Watts & Mrs. [William] Pelham passengers. The last, oh horrors! goes down to San Antonio with us on Wednesday. A stage though from Independence prior to the departure of Judge Watts from Santa Fé. Read Cunningham's life of Robert Burns.

NOVEMBER TUESDAY 1

If this weather continues how favoured we'll be during our travelling. Passed the day much as usual—loafing at St. Vrain's. Sent down this evening to Old Buchanan's & got 4 bottles of "Vino Carlow [Vino di Carlow] del Paso," 2 for the Dr. Made all preparations for tomorrow's start. Mail from the west in & our boys from Santa Fé having room enough to sit edgewise have gone on. Evening most delightful.

WEDNESDAY 2

Called by Parsons at 3 A.M. Up & off once more for home. Travelled 5 miles when Stage was upset, 3 on the seat & I undermost. Fortunately no one injured. Came 21 miles to San Lazario to breakfast. Day delightful. On the Rio Grande. From San Lazario [Elizario] travelled 24 miles to dinner at Smith's Ranch. Meal oh! most miserable, but 50¢ for everything. Travelled 36 miles to Supper at Fort Quitman—a station of U.S. troops (1 company) on Rio Grande. Cannot go on to night, as one of the team (taken here) is absolutely tottering with weakness. Spread myself on the counter of a six penny store & went to sleep. No beds to be gotten.

NOVEMBER THURSDAY 3 1859

Slept like a log from my fatigue. Three upon a seat none too large for two renders, this trip one more sorely uncomfortable than any ever taken. A wild horse to take the place of the exhausted one. The colt travelled off well. Reached the Eagle Spring at 4 P.M. Passed through a country today filled with little else than [sketch of three cacti]. Parched & burned beyond measure. Day deliciously cool.

FRIDAY 4

Slept most miserably last night. Crowded beyond measure. Came to the 'Ojo del Muerto' to breakfast at 6:25 A.M. Gave us a good breakfast. 60 miles from Eagle Springs & 177 from El Paso. Reached Fort Davis at 1 P.M. Dined with Lieut. Van Horn. Distance from El Paso 225 miles. Came through the "Wild Rose Pass" a remarkable passage & on to the Barilla Spring (25 m.) to Supper. Night clear & pleasant. Off for Comanche Spring our next drive—

SATURDAY 5

By snatches secured quite a fair share of sleep last night. One on our seat taking the floor gave us more room. Reached Comanchee [sic] Spring at 7:25 A.M. where we breakfasted. Here are stationed 1 company U.S. Infantry. The country we pass over to day miserable as New Mexico. Travelled all day to accomplish 40 miles. Came to the Pecos by night fall. Supped here. In again & off for the night. Quite cool. Met northern going coach at 10 P.M. & changed coaches.

NOVEMBER SUNDAY 6 1859

Night chill & I suffered very much. Crossed the Pecos at daylight. Reached Ft. Lancaster at 6:30 [or 6:50] A.M. No breakfast here. Must buy things to eat & have some coffee made beyond. 6 miles from Ft. Lancaster called a halt & had a snack. Travelled until 1 P.M. to Howard's Spring, 407 miles from El Paso, where we again take a cup of coffee. Feel most exhausted. At midnight reached the Head of Devil's River.

MONDAY 7

Slept here for an hour & a half—Distance from El Paso 451 to Head of Devil's River. Got breakfast at 5 A.M.—on wild Turkeys. Morning continues chill & cloudy. Crossed the Devil's River several times. Self quite sick[,] nauseated & headache. Reached Fort Hudson at 9 A.M. Change Stage & horses here. Travelled all day without eating anything. At the San Philippe [Filipe] Spring passengers supped. I could eat nothing. 153 miles from San Antonio. At 6

TUESDAY 8

At 6 A.M. Reached Fort Clark. Here delayed unnecessarily 2 hours. Up to this point had given me the middle seat, very kindly, by the passengers, but three soldiers getting on crowded all hands as compactly as bricks. Reached Turkey Creek at 9:15 A.M. Here encountered more than two hours delay getting breakfast. Weather cloudy but pleasant. Country much changed since leaving Clark. Soil rich & dark, covered with verdure & many new, to us, wild flowers. Passing on from Turkey Creek came to Uvaldais [Uvalde] (20 miles) the first veritable Texan village. To see white people once more a luxury appreciated by all. Told here of Indian depredations ahead. U.S. troops had a conflict with some few Indians but a short time since & but a short distance in advance of us.

NOVEMBER WEDNESDAY 9 1859

Came to a German's (Kirners) to supper at 11 P.M. Supper first-rate. Clean & well cooked. 50 miles from San Antonio[.] All of us slept but little during the night—in the joyful expectation of reaching San Antonio to day. Singing, with anecdotes, occupied nearly the entire sleeping hours. Morning was ushered in by all manner of noises, mostly however barn-yard, performed by the company. Reached another little Texan village at 6 A.M. 25 miles from San Antonio where we breakfast. Castroville rather a snug little place & our host with his wife little french people. Starting again at 8 A.M. Reached San Antonio at 1 P.M. San Antonio rather a stragling [sic] mixture of Stone (see Feb. 28th.

[February 28]: frame & adobe buildings. Some of the buildings constructed of a drab limestone are striking & architectural. After dinner Dr. & Self turned in for a nap & would have slept on until doomsday perhaps had we not been aroused by singing beneath us (quite a sweet voice asking "do they miss one at home &) at 6:00 P.M. Washed[,] took tea & awaited the coming of the coach for Powderhorn. Coach around at 9:30 A.M. &

we find 8 inside with our number. Rattle off in fine style which drops into the most laggard gait at the "suburbs" of the city. Night clear & moon full. Napped away the night. One lady passenger.

THURSDAY 10
At 6 A.M. reached stand & breakfasted. Road heavy but we move most uncon[s]cionably slow. Reached dinner Station (52 miles from San Antonio) at noon. Are told of Yellow Fever at Galveston. Apparent depth & richness of soil much increased. Country gently undulating & wanting little but water. At 8 P.M. came to Yorktown to supper (74 miles) where we were well treated & had the luxury of "ebo shins & gizzard foot" [racial epithet] waiter. Hammered away all night without sleep so crowded & uncomfortable.

FRIDAY 11
Night cloudy but air pleasant. Wind from the South. Reached Victoria [in Texas] at 8:30 A.M. where we take breakfast. Victoria an old place, now however improving. Are told here that Brownsville has been sacked by the Mexicans. Distance from here to the coast (52 miles. From Victoria the road lies upon a rich prairie much sunken in what is termed "hog wallows" [small depressions]. Reached dinner house at 12:15 P.M., 17 miles from Victoria. With change of Stage & mules we start at 1:30 for Indianola, traversing the worst road to be found anywhere we reach this place at 9 P.M. completing our 9 days & 10 nights of staging continuous.

NOVEMBER SATURDAY 12 1859
Our house very comfortable & all slept like the dead last night—up at 7:30 A.M. Find to our satisfaction that the Steamer leaves for New Orleans at 3 P.M. to day. Day hot. Indianola a small place on a fine beach. To frequently however ravaged by Yellow Fever. About noon a strong Norther with terrible power & chill drives all crowding around the stove. Steamer cannot leave to day. This perhaps fortunate for us as the cold will render stopping at Galveston safe.

SUNDAY 13
Slept last night like most deeply & sweetly. Morning so cold as to waken us early. Water frozen in the rooms. News from the vicinity of Brownsville indicates that Cortinas & his band are progressing into Texas with fire & sword. Folks here much excited. A party of 20 left here yesterday for Brownsville, now in possession of Cortinas' marauders. Word from the "Matagorda" [steamer] that she will leave at 11 A.M. Still a strong wind from the north. Underway at noon. Fare good. But few (20) passengers. After supper had a quiet [card] game of Eucre [euchre] & then turned in.

MONDAY 14
Wind much abated before bedtime last night. Slept soundly & well as but little sea was running & this morning is glorious as October. Stopped at the Galveston wharf about breakfast time where we remain 2 hours. Will not go up in the town as think it hardly safe. After a delay of 2 ½ hours at Galveston we move off. Water calm as a lake. While away the day newspaper reading. Distance from Indianola to Galveston 130 miles. After supper Jackson, Schaeffer, Holt[,] the Dr. & myself take a comfortable game of Eucre. Turned in at 9.

NOVEMBER TUESDAY 15 1859
Slept well & have not the least disposition to be sick. Up & breakfasted at 8 A.M. In Berwicks bay this morning. From Galveston 170 miles. Once a great harbor for Pirates. Water green as a lawn. Sugar plantations on either side. Reached the landing & New Orleans & Apelusas R.Rd at 10 A.M. From Berwick's B. to N.O. 80 miles. At 3 P.M. in New O. & at the St. Charles [Hotel]. Took dinner—(a formal, crowded & tedious party, though all very grand) bought ticket for Balto. & off via New O. & Jackson for home. Supped at Magnolia.

WEDNESDAY 16
Cars crowded all night. Fair at Jackson. Slept but little. Breakfasted at Canton [the terminus of two major railroads in Mississippi]. From Canton travelled to break in the Miss. C. R.R. by noon where we dined, here we take stage for 24 miles to termination of break, at "Duck hill" here we supped at 7 P.M. All day been in the Cotton country. Moved from Duckhill at 9 P.M. Road in good condition, but train moves slowly. Slept but little. Cars too heated. Cloudy & rain like.

THURSDAY 17
At 5 A.M. train halted at Grand Junction [in Tennessee] where we should have made a close connection with the Memphis & Charleston cars. Express in hand-car sent up for another Engine as that starting from Memphis broke down. Leave the Junction 2 hours behind time. Parted at J—with Dr. Newberry who takes the Mobile & Ohio Rd. to Cairo [Illinois] &c. The country to day not so pleasing. Less cotton & more sterility. Train moves like a sluggard. The vicinity of Huntsville an attractive region. Sup at H. & learn of the death of Carrie Kinkle [or Kishkle].

NOVEMBER FRIDAY 18 1859
Slept quite well last night. Cool & cloudy. At Stevenson [in Alabama], the terminus of Miss. Central R.R. we were delayed from 12:30 to 5 A.M.

(2 ½ hours) which makes up the 12 hours, to catch the Eastern going train, being that period behind time. At Chattanooga at, 8 A.M. we took breakfast & reached Knoxville at 2 P.M. where we dine. Things begin to look familiar. Rain & wind heavy. Train for Bristol soon off. Meet with an old acquaintance in the Conductor & much distressed to find Genl. [Shemberry?] See March 2nd [March 2] formerly one of my contractors a brakesman on the same train. At Greeneville we stop for supper. Supper house Vance's where I saw many old, familiar faces. Old Vance, his wife having died, married again but a Short time since & little Flora I found a finely developed, beautiful woman, was urged to remain one, but could not. Soon in cars & off for Bristol. Raining terribly.
Reached Bristol at 11 P.M. Here took the V & T [Virginia and Tennessee Railroad] Cars for Lynchburg. Rolled up for a sleep.

SATURDAY 19

Slept comfortably, as from habit I believe I could when on my head. Day finds us at the Alleghany Tunnel. Breakfast at Liberty (the best for months) & then to Lynchburg by 10 A.M. Taking the South Side cars we soon find ourselves at Farmville. There we got an admirable dinner. Soon at Danville R. Rd. junction, where [we] change cars. Reached Richmond at dark. Find the folks at the Armory at tea. All well. Telegraph Emmy.

MEMORANDA.

May	5th	Stereoscopic views	$4.25
"		Mallaird's Candy [caramel candy]	1.00
"		Dusseldor[f] Galeny	0.25
"		Segars [sic]	0.12
May	9th	Pocket comb	0.25
"	"	Livingston' life in Africa	0.50
"	10th	Telegraph to Balto.	1.85
"	11th	Dictionary	1.00
"	"	Theatre	0.50
"	12th	India Rubber Blanket	2.75
"	"	Buck Gantlets[buckskin gloves]	2.00
"	"	Boots	5.50
"	"	Slouch	3.50
"	"	India Rubber Coat	8.00
"	"	Suspenders	0.75
"	"	Express of Watch home	1.50
"	"	Gard	.37
"	"	Book of Emile Fuillet[a French author]	.25

"	"	Straps	.75
"	"	Segars [*sic*] 25¢. Bottle Catawba 75.	1.00
"	13th	Figs	.25
"	14th	Porter on Boat	.25
"	16th	2 Pair Blankets	6.50
"	"	Strap for Pistol & knife Sheath	0.50
"	"	Tea	1.50
"	"	Books & Pamphlets	0.50
"	18th	Pipes	0.20
"	19th	Kiawa chief	0.25
"			
"	23rd	Buffalo Robe	4.50
June	3rd	Tobacco at San José	0.30
"	6th	Postage Stamps	1.00
			$46.17

MEMORANDA.

1859		Brt. Over	$46.17
June	7th	Washing Clothes	1.62
"	9th	Concert	1.00
"	13th	Panoramma	0.25
"	"	Postage on Cap	0.25
"	15th	Washing Clothes	0.37
"	22nd	Stretching Boots	0.50
"	"	Fixing Shirts	1.50
"	"	Washing	0.50
"			
"	30th	Expenses to Galisteo &c.	1.75
"	"	Washing	0.37
"	"	Charity & Goggles	0.87
July	2nd	Candy	0.50
"	5th	Soldier's Pants	4.92
"	6th	Washing 60¢. Charity 25¢	0.85
"	7th	Tobacco box	0.25
"	11th	Wooden stirrups	1.50
"	"	Altering pants	2.50
"	"	Smoking tobacco	1.50
"	12th	Camphor	0.12
"	"	Washing	0.50
August	6th	Soldier, for mending shoes	0.25
Sept.	1st	" " " "	0.25
"	26th	Water melon at San Domingo	0.37 ½
"	27th	Navajoe Blanket	12.00

"	28th	Peaches, Grapes &c.	.50
"	"	Cutting hair	.25
"	29th	Grapes 25¢.	.25
Oct.	1st	Postage Stamp	.25
"	5th	Concert tickets	1.00
"	6th	Washing	1.00

MEMORANDA.

1859.			Brt. Over	$84.16
Oct	8th	P[f]eiffer's Pipe		$3.00
"	"	Handkerchief for Pomosamia		1.50
"	"	Lariat & Spurs		2.10[or 2.50]
"	"	Sam for washing		2.88
"	10th	Ear Rings for Emmy		13.00
"	"	Vial		.10
"	11th	Bow & Arrows		2.00
"	"	Tea		$22.00
"	"	Board Bill		26.00
"	12th			1.50
"	"	Fare to Fort Union		15.00
"	"	Dinner at Pecos		0.50
"	13th	Bill (supper, lodgings & breakfast) at San José		1.50
"	"	Dinner at Pecos		0.50
"	14th	Two Navajoe Tilmas for Charly & [co.?]		4.00
"	15th	Charity 25¢.		0.25
"	16th	Cora & Harry Whiting		1.00
"	17th	Board		7.50
"	"	Fare to El Paso		40.00
"	"	Cap for Henderson		3.50
"	"	Washing		.37
"	"	Dinner at Peno's		0.75
"	"	Bill at Algadones		1.00
"	"	Breakfast at Alamada		0.50
"	"	Dinner at Peralta		0.50
"	19th	Bed at Tomé 40¢. Breakfast at La Joya 50¢		0.90
"	"	Supper at Mexican's		0.50
"	20th	Dinner at Fray Cristobal		0.50
"	"	Cakes " " "		0.25
"	21st	Supper at Doñna Anna		0.50
"	23rd	Cigaretas 10¢ Candy 35¢. Ferry over Rio Grand[e]		0.70
				218.46

MEMORANDA.

			Brt. Over	$218.46
Oct.	27th	Candy 25¢		.25
"	28th	Ferry 25¢. Mexican Blanket 10.00		10.25
"	29th	Fare to New Orleans from El Paso		100.00
"	"	Segars [sic]		0.38
"	30th	"		0.25
Nov.	1st	" 2 Bottles "Pos" wine		2.50
"	2nd	Breakfast at San Lazario		0.50
"	"	Parson's bill		17.00
"	"	Dinner " Smiths' Ranch		0.50
"	"	Supper at Fort Quitman		0.50
"	3rd	Breakfast " " "		0.50
"	"	Dinner at Eagle Spring		0.50
"	4th	Breakfast at the Ojo del Muerto		0.50
"	"	Supper at Barilla Spring		0.50
"	5th	Breakfast at Comanchee"		0.50
"	"	Supper at Pecos		0.50
"	6th	Fruit Can at Ft Lancaster		1.25
"	8th	Breakfast at Turkey Creek		0.50
"	"	Supper at Kirners		0.50
"	9th	Breakfast at Castroville		0.50
"	"	Hotel charge at San Antonio		1.50
"	10th	Breakfast		0.50
"	"	Dinner		0.50
"	"	Supper at Yorktown		0.50
"	11th	Breakfast at Victoria		0.50
"	"	Dinner at stand		0.50
"	12th	Slouch hat		2.75
"	"	Segars [sic]		0.25
"	13th	Bill at Indianola		3.50
"	"	Texas almanac		0.25
"	15th	Cab to St Charles		0.50
"	"	Fare to Baltimore		<u>47.00</u>
				$414.59

MEMORANDA.

			Brt. Over	414.59
Nov	15th	Bus to Jackson R. Rd		0.50
"	"	Consuelo (novell)		0.50
"	"	Telegraph to Emmy		3.05
"	"	Dinner at St. Charles		1.00

"	"	Supper " Magnolia	0.50
"	16th	Breakfast at Canton	0.50
"	"	Dinner " " Break"	0.50
"	"	Supper " Duckhill	0.50
"	17th	Breakfast " Grnd Junction	0.50
"	"	Supper " Huntsville	0.50
"	18th	Breakfast " Chattanooga	0.50
"	"	Dinner at Knoxville	0.50
"	"	Supper " Greeneville [sic]	0.50
"	19th	Breakfast " Liberty	0.50
"	"	Dinner " Farmville	0.50
"	"	Hack to Armory	1.00
"	21st	" & Baggage to Centrl. Depot	1.25
"	22nd	" to home	1.00
			$428.39

Amount Expenses for traveling &c—returned by Government	271.90
Total spent during absence from May 7th to Nov. 22nd /59. =	$156.49

CASH ACCOUNT. — MAY.

Date.		Received.	Paid.
3rd	Recd of Lt. Ives	80.00	
4th	Passage of self to New York		6.00
"	Hack hire		1.00
5th	Hack hire to St. N.		0.50
"	Bill at St. Nicholas		2.00
"	Hack self & Fisher		1.00
"	Fare to Balto of do.		12.00
"	Supper at Phila do.		1.00
6th	Hack hire to home Self.		1.00
"	Bag[g]age Express		0.25
7th	Hack for self to Cars		1.00
"	Fisher's Bill in Balto.		5.00
"	" Riding to & from depot & Baggage		1.00
"	Self & Fisher fare to St Louis		52.00
"	" " Supper at Martinsburg		1.00
8th	Breakfast self at Grafton		0.50
9th	Bill self & Fisher Bellaire		3.00
"	Breakfast " " Zanesville		1.00
"	Telegraph to Dr. Newberry		0.75

"	Bill self & Fisher at Cincin[n]ati		1.50
10th	Breakfast " " at Vincennes		<u>1.00</u>
			92.50
12th	Carriage to St. Louis Arsenal & Back		<u>2.00</u>
	Amount Paid out		$94.50
	" Received from Ives		<u>$80.00</u>
14th	Recd from Dr. Newberry		$14.50
	Balanced		

CASH ACCOUNT.—JUNE.

Date.		Received.	Paid.
6th	Salary from Macomb to 30th June	$232.25	
"	Same enclosed to Emmy		$232.25
July 5	Soldier's Pants	4.92	

CASH ACCOUNT.—SEPTEMBER.

Date.		Received.	Paid.
30th	Salary from June 30th to date	360.00	
"	Soldiers Pants		4.92

Santa Fé

To	Algadones	45	
"	Bernalillo	6	51
"	Albuquerque	24	75
"	Peralta	18	93
"	Tome	10	103
"	Casa Colorad	15	118
"	La Joya	15	133
"	Sabino	16	149
"	Socorro	12	161
"	Ft. Craig	33	194
"	Fray Cristobal	8	202
"	Donna Anna	100	302
"	Las Cruces	6	308
"	Ft. Fillmore	7	315
"	El Paso	37	352

CASH ACCOUNT.—OCTOBER.

Date.		Received.	Paid.
31st	Salary from Sept.	120.00	

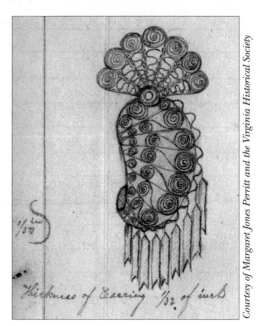

Sketch of the earring designed by
Charles H. Dimmock for
his wife Emmy.

JUNE BILLS PAYABLE.
1/50th in
Thickness of Earring 1/32 of inch

SEPTEMBER BILLS PAYABLE.

Date.	NAME.	Dolls. Cts.
27th	Capt Macomb (Paid)	10.00
28th	Vail (Santa Fé) Paid	1.00
"	~~Fisher~~ (Paid)	~~1.00~~

OCTOBER BILLS PAYABLE.

Date.	NAME.		Dolls. Cts.
√	Sam Wortley for washing (Paid)		$2.88
	Tea (Black)		
	Basin		
√	Waste paper		
√	Cartridges		
	See Whiting		
	" " " "	Crackers	
	Due Dr. N. for Basin		1.00 total
	" " " "	Cotton Cloth	.30 total
19	Due Dr. Newberry Bed at Tome		.40¢

"	" " "	Breakfast at La Joya	.50¢
20	" " "	Dinner at Fray Cristobal	.50¢
22nd	" " "	Breakfast at Cottonwood	.50¢

RECEIVABLE.

2nd	Loaned Dr. Newberry	5.00
3rd	Deposited with Johnson	165.00
4th	Loaned Dr. Newberry	1.00
5th	" " "	0.50
8th	Deposited with Johnson	100.00
16th	Loaned Dr. Newberry	1.00
18th	" " " Algadones	1.00
"	Dinner for Dr. N at Peralta	0.50
21st	Supper " " " " Doñna Anna	0.50
22nd	Ferry across the Rio Grande	0.25
Oct 9th	Paid hotel charge of Dr. at Antonio	1.50
" 11th	" " " " " at Victoria	1.50

NOVEMBER BILLS PAYABLE.

Date.   NAME.   Dolls. Cts.
         W. H. Jackson
                 San Antonio
                         Texas

DECEMBER BILLS PAYABLE.

[Log of Distances]

Ind.	to	Westport	12
W.	to	Indian C	12
I.C.	"	Cedar C.	10
C.C.	"	Bull C.	10
B.C.	"	Black Jack Point	8
B.J.P	"	Willow Spring—	10
W.S.	"	Rock house—	15
R.H.	"	110 Creek—	10
110 C	"	Dragoon C—	13
D C	"	Elm C—	13
E.C	"	Council Grove—	22———
			135
C. G	"	Diamond S—	15
D. S.	"	Lost Spring—	12
L. S.	"	Cottonwood Fork—	17 ½

C W F	"	Little Turkey—	18
L. T	"	Big Turkey—	8
Big T	"	Little Arkansas	18
L. A	"	Jarva's C—	9
J. C	"	Cow C—	9
C. C	"	Big Bend Ark—	18
B. B A	"	Walnut C	
		or Allisons Ranch	7 ———
			131 ½
A. R.	"	Pawnee Rock	14
P. R	"	Pawnee fork C	11
P. F. C	"	Big Coon	25
Big Coon	to	Little Coon	18
L. C.	"	Arkansas River	10
A. R	"	Fort Atkinson	10
F. A	"	Crossing Arkansas	16
C. A	"	Sand Creek	50
S. C	"	Lower Cimarron Sprg	8 ——
			162
L. C. S.	"	Barrell on the Cimarron	10
B on C	"	to head 18 miles Ridge	18
18 M. R.	"	Middle C Springs	11
M. C. S.	"	Cimarron	12
C	"	Upper Crossing	18
U. C	"	Hole in Rocks	8
H. R.	"	Cold Springs	10
C. S.	"	Cedar S "	16
C. S	"	McNeese's Creek	10 ———
			113
Mc C	"	Cottonwood Sp	11
C W Spring	"	Rabbit ear Creek	13
R E C	"	Round Mound	8
R. M.	"	Rock Crk.	11
R. C.	"	Whetstone Spring	8
W. S.	"	⎰ Willow Creek	10
		⎱ or Point of Rock Creek	
W. C	"	Breaks of Red River	10
B. R. R	"	Crossing of " "	12
C. R. R	"	Ocaté	10
O.	"	Dragoon Spring	10
D S	"	Burgwynn "	12
B. S	"	Fort Union	12

F. U   "   Santa Fé   105 ———
$$\begin{aligned}
&232 \\
&113 \\
&162 \\
&131\,\tfrac{1}{2} \\
&\underline{135\phantom{\tfrac{1}{2}}} \\
&773\,\tfrac{1}{2}
\end{aligned}$$

(Licapodium Dendrolobion

     At Ft. Lancaster
Quasia cure for Dyspeptia
Mix enough for one day,
Say desert spoonful

Left East Bank lat. 37.15N

Nascimiento

Roll Creston Gipsum [*sic*]

[Note: Dimmock made several random computations on these end pages.]

TOPOGRAPHICAL MEMOIR OF
CHARLES H. DIMMOCK

T erby Barnes found this important manuscript in the Rodgers Family Papers on a research trip in 1984 to Washington, D.C. She subsequently transcribed the document and shared it with me. (A typescript of her transcription can be found in the holdings of the Utah State Historical Society, Salt Lake City.) In 2007 I visited the Manuscript Division of the Library of Congress and made my own copy and transcription of the file, published here.

Dimmock wrote the 23–page manuscript on legal-sized paper, possibly supplied from the law firm in Maryland where he worked. In April 1860, Macomb "ran over to 'Balt[imore]' and …transacted my business with Mr. Dimmock." Macomb possibly obtained the document from him at that time. More likely, he picked up the 1860 manuscript map drawn by both men, now located in the Cartographic Division of the National Archives in Washington, D.C.

Why Macomb failed to enter Dimmock's topographical data in his report of the San Juan Exploring Expedition is open to speculation. One reason might be that Dimmock later joined the Confederacy in the Civil War which Macomb would have considered treasonous.

From the Library of Congress, Washington, D.C.

Topographical Memoir of the route traversed by the "San Juan Exploring Expedition" from Abiquiu, New Mexico to the junction of the Grand & Green Rivers, Utah; and the return by way of the San Juan River to Santa Fé, New Mexico.

Between Santa Fé—the rendezvous and starting point of the Expedition & Abiquiu, the distance and topographical features were so fully known, that it was deemed Superfluous to begin the notes of the exploration, until after leaving the latter place.

In the immediate vicinity of Abiquiu, and Camp 4 of the Expedition, the Rio Chama passes along the base of the Southern bluff enclosing it, leaving a valley of about one mile in width stretching across to the Trap dikes & sandstone bluffs on the north. The magical variety of outline & shape to be seen in the Sandstone formations around Abiquiu—from a distorted Titan, to the minute vagaries of a Chinese's fancy; from the castellated towers of architecture run mad, to the shadowy traceries of a Fairy's home—must lead every traveller through that strange region to wander awhile from the beaten trail. Above Abiquiu for 5 miles, beginning nearly opposite the village, the bluffs contract the valley of the Chama to a width of about half a mile. At this point the country opens, the bluffs receding to right and left, and the trail diverging runs parallel with the stream—Some 6 miles to north thereof—until the 21st mile from Camp 4 is reached. From this divergence the trail passes over an open country, gently sloping to the left, and enters the valley of the Arroyo Seco, a tributary of the Chama. At Camp 5—the 15th mile—the bluffs on the right come closely down upon the Arroyo, & are high, steep and rugged. A few miles beyond the stream becomes shut in on the left, and between these bluffs—footing against each other—the trail reaches Camp 6, at the Ojo del Navajo, where, as at Camp 5, there is found good water. Leaving the Arroyo on the right, the trail from Camp 6 follows a small stream, tributary thereto, for 3 miles—to its head—and rising upon a gently undulating Sage plain, with low hills on either hand, crosses a divide, at whose western foot heads the Cebolla, another tributary of the Chama. On the Cebolla, at the 36th mile, the Old Spanish trail, thus far travelled, is diverged from, and the line to Camp 7. on the Rio Nutria, passes over a Sage plain with low hills to right and left as before. Crossing the Rio Nutria—a small stream—the trail ascends a ridge, from whence can be seen a range of mountains some 40 miles to the right and Mt. Gallinas 8 miles to the left, and following a valley running at right angles to the Nutria, crosses—at the 47th mile—the ridge dividing it from the Rio Chama to which it is tributary. Descending the ridge for 2 miles, whose western slope is finely wooded, the Rio Chama is again met & crossed to Camp 8. The Rio at this point is about 50 feet wide, clear & pebbly-bottomed, with an average depth of 2 feet. Upon its bank some twenty distinct varieties of flowers, mingled in wildest profusion, were found, whose various & brilliant tintings mirrored by the stream gave a effect of rare beauty, heightened by a contrast with the sterility around. From Camp 8 a ridge, forming the western slope of the stream, is passed over & for 5 miles the trail traverses an undulating country, shut-in on the left by a line of ragged, unconnected mesas, varying from one to three miles in distance from the line; and bounded on the right by a gently descending ridge. The ridge on the right turns north at the 55th mile, & about 5 miles distant in that direction, is a high rocky bluff, while some 25 miles still farther north can be seen a range of mountains. Passing on, the line of broken mesas continues on the right & the rocky bluff upon the left until they converge at Camp 9 on the Laguna de los Cabellos. A depression in the pass, formed by the convergence of these bluffs is the recipient of rains shed from a considerable expanse of country, producing the Laguna, one mile in length and averaging about half a mile in width. Beyond the pass the bluffs subsiding recede in easy ascents and continuing for about three miles are substituted by a high & rocky mesa on the left and a steep line of slope on the right. Between these the trail passes over a succession of low summits into a well timbered valley leading to the * Nutria del Navajoe (* Nutria seems synonymous with our term of Creek, and is always an important stream.); and crossing it & a broken, arid country beyond reaches the Rio del Navajoe & Camp 10 at the 77th mile. The Navajoe here is about 30 feet in width and 2 feet average depth. Running parallel with, and a mile south of a tributary of the Navajoe, the trail traverses a series of small ridges—generally the spurs of higher ones on either side—& passes over a high rolling country to the head of a rapidly descending valley, from where the San Juan mountains, apparently ten miles distant to the north, are seen; and following down this valley—densely wooded & with a number of Superb specimens of the Silver Fir—the Rito Blanco is gained & crossed at the 88th mile. Of about the same dimensions as the Navajoe, the Rito Blanco rapidly passes, in a dirty white stream, between high, rocky & picturesque bluffs, deeply gorged by tributary Nutrias. Along its northern bank for 2 ½ miles, to Camp 11, the trail passes, when diverging therefrom it encounters gentle undulations, passing between high broken ridges—through whose gaps the San Juan Mountains continue visible about 15 miles to north—and reaches the valley of the Rio San Juan at the 97th mile. For 1 ½ miles along its northern bank the trail passes before crossing to Camp 12. The Rio San Juan, before the entrance of its large tributaries—fed alone by the rains and melting snows upon the mountains north—is about 100 feet wide & 2 ½ feet average depth. Its valley, here green & flower-gemmed opens a vista through which the lofty & volcanic pile of the San Juan Mountains are seen, umber-tinted & gloomy; their needled peaks of trappen rocks; courting the lightening in the clouds above them, spread eternal shadows over the exhaustless snows sleeping in their chasms. Across the stream from Camp 12 & a little above—in the flowery plain midway between the Rio & the bluff—is the Pagosa, a hot spring, surrounded by a natu- ral—crater-like, mound, circumscribing it to an irregular figure about 50 feet long by 40 feet wide. Lifting the water from an unfathomable open- ing, and impregnating it with chemical virtues, the escaping gases give an appearance of active ebullition, & imparting a heat between 140° & 150° Farenheit,* (* The testing Thermometer registering only 140° was found inadequate; the column filling the entire vacuum.) rise in a vapory column, visible for many miles. The flow from the Spring is subterranean until its immediate junction with the San Juan.

Deflecting from the Rio San Juan the trail, bearing westerly, mounts an undulating table-land. At the 104th mile a high ridge can be seen 10 miles to right, and a little in advance the Nutria del Francais—flowing into the Rio Piedra—is reached, down which the line continues, passing Camp 13, to the 116th mile. Shut in by elevated, Rocky, slopes, this stream winds through a narrow but fertile valley much the resort of neighbouring Indian tribes[.] From the point stated in this valley the trail crosses to the head of the Nurtia del Piedra and passing north of the Piedra Parada— the lone stern sentinel of ages, gurading the solitude of the hill-top—de- scends to the Rio Piedra. Following up the Piedra for about one mile the trail crosses to Camp 14 near the 123rd mile. Begirt by lofty ridges this stream will average in width 75 feet and in depth 2 feet. Entering the Piedra near, and to south of, Camp 14 is the Nutria de las Casas passing in a narrow gorge between steep bluffs. Up this the trail winds to its head spring & crossing a very elevated ridge pursues a tributary of the Rio los Pinos, through a miserably sterile country to within two miles of that stream, where the tributary turning South, it and the Nutria de los Pinos is crossed, & one and a half miles farther on the Rio los Pinos to Camp 15 near the 141st mile. Four miles East of the crossing of the los Pinos the Tunicha Mountains can be seen, far to the South west, and a high ridge 10 miles to north. At the crossing the Sierra la Plata appears 30 miles in advance, 10° west of north. Where the trail crosses the Rio los Pinos, the Stream is divided by an island—a quarter of a mile wide by about 2 miles in length—into two branches of 75 feet average width & 2 feet depth. With a bottom whitened by Sand & pebbles, the Rio los Pinos flows in a clear Stream between lofty pines Shading the most delicate trout abounding in its waters. Mounting the high-land west of the Stream a valley is followed to the 147th mile, when the trail turns more South & crossing a low ridge—from where high-land can be seen about 20 miles to left— passes over the Rio Florido to Camp 16. From Camp 16, at the 150th mile, a high ridge—bearing parallel with the trail—appears 10 miles north.— The Rio Florido, about 25 feet wide & 2 feet deep, is clear and trout-filled. Passing from the stream to the table-land beyond, the line strikes the old Spanish trail, two miles from the Florido, & continues on it, running parallel with the distant high ground to left. Striking upon the head of a ravine the trail follows down to the Rio las Animas. The ridge on the north converging forms one slope of the ravine & turning becomes the bluff bank of the river. In width the las Animas is 175 feet & 2 ½ feet average depth, Very clear & fish-abounding. Leaving Camp 17, at the 157th mile, the mesa bounding the western Side of the valley, & 250 feet above the stream is climbed & passed over into a broken valley, shut in on the left by a high barren ridge & on the right by gentle slopes. From this the trail traverses a succession of small spurs and mounting by an easy ascent to a well-timbered table-land—from where the country, on either side, seems much broken—continues on the same to the valley of the Rio la Plata. After descending from the Mesa the northern bank of the stream is pursued to about the 170th mile, & Camp 18. Flowing between the spurs of the Sierra la Plata on the north—from whence it springs—and the Mesa Verde on the South, this little stream, 20 feet in width, has "its line cast in pleasant places." Just at hand, presiding over the beauties at their base, towers that majestic cluster of peaks forming the Sierra la Plata. Lifted from waving grasses & countless flowers of the valley, vainly the eye peers among naked, hopeless crags for some gleaming of that metal the name of the Sierra indicates; until heavy and wearied it sinks in the conviction that the steel-clad Hidalgo must have seen with an eye of faith, strengthened by avarice, the inaccessible hoard deep buried in the bowels of the grand old mountain. A short distance in advance of Camp 18 the trail crosses the Rio la Plata & following along the foot of Mesa Verde passes the base of the Sierra la Plata, over low mountain spurs. Near the 181st mile quite a high divide is passed with elevated bluffs on the left—the mountain having turned north being some 8 miles distant—and the trail approaches the Rio los Mancos in a valley between gentle slopes. Some 3 miles distant from Camp 19 at the crossing of the Eastern branch of the los Mancos, the Mesa Verde is still seen to south & the spurs of the Sierra la Plata upon the north. Converging one mile to left of the trail, the two branches of the los Mancos are distant from each other, at their crossings about half a mile. Heading in the Sierra la Plata these streams are exceedingly clear, affording trout in abundance. In width the two branches average, respectively, about 20 feet & are 2 feet deep. Over broken ridges making down from the high land north, the trail continues from the Rio los Mancos for some 12 miles, running nearly parallel to a broad valley on the left, sweeping up to the Mesa Verde, now about 8 miles distant. Near here the Orejas [sic] del Oso & the Sierra Abajo, to north of them, are visible. Turning somewhat north, at the head of a ravine entering the Cañon of the Nutria del Dolores, the trail descends to Camp 20 on the bank of that stream, at the 198th mile. From the rocky cañon of the Nutria the line ascends at once to the mesa South of it and passing in view of the cañon—as it approaches & diverges in its sinuosities—of the Mesa ve de & the Sierra la Laté—about 15 miles to the Southwest—reaches the cañon of the Rio Dolores at the 202nd mile. Up the cañon of this stream, bearing from the north East for many miles, there is a view remarkable for the mingling of sterile, grandeure with verdant beauty. At this point the stream turns north-west & the trail descends to it, and Camp 21, a mile beyond. The Rio Dolores sparkling & clear, 70 feet in width, flowing in a rapid shallow & winding stream, through flowery meadows & rich green Cotton-woods, bending in leafy exuberance, seems but illy named, as too fair a scene for one to "come to grief." Rising from it however—leaving the stream uncrossed on the right. Ruins mark the summit of the mesa up which the trail passes, indicating from their great apparent age that centuries must have passed since from amid crumbling walls the voice of sorrow trembled through the valley. Over a gently broken sage plain, spreading far to the right, interspersed with stunted piñons, the trail passes. A broad valley on the left extending to the Mesa Verde—now bearing off to the South—continues to the foot of the Sierra le Laté. Near the 213th mile the line passes Camp 22—the Saronaro [sic]— near the head of a small cañon, the site of old & extensive ruins, & crossing, continues upon a plain reaching to high ground on the right, 15 miles distant, & to left for about the same extent. From this plain an uninterrupted view is gained of the Sierras la Plata, San Migual, [sic] la Sol [sic], Abajo, le Laté & Orejas del Oso. Falling into a rocky cañon about the 223rd mile, the trail passes through it for 3 miles, when mounting its steep side & leaving it on the left, another cañon, half a mile beyond, is taken & followed between rocky walls, from its head to Camp 23—at the Tierra Blanco. Leaving the cañon at the 230th mile—one mile from Camp 23—the trail again strikes a sage plain bounded by high ground about 15 miles to the right & stretching an indefinite distance to the left. A broad valley is seen on the right 6 miles distant & at the 242nd mile a rocky cañon close on the left into which the trail enters for a short distance & passing from it crosses another three miles beyond, approaching the Juajolote and Camp 24, at the 246½th mile. From the Juajolote—a cañon slimy with water-lizards—the trail passes up a ravine, with occasional rocky projections, to its head & traverses the interminable sage plain; contracted in some measure by a stunted growth of wood on both sides, three miles distant from the trail. About the 251st mile the country 10 miles to right appears elevated and the plain being passed over becomes undulating; this continues—the lines of wood having terminated—to the 256th mile at the cañon of the Ojo del Cueba & Camp 25. The trail here crosses the left branch of the Cañon del Cueba and is again upon the Sage plain broken by occasional depressions. Passing at the 259th mile a rocky cañon, three miles to north the trail descends a tributary of it & rises at its head a mile beyond. Meeting a deep, precipitous chasm the line descends along its rocky southern slope to the valley of the Cañon de la Pañitas, contracted by almost perpendicular walls—some 600 feet in height—to a width varying from a half to a quarter of a mile & continues past Camp 26—where in the cliff to north, Saurian fossils of exceeding interest were exhumed—with most inadequate implements—by the indefatigable ardor of an enthusiastic & accomplished Geologist* (*Dr. John S. Newberry)—down the cañon to the 270th mile where the line hugs the foot of the wall on the north, that on the South receding & the country in that direction becoming exceedingly broken. Along the foot of the north wall the trail follows until it turns to the north-East—near the 274th mile—falling back as the southern bluff of a cañon leading from that direction. On the northern side of a subordinate cañon, at the mouth of the one mentioned, Camp 27 at the El Tenejal, near the 275th mile, is passed. Around the country appears an intricate mass of irregular bluffs, detached buttes & Sinuous cañons. From Camp 27 the trail crosses a number of ravines leading into a principal one on the left, passed over about the 279th mile, & slowly diverged from—& encounters four tributary cañons, with their intervening ridges, before entering, at right angles to its course, the almost inaccessible cañon of the Ojo verde, debouching upon the leading one two miles to the right. At the Ojo verde a line of bluffs, seen six or eight miles to north along the trail from Camp 27, turns towards the Sierra la Sal some 17 miles distant, and a red Sandstone butte of considerable eminence, two miles to the South, marks with distinctness the cañon from Camp 27. Passing from Camp 28, the Ojo verde & the 286th mile, the trail at once ascends the side of the cañon reaching a rolling, elevated ridge, from where a valley six miles to right is visible, continues by a red sandstone bluff, 2 miles to left at the 289th mile, and a butte of the same formation close on the left a little in advance, to the perpendicular side of a cañon bearing nearly east & west. To accomplish a descent of some 600 feet, to the valley beneath, the trail turns somewhat north of East & winding around the intricacies of the bluff, by a path the trembling mule hesitates to pursue, follows up the side, slowly descending from ledge to ledge, for 3½ miles, ultimately reaching the bottom of the gorge. It may be proper to state that this descent is deemed impracticable for a train of packed mules & that the train with the military escort were left at Camp 28, and a small armed party of nine pushed on to seek the junction of the Grand & Green Rivers. Down the cañon averaging a half a mile in width—gradually opening as its mouth is approached—the line passes; the walls on either side increasing in altitude until towering, with perpendicular faces, they rise from one thousand to twelve hundred feet above the valley. Turning south at the 303rd mile the wall on the left recedes towards the Sierra Abajo, & in its place, as the trail advances, a wild of fantastic mesas & isolated buttes extend apparently for 10 miles to the left eroded into pyramids near whom the greatest of Gizeh would be dwarfed & castled by basaltic towers grander than that of Babel. Upon the right the perpendicular face of the cañon, broken by deep recesses & rounded projections, diverges gradually to the North, turning near the 307th mile—where it is 3 miles distant from the trail—abruptly in that direction.

Entering among detached piles of sandstone at the head of the Cañon Colorado, soon forming continuous walls from 400 to 600 feet high—broken by the enterance [sic] of side cañons—the trail winds through its devious mazes passing Camp 29,—crossing Labyrinth Creek, flowing through the narrow gorge, one hundred & twenty seven times in 16 miles—to the 321½th mile. From here to the junction of the cañon with that of Grand River—distant by an air line 2¼ miles—the perpendicular breaks in the bottom of the gorge, preclude the passibility of any farther advance.

The summit of a columnar sandstone pile, lifted high above the top of the left wall of the cañon & about two miles distant from the point of interruption, was ascended with much difficulty, and from it the turbid stream of the Grand River—twelve to fifteen hundred feet below—was visible; passing in devious & contorted course between sandstone walls,— from one thousand to twelve hundred feet in height, whose pilastered faces, in light & shadow, through all the changes of the sandstone series, from deepest red to lightest yellow, presented an appearance wonderful in the beauty of its originality. Across the chasm of the Grand River, over a country deeply serrated by cañons penetrating in all directions, whose valleys the rays of a meridian sun alone can reach, & whose intricacies can be only seen by the bird or the aeronaut , the cañon of the Green River, "opes its ponderous & sandstone jaws." To the left of the point of observation some 4 miles the junction of the two streams is represented to take place by a Ute chief whose intelligence, activity & ugliness, blended with

the lore of his native soil—as evidence by his person would seem all the at-
tributes necessary for an amateur topographer to whom credence should
be duly given. South of the stand point described, many miles distant,
the barren plain, arid and trembling from intensity of heat, is covered
by mesas broken into isolated pinnacles & clustered castled summits, so
architectural in effect that among spires, turrets & battlements the eye
seems wandering over the ruined glories of a heavened [sic]-burned city.
The total distance from Abiquiu to the Grand River, by the route just described, closely approximates 323 ¾ miles; & from Santa Fé 375 ¾ miles.

Returning to Camp 27—47 ½ miles from the Grand River, from which
to Santa Fé the distances will be marked—the trail turns from that camp
a little east of south & crossing several low hills, enters a Valley interspersed with sandstone buttes, having a line of broken bluffs on the right
& the high wall, which has turned South from the Cañon de las Pañitas,
on the left. Up this Valley to near its head the trail passes, when ascending
the high ground on the right, Camp 30 at the Cold Spring—between the
walls of a small cañon terminating just ahead—is reached, 62 miles from
Grand River. Bearing south, the line passes to a table-land, gently broken,
& crossing several ravines, leading down from the Sierra Abajo, runs
parallel with a broad valley six miles to left. Near the 67th mile the Sierras
Abajo, le Laté, la Plata, San Migual [sic] & la Sal are all to be seen. The
trail descends a gentle slope at the 70th mile & crossing Cherry Creek to
Camp 31, from which the Sierra Abajo is about 8 miles distant to west.
Low spurs of the Abajo, terminating in a broad valley on the left, 5 miles
distant, forming occasional rocky cañons, the trail encounters until at the
78th mile it enters a small valley, along which it passes, for one mile, to
Camp 32 at the Mormon Spring. Passing on the same broken country
continues to the 91st mile where old ruins mark the summit of a sage plain
which gently descends to the Cañon of the Ojo del Alamo, when at the
94th mile, the trail crosses the cañon to Camp 33. The country now becomes much broken on the right; and on the left, at the 98th mile a broad
cañon is seen, 2 miles distant, which the line approaching descends to by
means of a spur transverse to its course, and passes between its walls—200
feet in height—to the 106th mile; at which point the left wall of the cañon
turns South East. Within a quarter of a mile of the western wall the trail,
bearing a little west of south, continues to about the 108th mile where the
wall on the west recedes, that on the East being 4 miles distant, with
rounded hills intervening. Just beyond is the cañon of the Ritito del Sierra
Abajo, whose stream is descended to down a steep bluff and Camp 34,
near the 109th mile, is reached. Along & near the left margin, the line
follows the stream, crossing a tributary of it between the 111th & 112th

miles, where the Ritito bearing off to the right, the trail passes over the spurs from the mesas wall on the left & descending a broken ledge at the 115th mile again approaches the stream along which it continues, crossing it twice, to near its junction with the Rio San Juan; here the trail turns east entering the valley of the River to Camp 35, near the 120th mile. The cañon of the Ritito del Sierra Abajo is about 2 miles wide, much broken & enclosed by irregular rocky slopes. The Rio San Juan, at Camp 35, flows in a rapid muddy stream about 350 feet wide, bearing a little south of west. Its valley here, one mile wide, is enclosed by a rocky wall varying from 50 to 100 feet in height. Turning up its valley the trail runs near the northern wall, the stream close against that on the South. On either hand isolated mesas are seen beyond, and high raised above the walls of the stream; from one of which an extended view was gained of the far-distant country. At the 123rd mile the river leaves the bluff and approaches the trail, receding again at the 125th mile near where Gothic Creek enters on the farther bank of the Stream. Through a cañon on the left, a small stream crosses the trail at the 127th mile. From here to the 129th mile the stream is against the right wall which now terminates in gentle Slopes. An isolated mesa is to be seen at this point, 8 miles distant, across the Stream. Still along the foot of the northern wall the trail, passes to near the 132nd mile where it diverges to Camp 36 close on the stream. Along the left side of the valley the line passes from Camp 36, occasionally crossing the points projecting from the second plateau of the stream. Over the river the country becomes much broken by high isolated mesas & nearer the stream by irregular bluffs. Exceedingly sinuous in its course the river approaches and recedes from the trail, which following the left margin of the valley, passes ruins of obvious antiquity at the 140th mile, & traversing the foot of bluffs jutting down from the left, Camp 37, near the 146th mile, is passed close under the northern bluff, against which the stream flows. Climbing along the face of the bluff from Camp 37 the trail is again, 2 miles beyond, forced to travel a narrow ledge between the bluff & the stream. Upon the left the walls become high & steep and the country over the stream continues extremely broken. A bluff footing in the river is passed with difficulty at the 159th mile to Camp 38, opposite which, on the Southern bank of the stream, an extensive ruin presents itself. From Camp 38 the trail leaves the river and ascends a cañon, running North-East, to the high land above the valley over which it passes, with the river from one to two miles on the right, to near the 162nd mile, when descending a bluff, the valley & stream of the Rio los Mancos is crossed, the trail again ascending to the elevated plain beyond. The Rio los Mancos enters the San Juan one and a half miles to right of the trail, & from want of tributaries or evaporation has a volume scarcely larger than when seen at the former crossing. Within 2 miles of the river the trail continues for three miles approaching & descending to its valley about the 167th mile. Beyond the Stream the bluffs appear more regular & the plain above them less uneven, reaching back to the base of the Cariso [*sic*] Mountains, which with the Tunicha [*sic*] are not far distant. For one mile the line passes along a bluff, which the river twice strikes in its curvings & mounting again the plateau above, runs parallel with, & three miles distant from, a mesa on the left—which terminates at the 172nd mile—& with the river about 2 miles on the right, to which the trail falls near the 172nd mile. The country to south of the river is much broken by ragged mesas. To Camp 39, at the 174th mile, the trail follows, for one mile, the bluff of the stream & then nears its margin. On the summit of the bluff swept by the river, at the 173rd mile, a Fortification, crescent-shaped, defending the accessible approach, marks the point as some last desperate stand of a people advanced in civilization, long since obliterated by the savage hords [*sic*] around. The trail, from Camp 39, continues in the valley of the river to the 178th mile, where rising a spur to the high ground on the north, it descends, near the 180th mile, again to the immediate valley of the stream. A long line of irregular mesas are visible a little back of this point some 8 miles distant to the left. Midway between the broken slopes—one & a half miles north—& the river the trail keeps the valley to near the 184th mile when it is forced by the stream to mount the bluff near whose edge it follows to Camp 40, at the 188th mile, where the river receding permits the trail to descend. At or near Camp 40 the nearest and best view is obtained of the *Ship (*this is a peak in the Navajo Country called "the Needles"), bearing S. 35° W. & distant by triangulation 11.6 miles. This remarkable feature visible from beyond the crossing of the los Mancos—26 miles back—deserves a passing notice. Ejected from the long low mesa upon which it rests to a height of 1600 feet, standing alone, this mass of reddish brown trap, with its two spires & buttressed walls, requires no effort of the imagination, as seen from Camp 40, to distort it into a grander old Cathedral than Christendom contains. Its finialed spires, lit by the evening sun, when the plain at the base is lost in the gloaming, seems bearing the mark of divine approbation—a shrine where assembled nations might bow, forgetful in emotions evoked by its presence, of the petty schisms dividing the world. Seen in the distance at midday, looming from its reflected image in the mirage, the fitness of its title is apparent— a phantom ship mirror'd upon a trembling sea. Leaving the river from Camp 40 the trail passes between it and the slope on the north, crossing a projection therefrom—whence is seen a trap dike across the river, about 15 miles distant—and in Sight of a high mesa, 10 miles to left, approaches a line of volcanic upheaval at the 195th mile; along which it follows about one mile south—to near the 198th mile where the river breaks through the upturned Strata, which continues across the stream. Here the trail passes around the bluff—it receding to the left—and comes again upon the river at Camp 41 & the 201st mile. Diverging from the stream—divided here by an island—the line passes parallel with it—one mile distant therefrom—& crossing over a projection from the left, is near the river at the 205th mile. The character of the region across the stream continues much the same—the bluffs of varying heights, from 50 to 200 feet, Surmounted by occasional isolated mesas. Passing the 205th mile the line is left by the stream—the bluffs on the north moderate, & a river is passed at the 208th mile, crossing points projecting from the left, the line passes in view of a high mesa wall, 10 miles to north of the 214th mile, & reaches the Rio la Plata near the 215th mile. As with the Mancos the la Plata has here but an inconsiderable increase over its upper stream & empties into the San Juan about half a mile from the trail. From the la Plata the trail passes the point of a rounded hill on the left & follows the valley of the San Juan, to near the 218th mile, to Camp 42 on the Rio las Animas, whose junction is effected with the San Juan one mile to South. In this vicinity are the almost obliterated remnants of an extensive settlement, the abode—as indicated by dim traces of acequias—of an agricultural people. Following up the Las Animas—whose valley is here wide & cultivatable—for a short distance, the trail crosses the stream increased by the confluence of the Rio Florido above to a width of about 250 feet and an average depth of 3 feet—and continues up the valley of the San Juan. From the eastern bank of the las Animas the last view is gained of the Ship, now 38 miles distant. The valley of the San Juan becoming broader the slopes on the north are less abrupt, while those across the steam are high & broken. At the 226th mile the river is 2 miles South of the trail, which passes near the Casa de Montezuma—an old, well-preserved cobble stone building—at the 229th mile. Opposite here the Arroyo Chaco enters from the South, through a mass of whitish yellow mesas—and the trail strikes the river again at Camp 43, one mile beyond. The trail leaving Camp 43 passes within a mile of the stream, crossing at the 237th mile a point of bluff, against which the river flows, and rising from the valley, at the 239th mile, traverses the second plateau for 2 miles, & again descending reaches Camp 44 near the 242nd mile. Across the stream, on the East, Cañon Largo opens upon the valley of the San Juan & the bluffs near & around it are elevated & broken. After careful & extended explorations a practicable crossing of the San Juan—here bearing but little east of north—was discovered, one mile down the stream from Camp 44, where the force of its current is broken by several small islands. The average width of the river at this point of its course is about 250 feet and its depth 3 ½ feet; at the ford however, spread

by the islands mentioned, its width is greater. Crossing the San Juan with no inconsiderable difficulty & danger, the trail ascends a hill South of Cañon Largo & crossing the spurs breaking from the lofty bluffs, 2 miles to the right, gradually enters the valley of the cañon. From where the line enters to Camp 45, near the 251st mile, the valley broken by small ridges—is about 2 miles wide from bluff to bluff. At Camp 45 Cañon Blanco enters on the right, & beyond the trail finds the valley of Cañon Largo less undulating, with walls from five to eight hundred feet high. Passing up the Cañon its walls—broken by the entrance of side cañons—gradually decrease in elevation & narrow the valley—at Camp 46, near the 264th mile, to about one mile in width; the walls having an altitude of between three & four hundred feet. Still in the cañon the trail continues—which has narrowed at the 271st mile to a width of half a mile with walls not exceeding 150 feet in height—passing Camp 47 near the 278th mile—the cañon continuing to contract & the walls, about 75 feet high, are surmounted by masses of broken rock. To its head, near the 284th mile, the cañon narrowing to about one quarter of a mile in width is bounded by rock covered slopes. Beyond, the country opens, the line mounting upon a rolling tableland from where, at the 286th mile, a line of low broken mesas are visible on the right and a cañon one mile to the left, receding from the trail. Over gentle undulations from the ridge to north, the trail passes still in view of the mesas on the right—which terminate about the 288th mile—& descends an easy slope, with a valley two miles to the right and a ridge about three miles north, to the 291st mile & Camp 48, at El alto del a Utah. From the hill just descended a high broken mesa is seen some 15 miles to right. El alto del a Utah, across the valley, North-east from Camp 48, is a considerable hill, from whose rocky summit the Navajoes have hurled to sudden death their Ute captives. Leaving Camp 48 the trail bears directly for the Sierra Nacimiento—30 miles distant, & first visible from near this point—passing up a broad valley, with openings on the ridges enclosing it on either hand, to the 295th mile, where, close on the right, a high ledge of rocks, occupying the centre of the valley, becomes at the 298th mile subsiden [sic] to its gentle Southern Slope. To Camp 49—at the Cañada de las alimas, near the 306th mile—the valley is bounded by low hills & preserves a width of about one mile. Continuing, the trail—near the 311th mile—enters between high broken bluffs, whose convergence about the 314th mile—forms the divide between the waters of the Pacific & the Gulf of Mexico. Over this the line passes to Camp 50, six miles from the summit of the Sierra Nacimiento & 316 miles from the Grand River. From Camp 50 the trail changes its general direction, passing parallel with the Nacimiento—and 3 to 4 miles from its base—over the undulations incident to the vicinity, & crossing two tributaries of the

Rio Puerco, passes Camp 51, at the 328th mile. Continuing as before, somewhat East of South, two more branches of the Puerco are crossed within the next 3 miles, & a third near the 331st mile, where three deserted Mexican houses crown the hill on the left. A high mesa on the west of the Puerco terminates near the 334th mile & is 5 miles to right of the trail. Another tributary of the Puerco is passed near the 336th mile & the line from there to Camp 52 encounters a succession of small ridges. Upon the left the mountain is about 4 miles distant & on the right the country is broken by small mesas. The trail from Camp 52, near the 342nd mile, is along the left of a tributary of the Puerco, passing down its valley, with mountain spurs on the east & a broken mesa on the west, to the 346th mile, where the stream turns south, towards the Cabazon—now visible— and the trail reaches Camp 53, near the 354th mile, over a rolling country; the mountain still on the left and on the right a mesa trending towards the Cabazon. The San Mateo mountain is seen from this vicinity far to the south west; while, shaped like a round-topped Sombrero, the Cabazon is 13 miles from, & its summit 1311 feet above Camp 53. One mile beyond the last tributary of the Puerco, heading in the Nacimiento, is crossed, and to near the 358th mile, the line passes parallel with the mountain, 4 miles distant from its foot. Here turning nearly east the trail enters among its spurs—Some of which are purely of alabaster—& rises by means of them to a low crossing of the Nacimiento, which still extends some 8 miles to South. From the Summit, at the 362nd mile to the foot of a bluff, near the 369th mile, the descent from the mountain terminates, the line crossing the Rio Jemez, at the 371st mile, reaches Camp 54 just beyond. Leaving Camp 54 the line passes through the Pueblo of Jemez & over a broken country—with high bluffs from the Vias on the left & a valley to right—crosses a rocky spur, near the 381st mile & over low ridges reaches a valley up which it passes from the 387th to about the 391st mile, when encountering a spur, it rises, to descend again at the 392nd mile, and follows a cañon—opening upon the valley of the Rio Grande—to the 394th mile—its termination—reaching Camp 55 on the bank the Rio, one mile beyond. The lofty [S]andia and the range of the Placers are visible from about the 383rd mile & continue so, with but few intermissions, to Santa Fé; the high mountains back of that place becoming the land-mark towards which the trail is directed. Nearly opposite the Pueblo of Santo Domingo the Rio Grande is crossed—being some 300 feet in width & 4 feet average depth—and the line, passing through the Pueblo, mounts the mesa at the 399th mile, continuing on its level Surface, with high ground about 8 miles to the left, to the 403rd mile, when crossing the Rio de Santa Fé, a high mesa, cañoned by the Rio, is climbed and the trail advances to the 410th mile. To this point from the 406th mile, conical hills

Sketch of "the Needles," or Ship Rock, by Charles H. Dimmock

are near at hand on the right, & low elevations on the left; while from the 409th mile high Symmetrical buttes appear 16 miles to right, beyond which are the Placers about 20 miles distant. The Rio de Santa Fé, having passed to the right of the trail since its first crossing, is descended to down the rocky Mesa's side, at the 410th mile & followed one mile below to Camp 56. Crossing the Rio from Camp, the line passes up its valley. The stream departing from the trail to a distance of 4 miles, approaches it again at the 418th mile. One mile on Agua Frio is passed & the trail reaches Santa Fé along the Rio, whose Slopes on the right are gentle & those to left steeper & more elevated.

The distance from Grand River to Santa Fé is about 424 miles.

> Respectfully submitted
> Chas. H. Dimmock
>   Asst. Engr. & Topographer
> of the "San Juan Exploring Expedition"

To
Capt. J. N. Macomb
Corps of Topographical Engineers U.S. Army
    Commanding San Juan Expedition
        &c &c

LANDSCAPE VIEWS

Portfolio of Lithographs from *Report of the Exploring Expedition from Santa Fé, New Mexico, to the Junction of the Grand and Green Rivers of the Great Colorado of the West, in 1859*

PLATE I. ABIQUIU PEAK [OR CERRO DEL PEDERNAL], LOOKING WESTERLY

J. J. Young from a sketch by Dr. J. S. Newberry.

PLATE II. NEAR VADO DEL CHAMA, UPPER CRETACEOUS MESA

J. J. Young from a sketch by Dr. J. S. Newberry.

T. Sinclair & Son. lith. Phila.

PLATE III. LA PIEDRA PARADA [CHIMNEY ROCK], LOOKING WEST

J. J. Young from a sketch by Dr. J. S. Newberry.

T. Sinclair & Son. lith. Phila.

PLATE IV. THE PAGOSA & SAN JUAN RIVER, LOOKING EASTERLY

J. J. Young from a sketch by Dr. J. S. Newberry.

T. Sinclair & Son. lith. Phila.

PLATE V. Rio Dolores & Sierra de la Plata. From near Camp 21

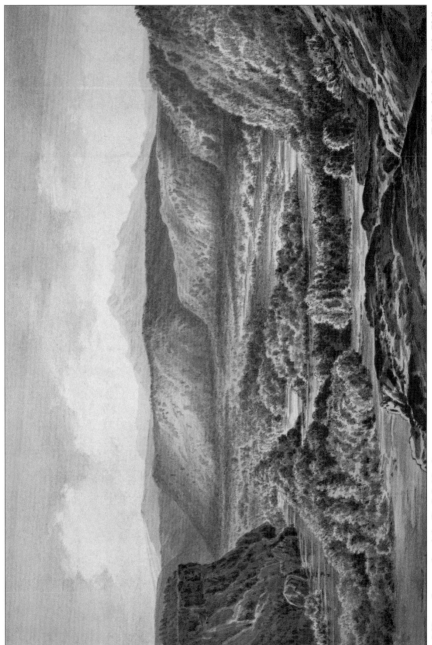

J. J. Young from a sketch by Dr. J. S. Newberry.

T. Sinclair & Son. lith. Phila.

PLATE VI. Casa Colorado & La Sal Mountains, looking northerly

J. J. Young from a sketch by Dr. J. S. Newberry.

T. Sinclair & Son. lith. Phila.

PLATE VII. HEAD OF LABYRINTH CREEK [LOWER INDIAN CREEK], LOOKING SOUTH-EASTERLY

T. Sinclair & Son. lith. Phila.

J. J. Young from a sketch by Dr. J. S. Newberry.

PLATE VIII. HEAD OF CAÑON COLORADO [SIXSHOOTER PEAKS]. EROSION OF TRIASSIC SERIES

J. J. Young from a sketch by Dr. J. S. Newberry.

T. Sinclair & Son. lith. Phila.

PLATE IX. LOWER SAN JUAN, LOOKING WEST. FROM NEAR CAMP 35

J. J. Young from a sketch by Dr. J. S. Newberry.

T. Sinclair & Son. lith. Phila.

PLATE X. The Needles [Ship Rock], looking south-westerly

J. J. Young from a sketch by Dr. J. S. Newberry.

T. Sinclair & Son. lith. Phila.

PLATE XI. THE CABAZON. FROM NEAR CAMP 54

J. J. Young from a sketch by Dr. J. S. Newberry.

T. Sinclair & Son. lith. Phila.

TRAP DYKE, POPE'S WELL, SOUTH OF SANTA FÉ, NEW MEXICO

J.S.N.

T. Sinclair & Son. lith. Phila.

THE PAGOSA, S.W. COLORADO

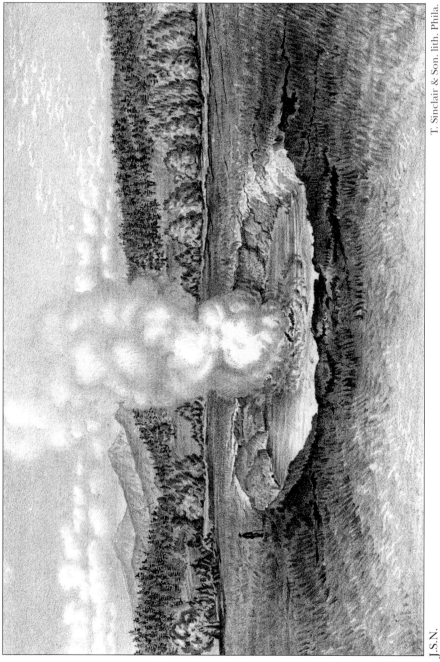

J.S.N.

T. Sinclair & Son. lith. Phila.

RUINS OF STONE HOUSES ON CLIFFS, LABYRINTH CANON

J.S.N.

T. Sinclair & Son. lith. Phila.

Abridged Diary of John S. Newberry
July 13 to
September 28 1859

D r. John S. Newberry apparently made the following condensed record from the expedition diary he kept in the field. The original unabridged version is now lost to history, and only a microfilm copy of his condensed work can be found.

Newberry inadvertently inserted into the abridged diary a number of quotation marks, which indicate that he was quoting himself. He penned much of his diary in telegraphic style and often wrote in incomplete sentences. But he included more elaborately crafted excerpts from his original diary in Macomb's published report.

The entries from Newberry's abridged diary, when added to the experiences recorded by Charles H. Dimmock and John N. Macomb, confirm the historical account of the survey. And they add minor details to give us a more complete picture of the expedition. Positions of dates and spacing of entries has been made consistent.

From the National Archives, Washington, D.C.

Recd at 78 Winder's Building on 11ᵗʰ July 1861. JNM

San Juan Expedition

Notes by J. S. Newberry

WEDNESDAY JULY 13, 1859
Santa Fé to Nambe 18 miles
Left Santa Fé at 2 P.M. Crossed low hills forming divide between Santa
Fé and Tesuque creeks. These hills are composed of gravel and are
sparsely covered with stunted Cedar and Piñon, soil sterile, except
along the Tesuque and Nambe where a limited area sustains a moderate growth of cottonwood, willows and other plants, when cultivated
by irrigation producing fair small crops of Corn and Wheat. Wheat is
now in full head about two feet high, all bald. Around the Puebl[o]
s are many Apricot trees loaded with fruit which is however small and
tasteless. Camp near Poquoque [sic] in a green meadow-like bottom of
which however the soil is quite saline. A little rain fell this afternoon [as
is] usual at this season.

THURSDAY 14ᵀᴴ POQUOQUE [sic] TO SAN JUAN 12 MILES.
Left Camp at 7 o'clock passing over country similar to that of yesterday. A
region of which the surface is much broken by hills of soft red sandstone
nearly destitute of vegetation and excessively barren; here and there the
verdant vallies of the tributaries of the Rio Grande form oases in the desert. Make Camp near the Pueblo of San Juan.

FRIDAY 15ᵀᴴ—CAMP 2 TO 3—10 MILES.
Left Camp at 8 A.M. forded the river, ascended and crossed the Chama,
camping 5 miles above the Cuchillo. Like the valley of the Rio Grande
about San Juan the lower valley of the Chama though narrow is quite
productive and with its fields of wheat and corn, its scattered ranches
with clumps of Apricot and groves of Cottonwood trees forms a beautiful picture, more beautiful from the contrast it presents to the surrounding sterility. We were today met by Mr. Pfeiffer[,] the Indian
agent who resides at Abiquiu[,] who is to accompany us part of the way
to the Colorado.

SATURDAY 16ᵀᴴ CAMP 3—4 (ABIQUIU 12 MILES)
We today continued up the valley of the Chama which is here beautiful and productive, though narrow and bordered by hills and mountains
which are exceedingly sterile. The alluvial bottom lands are cultivated
by irrigation and sustain quite a dense population. Some of the views

presented in our morning ride were more like home scenes than any we had before met with in New Mexico, so much so that they saddened while they charmed us. The houses and hamlets of the Mexican residences are frequently embowered in groves of Apricot trees from which their owners shook down showers of golden fruit, for which however they expected to receive an exhorbitant price.

Mr. Pfeiffer[,] the Indian agent[,] joined us early and escorted us to our camp in the Bosque near the Pueblo of Abiquiu. We afterward visited him at his residence where we found him surrounded by his Indian friends and where we were most hospitably entertained.

Trip to the hills—Beautiful glen. Castellated cliffs. Trap dykes. Ruins of ancient habitations.

JULY 17.

Party remain in Camp. We are joined by Lieut. Cogswell and our escort. Pueblo of Abiquiu. Senor Truxillo. Slaves among the Indians and Mexicans—Price of Eutaw child, a pony, their wildness and ultimate domestication,—beautiful view of the valley from Abiquiu—vivid green of Cottonwood and crops. Visit to the Cobra—Old Copper mines north of Abiquiu—picturesque valley bounded by cliffs of varied and brilliant colors—Old mines worked by the Spaniards on their first entrance into the country—galleries cut in sandstone with great labor and skill. Carefully walled and timbered—Copper not in veins but disseminated through the rock in balls and replacing sticks and trunks of trees—hosts of Bats—Old smelting furnace.

JULY 18

Remain in Camp. Purchase sheep. Experiment in subsistence of party.

JULY 19

Left Camp at 7 A.M. to visit Abiquiu Peak[,] the train moving up the Chama to Arroyo Seco—by a very rough ascent climbed the mesa of which the altitude is full a thousand feet above the Chama. This mesa is floored with trap and is connected with that of which the broken edge forms Abiquiu cliff—surface of this mesa which we crossed is covered with groves of Piñon separated by perhaps equal areas of prairie[,] the latter covered with grama grass now short and dry. Los Canones—Ancient ruined pueblo on detached mesa in forks of the valley—houses all built of dressed stone—about a dozen estuffas excavated in the solid rock— Los Canones the frontier Mexican town—depredations of the Indians— passed the night with Ponocino—his family—Mexican Cookery. Corn stalk[,] molasses & etc.

JULY 20.
Ascended Abiquiu Peak—its height about 9000 feet—its summit composed of trap rock forming a cuchillo—Summit covered with Pinon, its
slopes with yellow pine and spruce—View from the summit—passed the
night at Arroyo Seco.

JULY 21
Arroyo Seco to Nutria 28 miles.—the party having preceded us—Left
camp at 4 Oclk A.M. passing up the Arroyo Seco 12 miles following a
trail much obstructed by thickets oak to the Ojo del Navajo. Origin of
the name—thence crossed the mesa to the Cebolla and thence on to the
Nutria. Mesa generally rather barren, with much "sage brush" and here
and there clumps of Pinon. Valley of the Nutria fertile but narrow. good
grass and many flowers.

JULY 22—
Nutria to Vada del Chama—[blank] miles—Crossing low barren, sage
covered hills came on to the Chama flowing through a very beautiful
though narrow fertile, wooded valley. The hills on either side are high &
broken, their summits covered with forests of yellow Pine. The bottom-
lands are all susceptible of cultivation. The stream rapid & clear, about 30
yards across 2 to 4 feet deep, abounding in fish.

JULY 23. (CAMP 8)
Remain in Camp waiting the return of men sent back to Ojo del Navajo in
search of lost mule. Rain as usual—Write letters and send them back by a
Mexican who followed us thus far hoping to obtain employment.

JULY 24 (SUNDAY)
Detained in Camp by incessant rain. Dr. Newberry left Early in the morning with Neponocino and Temuche to visit the Tierra Maria at the Brazos
(forks) of the (del) Chama, [represented?] to be a delightful spot where
the branches of the Chama issuing from the mountains meet to form that
stream. The Mexicans formerly had a settlement there, now abandoned
on account of the depredations of the Indians. The streams which com-
bine to form the Chama are supplied by the drainage of the of the [sic]
southern and western slopes of the mountains bordering the upper Rio
Grande in the west, and the western declivities of the Sierra del Navajo.—
Clear, bright, trout stream.

JULY 25. VADA DEL CHAMA TO LAGUNA DE LOS CAVALLOS—C.
8—9. 9 MILES—
Today left the Chama passing over a rolling, and in places a somewhat broken surface—in our ascent to the Laguna de los Cavallos on the summit

of the divide between the waters of the Rio Grande & Colorado—The trail leads up a sort of valley or natural pass bordered on Either side by high and broken hills & mesas, the foot-hills of the Navajo and San Juan Mts. Most of this region is covered with open forests of large & handsome trees of yellow pine with glades of covered on which grew bunch grass or sage.

The streams are bordered with thickets of willow alder &c. with groves or continuous belts of the narrow leaved Cottonwood. Signs of deer, antelope, bear, & beaver are abundant, but at this season the larger game has for the most part sought the higher mountain vallies.

The Laguna is a small lake [set in?] occupying part of a basin on the hills, on the summit of the divide. Its shores are for the most part lined with rushes, marshy and difficult of access. –

It is said to have received its name from the drowning of some traders' horses which were swamped in its marshy margins in an effort to cross it. Rain. Lightening strikes near Camp—Views from Cliffs over looking the Laguna.

Height of divide 7600 ft
(about).

JULY 26 LAGUNA D. L. CAVALLOS TO THE RIO NAVAJO — (16 MILES)

Left Camp Early. Meet traders. Stamped[e] of Mexican sheep herders. - From the Laguna, [over route] [north?] the trail we were following led us through a picturesque & fertile country though too much broken to be pleasantly cultivated. As our approach nears the mountains, whose bases we are skirting the surface becomes more varied, the vegetation fresher & more luxuriant, the forests more continuous and the trees of larger size. It would be difficult to find anywhere more splendid timber than that through which we were passing during most of our march of today. The forest is [composed] almost exclusively of yellow pine with little or no undergrowth, and trees of 4[,] 5 & 6 feet in diameter, straight & smooth-trunked, were constantly in sight. Our Camp is situated near the entrance of a splendid magnificent wooded gorge through which the Rio del Navajo flows in its exit from the mountains. Rio del Navajo size, length,— its bottom-lands.

JULY 27. — RIO NAVAJO TO RITO BLANCO (14 MILES)

Country more broken & wooded. Gooseberries. Service berries. Spruces.—Indians. -

JULY 27. (CONTD.) —

"The Rio Navajo is a rapid stream now 30—40 feet wide 2—3 feet deep— now swollen by rains—which issues from a magnificent wooded gorge just above our camp, and joins the San Juan a few miles below. It here runs

through a most picturesque country of which the surface is beautifully varied—the hills often rising to the height of 1000 feet above the vallies[,]
covered with fine timber (<u>Pinus Ponderosa</u> & <u>Abies Douglasi</u>) <u>or</u> their
slopes with scrub oak—while the vallies are clothed with a dense coating of
grass. Large surfaces where the soil is drier are covered with bunch grass—
(<u>Festuca scabrella</u>) or "Grama" (<u>Bouteloua Polystachya</u>), the most nutri-
tious of all the grasses of New Mexico.—Here and there are sage plains of
limited extent—The bottom lands are occupied by thickets of Cottonwood,
willow, [thorns] honeysuckle (<u>Lonicera involucrata</u>) alder &c.
The soil is usually good, and covered with a continuous sheet of vigorous
& vivid green vegetation.—The climate is now wet—with daily rain—but
probably long droughts are not uncommon, and the winters severe—a
good country for stock—not for grain."
(Copy of ~~my note~~ the introduction to my geological notes of July 27. Dr.
N.) Size & character of Rito Blanco.

JULY 28 RITO BLANCO TO PAGOSA (8 MILES)
Over broken wooded country to the San Juan[,] here where it issues from
the mountains—in the rainy season fordable with difficulty.
Beautiful valley surrounded by wooded hills and mountains, surface
grassy & dotted with flowers, the winding river bordered by Cottonwoods
and willows—the Pagosa—40 by 50 foot basin. Water containing sulphur
& [gasses]—temperature 140° around the margin—Color deep blue—
pleasant & healthful to drink.
San Juan forded with difficulty. Soldier narrowly Escaped drowning—
Crossing of the sheep. -

JULY 29. ~~PAGOSA TO NUTRITA FRANCES~~
Remain in Camp to take observations.

JULY 30. PAGOSA TO NUTRITA FRANCES (12 M.)
Country same as yesterday—Visit of camp of Sobutah. Indians collecting
& drying service berries— They come to camp. Distribution of presents—
arrow shooting for [coat?].—Squaws dressing & painting skins.

JULY 31. NUTRITA FRANCES TO RIO PARADA (12 M.)
Country like that of yesterday, deluge of rain. Piedra Parada—Profusion
of service berries—Ford of Piedra. Encamp in rain—Rain Every day or
night since leaving Santa Fé.

AUGUST 1ST
Remain in camp to dry clothes—Rio Parada as large as San Juan. Very
rapid—Abundance of rattlesnakes—Visit of Indians of Delgaritos band.—
Delgarito himself.—Rain again—Get observation—Lat. 37° 13' 47"—

Aug. 2. Rio Piedra to Rio de los Pinos 17 miles

Visit Delgaritos Camp. Cross high and steep divide between the Piedra and Pinos, trail steep and difficult leading through dense thickets of Oak and Wild Cherry. Country west of the divide ~~more~~ bordering the Pinos and Animas more open and level covered with Sagebrushes and Clumps of Pinon. The Pinos a bold clear stream as large as the San Juan at the Pagosa. Visit of Cabazon and his band to our camp, distribution of presents.

Aug. 3d. —Rio de los Pinos to Rio Florido Camp 15–16.

Country open, comparatively smooth, higher portions dry with Pinon and Sage, lower and more level surfaces with good soil and a vigorous growth of grasses and annual plants among which the wild Sunflower is conspicuous. The Florido receives its name from the profusion of flowers which deck the pretty meadows lining its banks. The stream is about half the size of the Pinos[,] clear and cold containing an abundance of trout.

Aug 4th Remain in Camp

Several members of the party, Dr. Newberry[,] Fisher[,] Dorsey[,] Pfeiffer and the Indians make a trip of 35 to 40 Miles down the Animas to examine extensive ruins said to exist there. The excursion was a severe but interesting one, the ruins being extensive and in a good state of preservation. Similar in character to those subsequently found scattered in such numbers over the country bordering the San Juan. The geographical result of the excursion was the determination of the fact that the Florido is a branch of the Animas and does not flow directly into the San Juan as was before supposed. Below the junction of the two rivers the Animas passes through a formidable Canon, the sides of which form cliffs in some places 1500 ft. in height. Below the Canon the valley of the river is comparatively broad and fertile to the San Juan; there are evidences that this was once the home of a large population.

Aug. 5. Remain in Camp

In the morning exploring party returned from the lower Animas having been in the Saddle the greater part of the preceding day and night. They visited the Camp of Kiatano from whom in obedience to their ruling passion some of our Utes stole several horses with which they escaped to their own country and we saw no more of them. When this fact became known, Tumeche was dispatched with presents to remove any suspicion of a want of good faith on our part which might have been excited in the mind of Kiatano; on his return, Tumeche falls in with four lost Mexicans.—His extortion in taking their money and clothing for a small supply of food.

AUG 6. RIO FLORIDO TO RIO LAS ANIMAS 7 ½ MILES.

This morning Pfeiffer and his Indians left us to return to Abiquiu. Cross the mesa between the Florido and Animas striking the latter just where it issues from the hills. On the route we came again on the Old Spanish trail—Animas a clear cold rapid stream abounding in trout fully twice as large as any of those previously met with and at this time forded with some difficulty; it is fed by the drainage of the eastern slope of the Sierra de la Plata, the western of the Sierra de los Pinos and all the southern declivities of the mountain masses of which the northern drainage falls into the Uncompagre—fine trout caught in the Animas—Arrival of the lost Mexicans who had been sent for in Camp.—emotion of our packers at their reception—their history—sending back of men with donkeys to the Mexican settlements—fertile and habitable country bordering the Animas.

AUG. 7. RIO LAS ANIMAS TO RIO DE LA PLATA. 12 MILES

Route today through high broken country with picturesque wooded hills and fertile grassy vallies—divide between the two streams high[,] covered with Pine forest or thickets of Oak and service berry.—View from the divide back to the Sierras San Juan[,] Los Pinos[,] &c. and forward over the mesa country bordering the San Juan[,] the Sierra [Carriso], [Le Late], &c.—beautiful Camp in the valley of the La Plata—fine gramma grass—magnificent trees of Yellow Pine—the La Plata a small but clear sparkling mountain stream draining the southern extremity of the Sierra la Plata. This Sierra erroneously represented on all maps—its being a massive mountain chain having nearly a north and south trend—this the prevalent trend of all the mountain ranges of this region.

AUG 8. LA PLATA TO MANCOS.

To day cross the divide between the La Plata and Mancos a pass between the Mesa Verde and the foot of the southern slope of the Sierra La Plata—Mesa Verde a high table land extending from the Sierra la Plata to the San Juan—the slopes of its sides covered with green grass has suggested its name—Rio de los Mancos—Clear trout stream similar to those before passed formed by two branches nearly equal size which unite just below the crossing of the Spanish trail—about twice as lar fine trout caught. Mancos—Measurement of Yellow Pine. Camp 19. 150 feet high.

AUG 9. MANCOS TO NUTRITAS DOLORES C. 19–20. 15 MILES.

Up at 4 O'clock—Mercury 37°—leave Camp at 6. Route today led over a rolling country mostly covered with Pinon and Cedar with patches of Yellow Pine—with open spaces covered with wax berry or sage—Soil generally good but as we leave the mountains becoming drier the forest giving place to plains covered with sage—general topographical features of the region—the numerous rocky Mountain ranges giving out southward being succeeded by the interval of the table lands through which the San Juan flows—great plain country west of the mountains broken only by the canon vallies of the stream.—Sierra [Le Late] which we pass near—View Sierra Abajo and La Sal—detached mountain groups on the plain—Camp 20 on Nutrita, a small tributary of the Dolores running in a narrow valley bounded by Sandstone Cliffs—with but little arable bottom land.—Water good[,] grass moderate. -

Aug 10. Nutrita to Dolores Camp 20–21. 5 miles

Up and breakfasted at daylight crossing over rolling rather barren surface to Dolores,—a fine clear stream about as large as the San Juan at the Pagosa running in a narrow valley bounded by rocky cliffs—bottom land fertile with good grass.—Timber, Cottonwood, Willows and Yellow Pine.—Our Camp a noted stopping place on the Spanish trail, the last for an abundant supply of grass and water is obtainable with certainty going from the mountains to Grand river—extensive ruins of Stone structures on the hills overlooking Camp; (the same mentioned by Padre Escalante in 1774 [sic].)

Aug. 11. Remain in Camp to take observations.

Aug. 12. Remain in Camp.

Aug. 13. Dolores to Sarouaro 10 miles

Up at 3 a.m. by mistake of sentinel—Mercury 37. Route to day led over rolling surface—Sage plain with hills covered with Pinon and Cedar—Country generally dry and barren but strewn with fragments of broken pottery.—Our Camp on the site of ruined town.—Present supply of water and grass very meagre—these ruins very ancient.—Could such a population be now sustained here—has the climate changed[?]

Aug 14. Sarouaro to Tierra Blanca Camp 22–23. 17 miles.

A clear very hot day—country exceedingly monotonous—Surface nearly level—Vegetation Sage, with patches of Pinon and Cedar—Our Camp is at a spring in a ravine excavated in the sandstone floor of the Sage Plain—Water good in quality sufficient but not abundant in quantity—wood and grass rather scarce—White saline eflorescence [sic] on the cliffs—ruins near Camp—pottery strewed about as usual-

Aug. 15. Tierra Blaca [sic] to Guajolotes 18 miles

Left Camp at 7 a.m. passing over the most monotonous country possible—great Sage Plain with rare clumps of Cedar and Piñon.—very dry and sterile. The "Guajalotes" water holes or cisterns in the rock taking their name from the water-lizards which abound in there. Wood[,] water[,] and grass rather scarce and poor. Shower of rain at Evening.

AUG 16. GUAJALOTES TO OJO DEL CUEVA. C. 24–25. (10 MILES)
Today travelled over country precisely like that of yesterday.—Sage Plain
with clumps of pinon and cedar and a few scattered trees of yellow pine.
Camp beside a ravine like that at Tierra Blanca in which is a small spring
of sulphurous water. Sobutah returns at evening with letters. Wood[,]
water[,] & grass scarce.

AUG 17. OJO DEL CUEVA TO <u>CANON PINTATHO</u>? [CAÑON PINTADO]
C. 25–26 (12 MILES)
Route today led across sage plain till 11 o.c. then descend into deep valley with rocky sides of red & yellow sandstone—1000 ft. deep—follow this
down 3 ? miles. encamp at pools of surface water. Picturesque cañon. fine
grass—Dr. N. finds bones in cliff.
In today's march descend from great Sage plain into second step of table
lands.—

AUG. 18. CAÑON PINTADO TO TENEJAL. C. 26—27. (7 MILES)
Descend Canon Pintado to its mouth, where we reach the Edge of sage
plain.—On the south this plain stretches [round?] to the base of Sierra
Abajo. on the north to Sierra la Sal.—Views of these mountains—their
character.—Picturesque buttes of sandstone left by Erosion.—Tenejal
pool of surface water—many such in vicinity only & somewhat uncertain
source of supply of water in dry seasons—Curious & important provision
of nature—Casa Colorado sandstone Butte near Camp. (See view.) Wood
plenty. Water do. at this time—grass do.—

AUG 19 REMAIN IN CAMP.
Sent Indian[,] Campeau & Armijo to Explore route to junction of Grand
& Green rivers, and to San Juan.—

AUG 20.TENEJAL TO OJO VERDE. (10 MILES) C. 27–28.
Scouts report good Camp 10 miles west. Cross dry barren country to Ojo
Verde, a beautiful green bottomed cañon with steep rocky banks—fine
spring—good grass.—Encamp in heavy rain.

AUG. 21. REMAIN IN CAMP.
Indian returned last night. Campeau & guide this morning.—their
report.

AUG. 22. OJO VERDE TO LABYRINTH CAÑON.
Leave main body of Command in Camp. Start with Lt. Cogswell, Dr. N., Mr.
Dimmock, Campeau & 3 servants to visit junction of Grand & Green rivers.
Strike s.w. six miles constantly ascending—Perilous descent into canon—
follow it down to its mouth.—Emerge on third plateau.—Wonderful cliffs
& buttes of sandstone -enter Labyrinth Canon—its character, thickets,

stream bed quicksands, rocks—horrible time generally.—Canon formerly inhabited. [ruined?] stone houses in Cliffs. Camp 29 in Canon.

AUG. 23. C. 29 TO RIVER & RETURN—

Leave servants in Camp. follow down canon to Grand river & impassable falls—ascend cliff. Remarkable character of Country. Grand river its cañon—Dr. N., Lt. C., & Dimmock ascend pinnacle overhanging river.—hot & laboring climb, fine view, intersection of cañons short distance below supposed junction of two rivers.—Is said by Indians—junction inaccessible from our position—so with Grand river.—suffering of Lieut. C. & Dr. N. from heat & over exertion—return to C. 29.—

AUG. 24. C. 29 TO 28.—

Heavy rain during night. flooding of Cañon obtain shelter & refuge under cliffs.—Sergeant's mule runs off.—Difficulties of return.—interesting geological facts & fossils obtained by Dr. N.

AUG. 25. REMAIN IN C. 28.

Recur visit from Savariches ? Utes encamped near Sierra la Sal.—Their insolence & importunity dissatisfaction with the presents given them.—The heaps of tobacco given them by other Americans.
Party sent [toward?] San Juan report practicable route.

AUG. 26. KEPT IN CAMP BY HEAVY RAINS.

AUG. 27. RETURN TO C. 27. LA TENAJALES.—

AUG. 28. TENEJAL TO COLD SPRING. C. 27—30

Strike southward toward San Juan passing on East side of Sierra Abajo.—follow up an open grassy Cañada—which rapidly rises, the trail becoming broken rocky & difficult.—Camp 30—at fine clear cold spring near the surface of the great plateau of the sage plain.—Timber plenty. Pinon, Cedar, & yellow pine. Dr. N. & party with train? visited again today C. 26, and excavated more of the saurian bones, discovered there Aug. 17th.—They arrived in Camp 11 P.M., bringing bones of the extremities of large size and in good preservation.—Splendid aurora tonight.—

AUG. 29TH. COLD SPRING TO CHERRY CREEK C. 30–31. (8 ½ M.)

Route to day skirting East base of Sierra Abajo on this sage plain. View of Sierra la Plata—& San Miguel—La Sal—Le Late—Carisso [sic] &c. isolated character of Abajo, La Sal, La Late.—

AUG. 30. CHERRY CREEK TO MORMON SPRING C. 31–32 (8 M.)

Today's march similar to that of yesterday—over sage plain, crossing many deep & troublesome canons [washed?] in it by drainage from Sierra Abajo.—

Encamp in rain at small spring Evidently often serving as a camping place.—Dr. N. finds American silver coin.—Ruins in cliff over spring[,] broken pottery scattered over the country.—

AUG 31. MORMON SPRING TO OJO DEL ALAMO C. 32–33
Today our route led across country similar to that of yesterday & day before.—sage plain with patches of pinon & cedar. [extremely?] narrow & deep ravines. Ruins seen in several localities—extensive ones near Camp. all very old—Pottery every where—Water & grass scarce in ordinary times, now abundant from recent copious rains—has rained 26 days since leaving Abiquiu July 19.—
Get first view of Valley of San Juan & its peculiar scenery—mesas, buttes, pinnacles, &c. &c.

THURSDAY, SEPT 1ST. OJO DEL ALAMO TO RITO DEL ABAJO (15 M.) C. 33–34.
Country same as yesterday. Near present camp descended one step from sage plain mesa and are encamped in bottom of ravine [traversed?] by small intermittent stream flowing from Sierra Abajo.—Water milky and bad.—Grass good now [naturally?]— Rito lined with belt of Cottonwoods. Heavy showers—Magnificent aurora during night.

SEPT. 2D. RITO DEL SIERRA ABAJO TO SAN JUAN C. 34–35 (10 M.)
Follow down Rito to San Juan.—Size & character of San Juan.—Strange Country bordering the lower river.—Country of mesas, buttes—rocks sterile & desolate. Valley of San Juan Eroded in plateau region.—narrow belt of fertility with fresh vivid green vegetation. Grass, flowers, Cottonwoods, bounded by abrupt[,] often perpendicular[,] cliffs of red sandstone.—

SEPT. 3D. REMAIN IN CAMP.
Dr. N. & Fisher. Climb Cliffs.—Views of lower San Juan. probable [position?] of junction of.

SEPT. 3D. REMAIN IN CAMP TO RECUPERATE.
Dr. N. & Fisher climb cliffs—Views of the country bordering the rim [or river] below.—[Ruins?]—Country south of San Juan. High mesas—Navajo Country. Explorations by Maj. Simmonson, Capt. Walker, &c. &c. Remarkable [mountain?] primary & secondary [base?] with 3 shorter [bases?] inside of primary. {Eu. Brurstus optios?}

SEPT. 4TH. ON SAN JUAN C. 35–36
"Left camp at 7 a.m. passing along up bottomlands of river about 5 miles to mouth of Gothick Creek? Then [rise?] [over?] gravel hills to cut off a bend—thence [into?] the bottom lands again passing along base of

northern cliffs, sometimes ascending their sides—making our way with great difficulty—finally encamping in bottoms 13 miles from C. 35.—

The bottoms are here ½ to 2 miles broad, nearly level [const?] with clumps of "salt bush" & coarse grass; the river bordered with thickets of willow & pretty groves of Cottonwood; the soil somewhat alkaline but as good as that of the valley of the Rio Grande.—The river 100 to 300 yds. wide[,] rapid[,] deep & impassable.—

Broken pottery scattered Everywhere, and many ruined houses under or upon the Cliffs."-

SEPT. 5ᵀᴴ C. 36–37 (ON SAN JUAN)
Country same as yesterday, passed numerous ruins.

SEPT. 6. C. 37–38 (ON SAN JUAN)
Camp 38, just below mouth of the Mancos.—Days march very similar to that of yesterday. Difficult pass near Camp 38.—Ruin on opposite side of river.

SEPT. 7. C. 38–39 (ON SAN JUAN)
This morning left the river, ascended Cliffs of yellow sandstone which border the valley.—Cross the Mancos just above its mouth.—Ruins on Mancos.—Fine view of the Needles.—Ruins near Camp 39. [Double?] [semi?] circular wall on point of cliff.

Evidently for defence—a citadel for the inhabitants of the numerous dwellings on the bottom lands.—[Hue] south of Le Late, Carisso [sic] & Tunecha Mts., south side of San Juan.

SEPT. 8. C. 39–40 (ON SAN JUAN)
Today a monotonous march.—valley of river open.—Cross gravel hills. Numerous [ravines?] Striking views of the Needles on opposite side of river. Still finer view from Camp.—

SEPT. 9ᵀᴴ. 40–41. (ON SAN JUAN)
Monotonous march for 10 miles.—Then pass the "Creston"—Cliff of sandstones & Limestones the substrata of this region broken from their [connections and set] on Edge.—Pass difficult and [troublesome?] un-navigable.—Ruins near Camp.—

SEPT. 10. C. 41–42 (ON SAN JUAN)
In its general aspect the valley of the San Juan similar to what it is 50 miles below. More open than where one enters it. but timber less abundant.

Rain has been more abundant here and the grass in the valley and on the hills better.—Crossing of the La Plata.—Mouth of the Animas.—Open arable valley of latter stream. Extensive ruins near Camp. Traces of an acaquia [sic]—Once a large population living here.

SEP. 11. REMAIN IN CAMP.
Rained nearly all day—Mexicans find cornfield of Indians.—

SEP. 12. REMAIN IN CAMP.

SEP. 13. CAMP 42–43 (ON SAN JUAN)
March without incident.—Country without change. Just below Camp very extensive ruins apparently more modern than those below.—Arroyo on south side of river at one time supposed to be mountain of charcoal.—Buffalo berries.—

SEP. 14. C. 43–44. (ON SAN JUAN)
To day reached mouth of Canon Largo and the crossing of the San Juan.—Valley of the San Juan here much what it is below—a narrow belt, moderately fertile bounded by high abrupt or rounded hills, the edges of the table land from which it is excavated.—Soil at the ford alkaline but sustaining a dense growth of trees and shrubs.

SEP. 15. C. 44–45 (CANON LARGO)
This morning crossed the San Juan with considerable difficulty with the loss of several packs.—Crossing of sheep and goats—ford at the mouth of Canon Largo. this is a broad Canon one to three miles wide, cut out of the tablelands bounded by cliffs several hundred feet in height, traversed by a broad[,] sandy arroyo[,] flooded by rains but generally dry.—bottom nearly level and smooth with tolerably fertile soil sustaining pretty good grass and some timber along the arroyo.—Camp at mouth of a tributary canon coming in from the Southwest.—(Canon Blanco) followed up the canon all day, the bottom gradually rising—character remaining the same. Camp 46 the canon is nearly a mile in width—cliffs over 600 feet in height. Horses stolen from the Mexicans by Indians.—

SEP 17. CAMP 46–47.
Still following up Canon Largo which becomes more open.—Cliffs lower by the raising of the bottom—ruined houses noticed on the cliff about mid day.—Wood and water scarce—grass good.—

SEP. 18 C. 47–48
Last night first frost—morning cold and disagreeable.—today leave Canon Largo—come out on plateau—it here has a rolling surface with some sage[,] clumps of Pinon and Cedar.—grass good—wood plenty—water scarce and poor.

SEP 19. C. 48–49
Country very monotonous[,] gradually rising toward the Nascimiento

[*sic*] Mountain—the higher portions better timbered and further west—
Soil more fertile[,] grass better.—

SEP. 20. C. 49–50 CAÑADA DE LOS ALAMOS TO OJO SAN JOSE

To day cross the divide between the waters of the Atlantic and Pacific,
encamp at a fine spring near the base of the mountain.—Country passed
over similar to that of yesterday, but set with buttes of soft red and white
rock[,] apparently washed away from the surface of the plateau further
west.—Simple character—topographical relations of the Nascimiento
[*sic*] Mountain.

SEP. 21. C. 50–51

To day followed south along the western base of the mountain—Surface
varied with hills of moderate elevation—covered with heavy yellow pine
timber with many meadow-like vallies having an excellent soil[,] bearing
a strong growth of annual plants.—The Sandstone composing the hills
contains immense numbers of petrified trees of which fragments strew
the surface in every direction.

SEP. 22. REMAIN IN CAMP.

Small party ascend the mountain to find a pass [leading] directly to Santa
Fé.—return toward evening unsuccessful—heavy rain—country about us
very beautiful and fertile[,] probably cold in winter—has once been inhabited by the Pueblo indians as proved by the ruins near camp.

SEP. 23. C. 51–52.

To day moving south through a country similar to that of yesterday.—Pass
abandoned Mexican settlement from which the inhabitants were driven
by the depredations of the Navajos.

SEP. 24. C. 52–53

Still moving southward along base of mountain gradually descending—
country becoming drier—timber less abundant—consisting of Pinon
& Cedar with Cottonwood along the streams—gramma grass abundant
and fine.

SEPT. 25. C. 53–54 CHACOLI[1] TO JEMEZ

To day crossed by a steep and difficult pass the Nascimiento [*sic*] Mountain
to the Pueblo of Jemez.—in our approach to the mountain, crossed a
series of rocky hills composed of the strata underlying the country bordering the San Juan, among these, red sandstones, and white gypsum

---

1.   Lieut. James H. Simpson in his 1849 expedition noted that the "Rio de Chacoli" was "a small
     affluent of the Puerco, upon which we encamped." See Frank McNitt, ed., *Navaho Expedition:
     A Journal of a Military Reconnaissance from Santa Fé, New Mexico to the Navaho Country made in
     1849 by Lieutenant James H. Simpson,* (Norman: University of Oklahoma Press, 1964), 26.

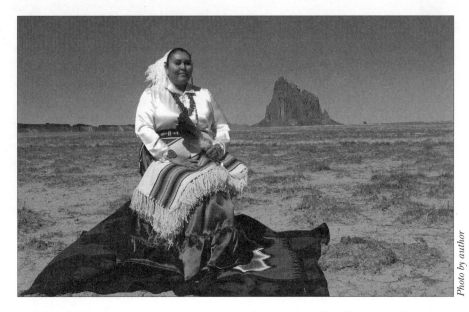

Photo by author

Splendidly arrayed in Navajo attire, Dosha Dee Dee Bradley poses for her senior picture near the base of Ship Rock in northern New Mexico. It's ironic, given the large Navajo population centered near the monument today, that Macomb's explorers did not see any of the tribe. Passing within sight of the landmark in 1859, diarist Charles H. Dimmock wrote: "Report of Navajoes in the vicinity, not believed."

conspicuous—the same rocks reappear on the east side of the Crest—Pueblo of Jemez—grizzly bears—Francisco Horta.—

SEP. 26. C. 54–55 JEMEZ TO SANTO DOMINGO

SEP. 27. C. 55–56 SANTO DOMINGO TO—

SEP. 28. C. 56–57 — TO ARROYO HONDO.

1859 Letters of John N. Macomb, Jr., to His Wife, Ann Minerva "Nannie" Rodgers Macomb

Macomb used his correspondence in part to create his summary report of the expedition. Fortunately, his wife Nannie saved the letters. It appears that she subsequently donated the collection to the Library of Congress.

I have removed most of Macomb's personal comments, unrelated to the expedition, from the following letters.

* * *

Santa Fé, N. M. 4th June 1859.

My dear Wife,

....I am just beginning now my preparations for the summer's work—that is as well as I can in the absence of pretty much everybody on whom I depend for Carrying out my orders. The Commander of the Department has been absent from here for the last four weeks—and I suppose when he returns I shall not find in him a very zealous co-adju[s]tor in regard to my campaign for it just breaks up one which he was preparing, and in which he expected to employ me, in view of the fact that my road business was about drawing to a close. To day our mail which left Independence in the middle of May, is due & I suppose that <u>my assistants</u> will be the passengers filling the coach—they certainly will fill it if they all came and bring with them the requisite articles for their summer's campaign, and the various

From the Library of Congress, Washington, D.C.

instruments that were to be sent out by them. This is just the time for me to congratulate you on having had the patience to remain at home; for it you were here, it would at once become a very serious question as to <u>how</u> you should take care of yourself and the <u>bairns</u> in my absence; and I should be leaving Santa Fé with a heavy heart in consequence—whereas now I can leave here, with the regret to be sure that I am for the time cut off from the receipt of your letters; but at the same time with the comfortable and comforting assurance that you and ours are as well established as possible under the circumstances—& infinitely better off than you could possibly be at any point west of the Mississippi river!

Well the stage came in about noon and I have seen and conversed with Dr. Newberry and Mr. Dimmock—with both of whom I feel well pleased, and I trust that we shall go smoothly through the season and think none the worse of one another at the close up of it.—According to the experience of <u>you and me</u> we should on the contrary think all the better of one another—Should we not? I have received your beautiful picture and find it an exceedingly good likeness; but, as beautiful as it is, it cannot make me love you any more than I did, for you had already all of my poor heart, as I know that I have all of yours and oh! How happy and cheerful a consciousness of this State of the Case has kept me in the long and weary time and distance which separates us. How it cheers us both in the path of duty does it not? I trust that the remainder of the time will pass more rapidly than has any one of the long months gone by. But there is much to be done before I can fix upon a time for turning my head homewards. I can only say that before there was any contingency [named?] for me to work up to, that the duty out here was an up hill business; but I feel now as if I had reached the top and that road home leads over a pleasant <u>descending slope</u>, down which we can drive at a merry trot. I remember when I was down at Fort Craig that I had two lines, each of four miles long, to measure back into the country from the river bank and it seemed, at both of them, very slow work for the first two miles and the <u>tallies</u> accumulated but slowly; but after passing the middle point how quickly did we attain the goal. Thus in life itself how long did seem those days and weeks of childhood! Happy though they were. My memory is chiefly with the pleasant scenes and incidents of the ~~past~~ the child life, still, with gratitude do I say it, these delightful recollections constitute but a small item in my present happiness when I think of my darling <u>wife</u> and children at home.

....

Hoping to hear from you in a week I remain your devotedly attached husband

J.N. Macomb

Sunday afternoon 5 P.M. A small Mexican Vagabond, one of my pet beggars, has just brought in a few bruised rose leaves which after the fashion of the Country, he dignifies as "Rosas de la Castilla!" I place them with Gus' [Agustus Macomb's] dry flowers for the sake of their sweet parfum. Adios.

*   *   *

Santa Fé, 19th June 1859.

My dear Wife,

...I suppose you think I am a long time in Santa Fé—the truth is I never saw a place where in it is so difficult to get what is required for one of these mountain trips. I have to be sure an order (a most <u>liberal</u> order) upon the Department to <u>sell</u> to me such things as can <u>be spared</u>! And you may depend upon it that they can spare but little on such an order. The Quartermasters Dept., in wh. I relied to furnish me, at cost, with mules has none to spare so that I shall have to look around and buy them here and there. Ever since Capt. Marcy came through here 18 months ago and bought up all the spare stock animals have been scarce here. It is a mistake to suppose that any of the <u>notices</u> which preceded my <u>order</u> to organize this expedition, were of sufficient authority for me to act upon except as regards mere personal preparations, and I have been ready myself pretty much all the time. The important part of the duty is now going on briskly enough and the expedition can only last a certain length of time on account of the limited supply of money, by wh. entirely I am to govern my movements. By the above I mean to say that the <u>expenditures</u> were begun sometime since and at a pretty lively rate too and to judge by some of the appointments made for me—expenditure seems to have been the great end in view! I have just made an agreement with a man who is to purchase mules for me, and to <u>pack</u> them (not in salt) but to load and unload them and see that they are properly taken care of in the field &c &c. and now I think my preparations will go on swimmingly and that I shall be able to ~~stat~~ start quite as soon as the Commander of this Department can furnish me with the requisite escort.

I feel very much indebted to Major Sibley for his timely suggestions to the Secretary for without the homeward tendency of the expedition the whole thing would be utterly distasteful to me. I look upon all of this region, I have yet seen, as being worth less than the cost of examining it. I was glad to make roads through it because it is a desideratum for all that <u>have</u> to pass through the country, to do it in as quick time as possible. I cannot imagine that a large population can ever be sustained here—here it is the end of June and scarce anything growing yet! To day we have had the thermometer at 95° in the shade! It is so dry here this summer that

I think there will be a deal of suffering next winter for want of the usual scanty crops.

I expect to go out by way of Cañada and Abiquiu where I was working a road last summer. My first route is to be over a part of the old "Spanish trail," which I have heard very favourably spoken of in regard to supply of grass, water and fuel—I shall endeavour to avoid the dry Country that Mr. Ives fell into, or to visit it in the <u>rainy</u> season.

I shall miss exceedingly our regular communications every week; but the bright prospect of the Christmas dinner <u>at home</u> will I trust enable me to wait patiently for the good time in prospect.

...—I must not forget to thank you for that <u>patent</u> drinking cup—the kindly drops of the "water of life" it contained were seized upon and I have them in my pocket book to refer to occasionally in the field—where we can take but few books. The <u>Art of travel</u> too came duly to hand—I expect to trust my self in the ~~hads~~ care of experienced travelleres of this country and to plod along absorbed with my Survey & astronomizing; and to practice but few arts of travel on my own account!

I feel much harrassed with the anxieties of the preparation to write a lively letter so I must say adieu my dear Wife. Ever your own

J.N.M.

*   *   *

Sunday evening 3d. July '59

My dear Wife,

This has been a day of interruptions with me—I wished to write to you at an early hour to day—and here are the shadows of evening again closing in upon me and the letter has <u>dwindled</u> down to this note!

As I was about to begin to day in came one of my pet beggars with a bunch of poor pea blossoms & I soon put him off, after duly caring for his pretty gift which is still blooming in my only <u>glass</u> tumbler, I soon made the poor boy's heart glad by the gift of the oldest pair of black pantaloons in this part of the country! Thus the last pair of my <u>old</u> cloth <u>nethers</u> have disappeared. Well I had no sooner seized the pen again than in came my <u>hostler</u> with "Captn. I cant get any waterhole to soak them raw hides in" well I told him to <u>hold on</u> and I would get the use of one—so my friend the Mayor Domo of the Obispo gave me the use of a small muddy pond in the corral of the <u>palacio</u> & in went our hides in the course of the day! but long before we could effect that cherished object various other interruptions occurred. Let me un-mystify you a little as to the important end of soaking <u>rawhides</u>. you see we are to have a lot of <u>packing</u> <u>lines</u> made to morrow out of these hides; & they must be softened over night before they can be cut up! Well in came a man reporting himself to me as in charge of three six mule wagons from Major Rucker's, Qr. Ms. Depot, with all my provisions & camp equipage for the summer! These had to be received and stowed away at once! I have now some of my young gentlemen keeping guard over these stores and shall have until we can depart from this City for there is not a reliable lock in the Castle I have rented, on the other side of the Parroquia from my quarters, to keep these things in until the day of my departure from this City.

...I have fixed upon the 12th of July for my departure from Santa Fé for the <u>interior</u> whether we work up to it or not remains to be seen. There are some 20 mules and a few donkeys to be purchased yet—and the holders think that we want them more than they Do & charge for them accordingly. I have bought some <u>44</u> mules already & upwards of <u>6000</u> pounds of provisions so I feel as if I were really in business again—the fact is that the road work was a mere recreation & I <u>think</u> I grew somewhat lazy under it. I hope now that I am likely to be fully occupied I shall grow bright again!

There is no use of our counting upon any set time for our re-union[.] We must patiently and gratefully abide our time and continue to be thankful for our many blessings. I love you dearly but I must quit & retire so good night...

*   *   *

Santa Fé, 10th July '59

My dear Wife,

...You will be pleased to know that now I feel very much relieved—having in the last week finished up my quarterly accounts and my annual report on the road question—this last was something I felt I ought to do for the sake of the old roads over which I have travelled many a mile pleasantly. The fact is that with so much that is pleasant to think of at home I should be ungrateful to get along otherwise than pleasantly.

I could not help feeling rather overpowered tho' for a time in relation to the outfit for this exploration with but little prospect of discovering any thing worth knowing—but Dr. Newberry says the country must be explored & the Govt. ought to pay for the expense so I have given myself less anxiety on the subject of late and I feel now with my seventy mules & eight <u>burros</u> to say <u>nothing of Donkeys</u>, about as easy as I did with a single pair eighteen month[s] ago. I have fixed up[on] Tuesday 12th, day after [tomorrow] for leaving here—Wednes[day] of this week at further cost must see us clear of this town for a few months <u>any how</u>.

So after you get this little note you must make up your mind to get along without hearing from me for a long time. I shall ask my young friend Rojer [*sic*] Jones to take care of my letters &c for me—in fact I have aske[d] him & he has promised to attend to it—as he is on duty here at the Hd. Qrs. Of the Department of New Mexico—he will be very sure to know of any chances of communicating with me.

I hope that you and the children will enjoy yourselves throughout the summer & re[turn] for the Winter to Washn. in [?] accustomed good health. I am sorry I did not hear from you by the last mail but I hope something may come by the next & that our messenger, whom we shall leave here for the purpose, will bring it along to Abiquiu the last settlement to the Northwest of this on our route.

I must say good night for sleep overcomes me.

God bless you all my dear wife and children[.] ever your own

John N.

* * *

Friday 5th August 1859.

My dear Wife,

Since my hurried note to you on the 25th ultimo, which perhaps will never reach you for it went from my camp on the upper ford of the Chama in a rainy time and was probably reconverted into pulp long before it could have reached the Post Office; well since then we have come on bravely—swimmingly I may say, for we have had much rain and have forded many noble streams. We have passed through a very interesting country, to me at least after my long residence in the bald region of Santa Fé, I find the sight of these green hills & flowing streams and fine pine trees a most refreshing sight. Since I was at Fort Stanton two years ago I have not seen such rains as we have had for the ten days we were in the mountains. We are now in clear weather again, and upon the whole find it rather pleasant than was the rainy time we passed through. For once I am obliged to give up my preference of mud for dust. For when we live upon the ground it is certainly more agreeable to step out of bed into the dry Dust rather than into the mud. I doubt if we get rain again for some time after the quantity that has fallen. I must now tell you where I am—Well my Latitude is 37° 13' N and Longt. about 108° 10' W. I suppose by our route some 220 miles to the N. W. of Santa Fé. Our whole party has enjoyed excellent health. Our mules, of which we have 69, and Burros of wh. 8, have enjoyed the fine mountain grass and gained strength & flesh upon the journey. But oh what a loss of time this sort of travelling seems. Always packing & unpacking. I only enumerated above my animals the escort has as many more. I am very well pleased at the fact of having my friend Mr. Cogswell along in charge of the escort—You will remember his name as the one associated with mine in the Fort Stanton Surveys two years ago. We have messed together ever since I came into Santa Fé on the 27th May 1857, and I wish very much he could go with me into the states after our summers journey. We have seen and talked with many of the Utah Indians and they profess to be friendly. Still we keep a good look out upon our animals lest the temptation should prove too great for these sons of the forest to steal them.

We have just heard rumors of a fight between our soldiers & the mormons in the Salt Lake City—these rumors are brought by Indian traders who came into our camp yesterday on their return from the great rivers we expect to visit—the reports are so extravagant we can scarcely believe them—they speak of battering down houses & killing women & children—so unusual a course for us that I cannot credit the reports—yet the description of the effects of the great guns so accurately given by the Indian reporters would seem to give a color of truth to the story after all—for without witnessing such scenes the Indians could hardly contrive such a story—but you will know the truth about this matter before this can reach you.

We see many beautiful flowers on the way "flores de estada" a very few of which I inclose for the dear children[.] I have some, a few, others in press which I hope to bring to my Gus, as I wish to see him enjoying the sight and possession of them—You will observe that the inclosed are the same sort as those, or some of those, sent from Stanton.

I can only tell you that we are all well here and full of hope that the winter will find us at our homes. I hope you may continue in the blessings of health and happiness and peace and plenty and that I may find the little flock all well and blooming on my return. I feel so well that I often think I must be profitting by your prayers for my well being. ever your own devoted husband[.]

J. N. Macomb.

*   *   *

Santa Fé, N. M. 30th Septr. 1859

My dear Wife,

You will rejoice with me that I am once more safely on the East Side of the Rio Bravo Grande del Norte! I reached Santa Fé on the day before yesterday having been absent just eleven weeks during all of which time I believe we were never very far from <u>Water</u>. I mention this first because it seemed to be among your chief fears that I would suffer with thirst—& to guard against this evil you had so ingeniously provided a <u>sectional</u> cup!

as if a cup were likely to be of much use where no water was! Well we had plenty of water, for where there was no water usually we were beautifully rained upon and thus spared all suffering in that score throughout our 77 days of absence.

You must be content to know that we had a delightful trip of it & all returned in good health & spirits. I am now surrounded by the luggage & am more or less disturbed by the process of packing and unpacking & occasional calls upon me for money &c to say nothing of my anxiety to sell the animals & other public property we have used on the expedition. So you must not expect any great things from me yet awhile. You will be pleased to know that my friends here gave me a warm welcome on my return and that I was greeted on my arrival by your two letters (last date 26th August) and a very nice letter from our niece Fanny who gave me good news of all our friends at & about Esperanza.

…I found my old quarters at the Bishop's palace just as I left them, with the exception that my attentive friend the french Major Domo had caused the room to be swept & had placed upon the table a beautiful bouquet of his own arranging so that the place is now fragrant with sweet flowers. This was a very pretty compliment on the part of my french friend and I shall ever remember it with pleasure.

This is Sunday evening 2nd October. Since I began this letter I have had a great deal to attend to & I may say I have attended to it, but I must now prepare to close this that it may go into the office before seven o'c. tomorrow morning. I found to day that I was shutting myself up rather too much so I started off for a walk this afternoon and called in on the way & took Capt. Wainwright & the children with me. We went up to old Fort Marcy which overlooks the town & the country for many miles to the South & West. Here we enjoyed the beautiful sunset and soon returned— this is a short walk; but as the height is about as great as that of the Castle where our friend Majr. Williams used to live is above the old "Dormitory," the exercise is good to mount & ascend. It requires more of an effort to over come the same height here than it does at Mackinac.

I wish before leaving the country to make a visit to my friends at Albuquerque and I must try and do it this week; their kindness to me has known no bounds since I have been here. Well, my dear wife, I have been so long without writing that I am quite out of the way now—resting from this seems not to bring about the restorative effect which we find from our natural repose! I reckon the plain truth is that nothing ever could make a letter writer of me at all events. So I'll quit merely remarking that you may write a note to me & send it to the care of Captn Van Vliet at Fort Leavenworth[,] Kansas and I will ask him to keep anything that may come for me during my journey.

...I cannot tell yet exactly at what time my train will set out from Santa Fé, but I hope it will be before the middle of October.—I wonder if my friend Major Smith has found out where you are yet & if he has succeeded in seeing you. He is a nice man—raised in Norfolk, Va. He left here for the states when I started for the Wilds of Utah. I doubt if he will return to New Mexico & I trust I never shall. With love to all I remain your devoted husband[.]

J.N.M.

*   *   *

Santa Fé, N. M. 6th Octr. 1859.

My dear Wife,

...We are all agog here for the arrival of the mail which still lags behind although it was due 48 hours ago. Saturday 8th October. Well that mail from Independence is not yet here although due <u>4 days</u> now, but I have just recd. your very welcome letter of the 9th of Septr. wh. although marked by you via Independence came by the <u>over</u>land & then from El Paso by our weekly Southern mail—so you see it is very quick after all—only 4 weeks from "Bailey's".

In regard to the mail by the Independence route we have as usual in Cases of detention various surmises as to the cause—we have pretty generally settled down upon the idea of high water in the arkansas river, as a friend of mine [Joab Houghton] has lately returned here from a visit to Pike's Peak and on his return found very high water <u>up on</u> the Arkansas.

...This is a [lurid?] region I assure you & you can never find out the full extent of how they drink and gamble in this country till you see me again.

I have drawn my pay to the end of October, (for the last four months) and I hasten to send the chief part of it to you ....

...I am very busy now; but I will leave this open until Sunday night in case an idea should come along mean while.

Well here it is Monday night the 10th Oct. & the mail from Independence not yet arrived. This letter should have left here this morning but the mail did not go on acct. of the now arrival of the other one. We have just heard of the safe arrival at Fort Union of some ladies at Fort Union from Leavenworth. They came out under the escort of Major J. L. Donaldson & his wife & Col. Bonneville's wife & daughter, make the party.

...Tuesday 11th. I have just finished packing up for a visit to Albuquerque and it is now but half past five o'clock; so you see if I get home this winter you may expect occasionally to hear the dulcet notes of the great waiter I used to beat the reveille upon three years ago. You will hear from me again—that is I will write before I set out upon my journey homewards. With love to all I remain your ever devoted husband and lover JNM Oct [no?]

*   *   *

Sunday night 23d Octr. '59

My dear Wife,

I am <u>that</u> tired with packing up and preparing for the long journey before me that I can scarcely keep awake long enough to write you a little letter.

I have this day re[ceive]d. a Copy of the orders to my escorting Lieut. by wh. I learn that that officer will have 3 non commissioned officers & 35 men which with my own party will make up about 52 persons[,] So that I hope we shall be able to get through safely and expeditiously.

I expect a detention of not more than a week at the South West Corner of Kansas, where I am directed to do a small piece of work. I have bought two wagons and a Carriage (Jersey) to bring in my party & I expect besides to ride in the old vehicle I have used here ever since I came with <u>power</u> in this country.

This carriage riding is all very well when you can do it at the public expense; but I should have been obliged to stay sometime before I could have got a comfortable outfit at my own cost.

I have been around tonight to see some of my friends and to say adieu.

…I bought about $300. worth of provisions for the trip for our party & I think I shall yet spend something more. My funds are getting low; but I hope to sell my animals & wagons for something at the other end of the route, and to come in out of debt. I suppose you must now be comfortably settled at <u>361</u> H street again.

I hope to leave here in the course of the next <u>48</u> <u>hours</u> and to go over to Fort Union where I shall be joined by my ~~es~~ escort. We have <u>guns</u> and <u>pistols</u> enough to make it very uncomfortable for the indians in case they should determine to attack us; but I hope we may go as quietly through the country as it has thus far been my good fortune to do.

Well I must say good night.

Ever your own devoted <u>husband</u>.

…Well again I say goodnight, with love to you all at home.

Letters of John S. Newberry to Spencer F. Baird, Smithsonian Institution

The following letters provide fresh insights into the Macomb Expedition and Newberry's activities related to the survey. Newberry shared a close friendship with his mentor, Spencer F. Baird, and named his third son after him.

Newberry's handwriting is very difficult to transcribe. Hastily written, his letters reveal the energy that he devoted to his work.

* * *

On the Prairies
May 17th, 1859

My Dear Baird

We left Independence yesterday all right, and are now fairly en route— It has rained almost constantly since we left Washington, and the roads are <u>awful</u>!

We have a coach all to ourselves and are progressing as comfortably possible under the circumstances—

I scribble this while the boys are going to bed & can only say—We are all right so far, and beg you to write me from time to time at Fort Defiance.—With kind regards to Mrs. B.   Yours affectionately

J. S. Newberry

From the Smithsonian Institution Archives, Washington, D.C.

*   *   *

Santa Fé
June 4, 1859

My dear [Spencer F.] Baird

We arrived here safely yesterday—Had rather a fatiguing journey across the plains, but have all been well[.]

Have seen Macomb, and like him very much, but as we suspect he might be slightly improved –. If you had him at the Smithsonian for a half day and could talk zoology into him all the time, I think he would be better prepared to go into the field than he now is[.] His interest in natural science is no[t] quite decided but general & abstract –

It's doubtful if we go to Ft. Defiance[,] more likely to Parawan [*sic*] & perhaps to Salt Lake –. Shall probably know by the end of the week –. Navajoes are again at war, and we are on [short rations]. Macomb has mad[e] application for 300 men as escort so we shall probably be safe but will be restricted in our movements.

Kind regards to Mrs B. & the Club.

Yours hastily, J. S. Newberry

*   *   *

Rio Florido
Lat. 37° 13'—Long. 108°
Aug 3d, 1859

Dear [Spencer F.] Baird[,]

Tomorrow morning I am off to an ancient Pueblo of great interest—near our present camp—& on our return—if we return, for it is a trip of some danger—Pfeiffer the indian agent returns to Santa Fé and will take our letters.—I have therefore lots to do—but take time to send you word from this far off region—to let you know that I do not forget you and the Old Smithsonian—however completely I may be forgotten there.

We are now more than 200 miles N.W. of Santa Fé in a region never before explored by whites, and a beautiful region it is.—as beautiful as any part of the continent, high cool, just now very wet, a region of picturesque mountains.—pine forest, grassy & flower decked vallies—with clear cold trout streams—with botany very like that of our northern states—a cretaceous geology of <u>great interest</u>—a fauna very meager. but similar to that of the great basin, generally.—Blacktailed deer. Elk. Antelope. black and grizzly bears.—badgers, coyotes—all very rare.—no rabbits, no squirrels—few birds—Stellar Jay, [Picicorvus], Melanerpes laquatus, Crossbills, Pine grosbeck, crows, magpies, ravens.—few hawks—buzzards &c.

It has rained every day or night since leaving Santa Fé—and I have been able to do little in the way of [preserving?] birds—we are [entirely] too [late] for eggs[.] I shall do however <u>all I can</u> though I have no help, and few facilities.

We hope to be back in Santa Fé by Oct 1ˢᵗ, and in the States in November

We are among indians—but so far all are Utahs & friendly[.] We hear rumors of war from the indians but hope to get through safely.—.

Give my love to Stimpson Foreman, Schaefer, & etc.—as well as my respects to Prof Henry[,] Mrs. Baird & other friends & [illegible] me here as Elsewhere.

Yours faithfully
J.S. Newberry

*   *   *

Santa Fé N.M.
Oct 1ˢᵗ 1859

My Dear Baird

We have just returned from our San Juan trip, all in good health, and having had a very successful and[,] barring the rain[,] a delightful excursion –.

We were gone from here only about 75 days, and of those it rained over 50. So you may judge we had rather a moist time.—. I had the greatest possible difficulty in preserving zoological & botanical specimens, and indeed for a time nothing could be done in either dept. and specimens before collection were ruined.

In geology I have been more successful than I dared to hope[,] obtaining complete sections of all the rocks of this region from the base of the carboniferous (at the granite) to and into the Tertiary.—

Our route led N.W. along the southern bases of the Navajo, San Juan, Pinos, La Plata &c. Mts.—some 400 miles to the junction of Grand & Green rivers—Most of this region is delightful—fine pine forests with beautiful green & flowery vallies—traversed by trout streams coming down from the mts. The prevailing geology cretaceous of which formation I was able to make a very complete analysis –. from base to summit some 3500 feet.—The Colorado I found running in a deep canon and bordered by the wildest and most fantastic scenery to be found on the surface of the globe—Less grand but far more varied & [interesting] than that of the lower part of its course—How much much [sic] difficulty we had in forcing our way to the junction of the Gran[d] & Green rivers you may be able to infer from my sketches—of which I have lots.

In the Triassic? sandstones of the banks of Grand river—I found a great saurian—of which I was able by great effort to exhume & [bring?] away— the bones of one extremity nearly entire—the remainder with [its?] teeth still remaining buried in the cliff –. The femur is 31 inches long & very ponderous—It is not Pleurosaurus .—. Ichthyosaurus or Iguanodon—but what it is I cannot say –. I shall submit the bones to Dr. Leidy—Fortunately all my large collections of fossils were brought in safely, though often in great danger in fording large rivers[.]

From the junction of Grand & Green rivers—we struck across to the San Juan near its mouth –. Thence we followed up that river 150 miles— then struck off to Jemez, & so in—

The San Juan is a fine stream as large as the Rio Grande below here its valley productive & once inhabited by a very large population—as, the ruins of pueblos were scarcely out of sight while we were near the stream[.]

On the whole the trip was exceedingly pleasant & profitable to me—I was uniformly well & worked hard, very hard –. But every day paid. I have now seen enough of New Mexico & am ready to go home.—. In Zoology I did everything possible, but I fear you will think that very little—We remained here six weeks before starting out and I could not find a single bird's egg after we reached the field (July 20)—We start in across the plains in about 2 weeks.—& hope to reach home by the middle of Nov.—
                    Till then adios.
                              Yours affectionately
                              J.S. Newberry
    PS. A thousand thanks for the letters & papers you sent me—& [?] to Washington [?]

                    *   *   *

                                        Cleveland O
                                        Nov. 25, 1859
My dear Baird[,]
    I arrived here safely & well on Tuesday last after a long and wearisome journey from Santa Fé by way of El Paso, San Antonio, & New Orleans—
    I am happy to say that I found Mrs N & the boys as well as I could wish—Spencer Baird particularly is to use a book phrase—all the fondest parent could desire—healthy, handsome, smart and about as amiable & good as his great name sake—I think he will not disgrace his name—
    We had a very pleasant & interesting expedition, and in geology partic- ularly the results exceeded my expectations—In Zoology my efforts were rendered nearly fruitless by the barrenness of the field and the constant

rains[.] I fear you will be disappointed in my collections—but I assure you I did my <u>possible</u>—

I hope to be with you within a month with Capt. Macomb & the collections—He is coming slowly across the plains to Ft. Leavenworth.

I take great pleasure in returning my sincere thanks for your kind letters, and the papers you sent me at Santa Fé—Both were inexpressibly welcome—

Please present my respectful regards to Mrs. Baird[,] Genl. & Mrs. Churchill[,] Prof Henry &c.—& believe me.—[Como Siempre]—

Yours affectionately

J. S. Newberry

*   *   *

Cleveland O.
Nov. 27, 1860

Dear Professor,

I have just received your inquiry about the plants.

Ives' are done with and may be included in the general collection.

McCombs plants you engaged to send to Dr Torrey last spring did you not? I will write to Dr. T. immediately about them and see if he can catalogue them for our report. If not, Dr Englemann will take them up at once. They had perhaps better be left for the present.

We are all well.
Kind regards to the Smithsonians
Affectionately
J.S.N.

LETTERS OF
FREDERICK W. VON EGLOFFSTEIN TO
JOHN N. MACOMB, JR.

T he following correspondence illustrates the careful development of Egloffstein's monumental map of the Macomb Expedition. It represents a compilation of several survey maps and other pertinent primary sources. Nevertheless, it is based primarily on the 1860 manuscript map of the expedition, drawn by Capt. John N. Macomb and Charles H. Dimmock.

The map's evolution occurred over a two year period during the Civil War. Construction of the map began at the outset of the war. And though the cartographer held emigrant status, he joined the Union effort, served as an officer, and was severely wounded in battle. These events delayed the map's completion until mid-1863, followed by its publication the next year.

From the National Archives, Washington, D.C.

*   *   *

Recd. and ansd. 16th May '61
1231 Chestnut Street
Philadelphia Pa
May 10th 1861.

Capt. J. N. Macomb
Corps Topl. Engs. U.S. Army
Washington D.C.
Sir,

I have the honor to report myself to you from Philadelphia, where I have located myself after due consideration at No 1231 Chestnut Street. This office is a few doors below the best photographic establishment in the city (and perhaps in the United States)—and not too far from my printer and the ruling machine, both occupying the same premises.

I have taken up your map while the photographer is going on with Capt. John Rodgers Sea-chart now promising a speedy termination.

The letter engraver, whom I also selected from among a number of unengaged competent men, intends to take up your plate at the end of this or the next week. I prepared a tracing of the lettering of all spanish words, which I will send you for examination, when finished, to guard against misspelling—Awaiting further instructions at your pleasure[.] I have the honor to remain

most respectfully your obedient servant
F.W. Egloffstein

*   *   *

1231 Chestnut Street
Philadelphia Pa.
May 30th 1861.

Capt. J. N. Macomb
    Corps Topl. Engs. U. S. Army
        Washington D.C.
Sir,

I take much pleasure in acknowledging your letter dated May the 28th accompanied by the list of altitudes. I shall construct a profil[e] of the same and send the same to your Office at the earliest practicable period.

In making out the proof for the lettering I was forcibly convinced of the propriety of giving a hurried copy of the whole map, on tracing paper, to enable you to consult such of the Officers, passing through Washington, who have travelled over that region. Moreover I have given a touch of india ink shading to the mountains, with the view of giving at once character to the masses of highlands. Being under the impression this additional work will in the end save many corrections, otherwise <u>unavoidable</u>. This tracing will enable you and Dr. Newberry to make at once valuable suggestions, where I should have failed to come up to the proper understanding. I will send this matter I think by next Monday. Had you been in possession of such a preliminary map, I am sure, we might have gained much valuable information and profited by the criticism of [?] Capt. W. D. Whipple has been at my Office, examined the map, and left a mem[o]randum to that amount on the uncovered map. I had just gone to the photographer next door and left the Office open, expecting the Captain every hour, according to your kind notice. This was unfortunate, but also unavoidable. Perhaps the Captain will see your map in Washington, as he left word of his intention to leave the City the same day at 3 O'Clock P.M.

I enclose a memorandum of the chief engineer of the Pennsylvania Central Railroad, with the latest and only additional information regards Mr. Blackwell. A young man, Clerk of the Continental, and now absent, is in charge of certain property belonging to Mr. Blackwell. When the same returns I may hear more and reliable information.

I am much pleased with the events of last week and hope for the speedy restoration of the "status quo" in the whole South. I am very busily engaged in finishing your tracing and delayed this letter until this evening, which may cause it to be delayed at the postoffice, should I not reach there before nine O'Clock this evening. Please let me know if Capt. John Rodgers is in the city of Washington or ordered to sea, as I intend to write to him, on business shortly. The Captains map is progressing but I can assure you I had yet many considerable difficulties to remove before I could do another step. This new process, when once fully mastered is as simple as all real valuable improvements.

Most respectfully
Your obedient servant
F.W. Egloffstein

*   *   *

Recd. & ansd. on the
11th June
See Pa. ck. bk. Wr.B8.

1231 Chestnut Str.
Philadelphia June 2nd
1861.

Capt. J. N. Macomb
Corps Topl. Engs. U.S. Army
Washington D.C.

Sir,

Your kind letter of the [21st?] instant I have the honor of acknowledging to day. I have sent yesterday the promised map on tracing paper under Major Bashi's address, directed to your Office; and also a short letter accompanying the same. I will now add a few remarks to the same, begging your permission to be as explicit as practicable.

This map is intended for your special use and I beg you to have it inspected and criticized by every body interested in that section of the territories. I have no doubt, but <u>many of the Officers</u> engaged in the Navajo war will pass through Washington just now and add by their private notes, comments, or recollections, to the skeleton now embodying the main lines of travel.

I had not time enough to tint the level plain, which deficiency will be easily corrected by a comparison with one of Lt. J.C. Ives's maps, showing part of the S. W. corner of your map. The [underfeatures?] of the map are rather light, or somewhat neglected, which you will kindly excuse, and explain to others, for I intended but to give a general idea of the masses of highlands, contrasting with the valleys and mesas in bold relief. The trails of parties passing over the country previous to your expedition I have marked in blue lines and the red lines will show at once the great amount of original work your map is furnishing, thus making a contribution to geography, which otherwise would have been burried [*sic*] perhaps forever in the reports and archives of the War Department.

The altitudes [elevations] are left out, as are many trails and names, which will be engraved, on the map, subject to your examination of the [running?] proofs, which will regularly reach your office, as the work progresses.

In marking this tracing I beg you to make out a list of corrections, on a piece of paper, instead of marking it on the map, which I will take care to correct on the original and also on the plate. The tracing thus remaining in your possession for further additions and changes. Many portions of the map are premature and the regular work on the original will improve greatly. For instance the San Juan Mountains, the Uncompahgre mountains and the main chain of rocky mountains North of your wagon road to Gunnison's trail, as I have not as yet made use of all the landscape views in our possession.

Your work and that of Capt. Gunnison connects at the Salt [La Sal] Mts. in longitude; Col. Loring's map connecting the two lines of travel diagonally across the San Luis Valley verifies this construction. Thus the whole of Capt. Gunnison's work is moved a few miles (3.75 [m?]) to the East, which agrees with the land office work of the upper del Norte, the latter being 15 <u>m</u> to[o] far West on Gunnison's map. Ives's and Whipple's work remain also unchanged as a body, but subject to the longitude of

Santa Fé and Albuquerque, so well determined of late. As regards the title I think the word Colorado Tery. could be added to Utah and New Mexico. The name of the former Secretary of War has been remarked by others being <u>out</u> of date. But this might be altered in substituting "<u>the bureau of Topl. Engrs. War Department</u>." However this is a question beyond my sphere and of no other than momentary importance, as your map will stand on record, I hope, for many generations after the settlement of the present political difficulties [Civil War]—

The blue river, or Na-un-ka-rea river has been called "Upper Colorado" by the settlers of Colorado Territory giving rise to the name of that territory; I have therefore added both Grand river and Upper Colorado. This river rises at Long's peak and is fully as long as Green river, deserving the main name Colorado as it drains the whole mountainous district between the del Norte and the Platte, snow capped mountains of alpine character; Green river being less formidable in every respect.

There is much to be done on your original map and the tracing is far more developed than the present accurate construction of the work in reality; which will explain some slight changes to occur in proofs from the plate itself in future. Dr. Newberry will be enabled to suggest many valuable points, since this tracing is at your command. I would like much to have your candid opinion of that general effect of the map. San Francisco Ms., Mt Taylor, Albuquerque Mts. Sierra la Plata, Spanish Peaks, Pikes Peak are scarcely as high as the Cañon of the Colorado near Padre Crossing is <u>deep</u>. I will have to reserve much power of shading therefore for this contrast and the minor canons will appear weak, although much bolder than on this sketch.

I hope this attempt will proof [*sic*] to you my desire and anxiety to make your map—a document of much value and an ornament to the bureau of topographical engineers. Much will depend upon my present success of the heliographic process. I hope for the best and will work my way indefatiguably—to accomplish this great object.

In leaving Washington you had the kindness to pay me up to the 1ˢᵗ of June. Moving to Philadelphia, and establishing new Office &c. have consumed much money and I am obliged to beg you for one month salary, my means getting rapidly exhausted.

I am glad to hear Commander John Rodgers will be here. I hope to have something ready to please him as I feel much indebted to his encouraging this new process of engraving and topography.

Most respectfully
Your obedient servant
F.W. Egloffstein.

* * *

19th June ansd. and
sent 2 copies Emory's   1231 Chestnut Street
report and one map only   Philadelphia Pa
by Ed. [?] <u>via Continental</u>   June 12th 1861.
                    [?]
Capt. J. N. Macomb
Corps Topl. Engs. U.S. Army   and wrote again on
Washington D.C.   21st & 22nd authorizing
                                                     expense of $5 or $6 for maps
                                                     &c of use to us.

Sir,

Your letter enclosing a check of one hundred and twenty five dollars for this month salary I have the honor to acknowledge.

I am happy to hear your expenses as favourable an opinion of the tracing, which I have hurried much more than I wish to do otherwise; but time is precious, and you will have in a reasonable period running proofs of the work.

I understand Major Sheppard is in this part of the country, I fear it is not the same gentleman, who directed several expeditions from Fort Defiance through Navajo strongholds as the trails on our map prove.

If you should be able, Captain, to gather a few maps of the mining districts around Pike peak, there are some published, the work would gain much in value, and secure to the chart a certain longevity, so desirable after the endless labor of compiling the material, which is scattered over so many Offices, embraced in so many correct and erroneous maps.

I propose now to make a slight tracing, or as well send one of the <u>final proofs</u> to Mr. Pfeif[f]er in New Mexico, in order to get from him and through him the most reliable information of the San Juan Mountains, further a delineation of the parks of the upper Animas, Dolores, and Uncompahgrea Rivers. The construction I have so far given is vague and may be modified by future developments of that mountain district.

I take much pleasure and pride in combining the material on hand in the most solid, compact and correct way. Few maps have ever been constructed with more care to preserve the material of each party, exploring in their own fashion and mapping in their own language. We see the marked differences for instance in comparing the maps of Capt. Simpson, Emory, Whipple, Gunnison & Ives with your own. Every map has its own character, difficult often to read and impossible for one who has not been over the ground himself or close by. This new style of topography whether modeled or merely imitating the plaster model, reduces these different languages of mapping in <u>one</u>, plain and readable.

There are many weak parts of the map, and as gold may be discovered in almost every section of that country, I fear the consequences; an early "exposition" of the errors embraced in the construction.

I hope to gather much more material before the work is ruled, or the last tint put on the top of the heliographic engraving. As soon as some proofs are advanced, to exhibit the skeleton geographical positions and triangulations, it would further our map much, if copies (preliminary) could be sent to New Mexico and the Pike Peak country or Colorado Territory, to such persons as Governor Gilpon, his Surveyor General, Mr. Henderson, Kid [sic] Carson, Leroux &c.—two at a time with the request to return one corrected copy to your Office.

It is strange how little our War Department Maps are distributed. Even the Army Officers are often met with in the field, commanding large bodies of troops not being in possession of the necessary maps already published for year past. If we can get an answer but from half of those addressed, the work would gain much in correctness and popularity. Your name is so well known in New Mexico and so highly spoken of, that there would be much readiness expressed in aiding in the construction of the map, by all parties who have travelled and explored in that region.

If you should come in sight of one of the oldest maps of New Mexico, published perhaps ten or twenty years ago, for instance "[Josiah] Greggs map" on the scale of 57 miles to the inch, embracing the country from the Western boundary of Missouri to the 108th merid. I would feel much obliged for the use of the same during a few days. On those old maps many valuable features are delineated which disappear on the recent publications.

I would like much to have the use of Emory's map for a few days only. Many of the Officers are in possession of a copy, perhaps Dr Newberry has a copy also. I do not trouble you in vain, and sorry as I am to ask you an unpleasant favor, perhaps the increased correctness of your map will repay you many folds for your troubles.

I saw to day for the first time Col. Meig's photograph on Chestnut Street. It is grouped with "the patriots" headed by the General in Chief, Major Anderson, President Lincoln, Mr. Dayton and a few others, in all twelve persons on one card. Opposite to this picture was another collection headed "the traitors" portraying twelve of the southern personages, only too well known.

Most respectfully
Your obedient servant
F. W. Egloffstein.

*   *   *

Recd. & ansd. on
The 1ˢᵗ July 1861.
    JNM.

1231 Chestnut Street
Philadelphia Pa.
June 28ᵗʰ 1861.

Capt. J. N. Macomb
    Corps Topl. Engs. U.S. Army
        Washington D.C.

Sir,

After having had the honor of seeing you at your Office in Winder building on Monday[,] I went in search of the Secretary of the Interior. But all was in vain, as Mr. Caleb B. Smith was not accessible. The next day I failed again to be admitted, when I called on the Prussian Minister, Baron [Frederick von] Gerolt, who kindly consented and presented me to Mr. C. B. Smith. I had as much success as could be expected under such favorable circumstances. The Secretary [of the Interior, Mr C. B. Smith] who had never seen maps of the new style, expressed his desire to have his map engraved like your present map of New Mexico, which he admired and inspected for at least one quarter of an hour. I left your kind letter and an estimate of the map of the Texas boundary survey in the Interior Department for final decision.

Baron Gerolt exhibited much interest in your map which he thinks is the first complete map of the most interesting part of Nord America ever published. As your map and the [Texas] boundary map join at Santa Fé, they will form a set of geographical maps much wanted in the scientific and travelling circles of Europe, and carry your name all over the world, where geography is cultivated. I hope that you will be able to secure two or three thousand copies besides your report, for distribution to the Universities, Academies, Geographical societies, Scientific institutes &c. of the United States and Europe. Baron Gerolt told me he sent originally Frémonts first map to the King of Prussia and Baron Humboldt; in consequence of which the King ordered the famous large gold medal of the knights of the "order of merit", to be presented to Frémont, the latter taking well care of having this presentation know all over the United States and Europe.

Fine thick paper impressions will cost you according to the quality of paper from 150 to 200 dollars per thousand, which will be well invested, as otherwise, your map would be bur[i]ed in a few libraries, never to be heard of again.

As I returned to Windersbuilding [*sic*] I was called for by the Office of Capt. A. A. Humphreys, who insisted upon my reading Mr. Ives's proofs, unattended to for many weeks, and otherwise to be sent back again without notice to the superintendent. Dr. Newberry had left, Mr[.] Young who was asked to read the illustrations had left with Capt. A. W. Whipple. I finally consented for two reasons: First the woodcuts (70 in number) were too bad to pass without comment, second Capt. Humphreys paid my travelling expenses, or 8 dollars for two days work. Consequently I left Washington Thursday and report myself to you this Friday evening in my Office. Hoping this delay, caused by business otherwise unattended to by any of the Officers will not displease you. I am only sorry not having been in my Office in case you should have come on from Washington yourself to see me.

I left your tracing in the hands of Capt. J. P. Woodruff on leaving Windersbuilding [*sic*], wrapped up in brown paper and addressed to yourself.

Your kind letter of the 21st June I received on my return and acknowledge the receipt of Col. Emory's map and two volumes, which I will return during the next week. I found on my return a well ruled glassplate [*sic*] for the final printing of Com. John Rodgers map, of which I have promised to send a proof to Cincinnati early next week.

I will and have to tax my full energies once more to push those two plates through, especially since the Texas boundary map will perhaps make it necessary for me to return soon altogether to Washington notwithstanding the summerheat of Washington nights.

I will soon write to you of my further progress and the pleasure it gives me to accomplish the task before me. Please be assured, Captain, of my sincere thanks for our kind assistance in this new contract for the boundary map.

Most respectfully
Your obedient servant
F.W. Egloffstein.

*   *   *

Ansd. on 12th July 1861   1231 Chestnut Street
                                                Philadelphia Pa.
                                                July 7th 1861.

Capt. J. N. Macomb
        Corps Topl. Engs. U.S. Army
                Washington D.C.

Sir,

Your encouraging letter of the 1st July I have the honor to acknowledge. I have since labored with some success on both your and Capt. John

Rodgers maps. Constructing your profile I find the barometric h[e]ights of the lowest altitude on Labyrinth Creek corresponding very well with Capt. Gunnison's datas [sic] at the crossing of Green river. Your lowest position is 3.156.18 feet below Santa Fé, or the latter taken at 7000 feet above the level of the sea, 3.843.82' positive altitude. I suppose the level of Grand river is about a thousand feet below this station which will give about 3000 feet. Captain Gunnison's observation at the crossing of the Grand river is 4440 feet above the sea 80 miles north or above your position; his crossing of Green river is 3828 feet. This corresponds well and I see no reason to doubt the reading of your barometers, or the computation of the same, which is very satisfactory.

I will send you the profil[e] with an impression of your steel plate shortly, when I will add a few remarks of minor points on the route.

In engraving the various trails I have considered to mark your wagon road in double lines thus ========. Please let me know as soon as convenient which is the whole extent of your roads. I suppose your roads commence at Fort Union via Apache Cañon to Santa Fé, thence along your trail via Santa Domingo, Algadones, &c. to Albuquerque. Did you cross the Rio Grande, or run a road west of the river? I have a vague idea of your having surveyed or built a road toward Albiquiu [sic] forming the now desirable connection between Santa Fé and the Pagosas mining district. Your wagon roads and the Public Surveys are important elements of the map and I will take care to engrave the same so, as to direct the eye of the reader to the same, without compromising the harmony of the whole map.—

I intend to lay down a little mountain work upon the plate serving as a skeleton for general information, however primitive for I am very anxious to get some impressions on the way to New Mexico during this summer, so we have a return and criticism from that region. The San Juan Mountains as well as the Sierra Blanca between Taos and Fort Garland have been much visited lately and many persons in New Mexico are able to furnish additional information, regards the upper valleys of the streams tributary to the Del Norte and the Canadian rivers.

I am sorry it got so late this morning that I have to close these lines in order to mail them in time. The days are so long and half past six in the evening finds me generally leaning over my steel plates, the only children I now pos[s]ess, and take care of.

I have to ask you also for the month of July salary, as my funds are exhausted, much owing to my trip to Washington and the various accidentals [sic] pertaining to the same.

If we should have rainy weather I will be able to send you soon an impression. On clear days, much time is lost in watching the photographic operations.

> Most respectfully
> Your obedient servant
> F.W. Egloffstein.

*   *   *

– Private—   1231 Chestnut Street
Recd. on 13 July '61   Philadelphia Pa
                                              July 10th 1861.

Captain J. N. Macomb No inclosures [*sic*]
        Corps Topl. Engs. U.S. Army
            Washington D.C.

Dear Sir,

I enclose a few impressions of the first Island of Commander John Rodgers map, now printed.

His specimen, imperfect in some respects and nearly an agua fortis proof, is however a satisfactory proof of the success of the heliographic process.

If examined by means of a magnifier you will see the delicate tint lines or grain of the work, my invention and forming a valuable new style of engraving.

I have sent impressions to Cincinnati to give I hope satisfaction to your brother in law, Commander John Rodgers, who has kindly encouraged me to master the difficulties of the experiment, which herewith closes. The rest is mechanical work which will require but ordinary diligence to give satisfaction. My photographer, the celebrated stereoscopist Mr. Langenhelm gives me additional assurance, that I will be able to print thus on steel any given stereoscope.

I would like to return to Washington as soon as this plate is done, when I will have the pleasure to print on steel your portrait and that of Col. M C. Meigs.

Should you have a good photograph handy please send it on, as it would not take a moment more time, whether I print or expose to the sun, two, or half a dozen pictures, save the laying of the [e]tching ground, a few minutes operation.

> Most respectfully
> Your obedient servant
> F.W. Egloffstein.

*   *   *

1231 Chestnut Str.
Philadelphia Pa
July 16th 1861.
Tuesday.—

Captain J. N. Macomb.
          Corps Topl. Engs. U.S. Army
                Washington D.C.
Sir,

I have the honor to acknowledge your favor of the 13th a.c. enclosing the draft of $125 1/100 on New York Sub-treasury, for which I beg to accept my sincere thanks.

The triplicate vouchers accompany these lines. I am happy to learn of your arrangement, as regards the two days voucher, which I made mention of to you in my last before letter. I thought there might be some discrepancy in the monthly accounts, so I informed you of the same, notwithstanding the protestation of Mr. Smith Thompson to the contrary. You know from experience so much better how to arrange these matters of liquidation. I have been a few hours in Washington, on Monday, going and coming so rapidly as not being able to see you personally. Called for to attend the summons in the matter of engraving the Texas boundary map, I suce[e]ded to prearrange a favorable result for taking up the new contract in about two weeks hence.

I am fully satisfied with drawing one more month of salary for drawing your map, when I hope your appropriation will be sufficient to cover the original amount of 800 dollars for the engraving. Perhaps if money should be left to your account, the item of lettering, might be defrayed out of the same, this latter however depending entirely upon your own approbation or such arrangements as you feel pleased to make.

Have the kindness Captain to let me know the full extent of your wagon roads in New Mexico, so I am under the impression there are some of your improvements on routes of travel <u>West</u> of the Fort Union and Santa Fé road.

I had certain offers made to me lately, to engage in volunteering, which I however respectfully declined, giving at present more than ever attention to topography. I sent you a little specimen of part of Commander John Rodger's map on last Friday. My unexpectedly fortunate success in heliography will <u>also</u> secure this process to <u>your map</u>, even without modelling the work so elaborately. Everything will turn out right and your engraving and map stand for many generations on record as an ornament to yourself and the bureau. I have the honor to be most respectfully

Your obedient servant
F.W. Egloffstein.

*   *   *

Recd. on the 28th Oct. '61

1231 Chestnut Str.
Philadelphia Pa
October 26th 1861.

Major J. N. Macomb
        Corps Topl. Engs. U.S. Army
            Washington D.C.
Sir,
   I have the honor of submitting to your examination a proof of your map, exhibiting the lettering thereupon.
   The title is not as yet cut in full for the reason of changes, which may deem advisable.
   I will have the honor of calling on you in Washington during the next week, hoping to receive further instruction from you. I felt very sorry of having been absent from my Office, when you called on me during your short tour through this city.
                         Most respectfully
                         Your obd. sert.
                            F. W. Egloffstein.

*   *   *

Recd. on 1st Feby 1862
opened by some other [?]

                         F. Nicholas [St?]
                         January 22, 186[2]

Col. J. N. Macomb
Corps of Topl. Engs.
        Washington,
Dear Sir,
   Your two letters have reached me on my return to this city from a tour in the interior states.
   I will send you a proof of your map, the same being much advanced, the work along the outward and homeward trail is finished and much besides, to make a handsome display.
                         Most respectfully
                         Your obedient servant
                         Baron F. W. Egloffstein.

*   *   *

Washington D.C.
May 30 1863

Colonel J. N. Macomb
        Topl. Engrs. U.S. Army
Dear Colonel,

You would much oblige me by sending that letter, you once required from Dr. Newberry, as Prof. Baird can not give me the copies of the Colon[el's] Report without Newberry's order.

Your plate is doing well and you will receive a good impression of the same during the week.

                I have the honor Colonel to be
                        most respectfully
                                your obedient servant.
                                        [illegible] F. W. v. Egloffstein.

[Note from Macomb]: Wrote a request to Newberry to send to Egloffstein an order on Profr Baird for the works, as many copies as he may have determined [illegible].

BIBLIOGRAPHY

Unpublished Sources

"Ancient Pottery from New Mexico, Collected by Dr. J. S. Newberry," accession number 027, 1860, Record Unit 305. Office of Registrar, U.S. National Museum, Smithsonian Institution Archives, Washington, D.C.

Bergman, E. H., Commander of Camp Plummer, to J. H. Carleton, Commander of New Mexico Military District, Santa Fé. Report of a Reconnaissance to the Animas River to Locate a Site for a Military Post, March 15, 1867. Center of Southwest Studies, Fort Lewis College, Durango, Colo.

"Capt. J. [N.] Macomb," accession number 291, 1860, Record Unit 305. Office of Registrar, U.S. National Museum, Smithsonian Institution Archives, Washington, D.C.

Colonel John N. Macomb to Colonel S. H. Long, Washington, D.C., October 28, 1862. Microcopy No. 506, Roll 53, M. Letters Received, Bureau of Topographical Engineers, War Department Records, Record Group 77. National Archives, Washington, D.C.

Crampton, C. Gregory. "Mormon Colonization in Southern Utah and in adjacent parts of Arizona and Nevada." Unpublished manuscript. 1965.

Dimmock, Charles. Papers. Special Collections Research Center, Swem Library, College of William and Mary, Williamsburg, Va.

Dimmock, Charles H. Papers, 1850–1873, Section 1, 1859. Diary. Virginia Historical Society, Richmond.

———. "Map of Explorations and Surveys in New Mexico and Utah, made under the Direction of the Hon. John B. Floyd, Secretary of War," 1859. Manuscript map. Record Group 77, W81, 1 of 5, 2 of 5, 3 of 5, 4 of 5, 5 of 5. National Archives, Washington, D.C.

————. Papers, 1850–1873, Section 6, 1859. Sketchbook. Virginia Historical Society, Richmond.

————. Topographical Memoir of the route traversed by the "San Juan Exploring Expedition" from Abiquiu, New Mexico to the Junction of the Grand & Green Rivers, Utah; and the return by way of the San Juan to Santa Fé, New Mexico. Series I, Box 21. Rodgers Family. Papers. Manuscripts Division, Library of Congress, Washington, D.C.

Hayden, Martha C. Interview by author, September 4, 2007. Utah Geological Survey, Salt Lake City.

"Instr. on return 30th Sep. 1859." [Letters Received, Bureau of Topographical Engineers, War Department Records, Record Group 77.] National Archives, Washington, D.C. Copy in possession of author.

[Ives, Joseph C.] to John N. Macomb. "Memorandum to accompany a map furnished to Captain J. N. Macomb, Topl. Engrs., for his assistance in the exploration of the San Juan River &c.," [April 1859. Letters Received, Bureau of Topographical Engineers, War Department Records, Record Group 77.] National Archives, Washington, D.C. Copy in possession of author.

Letters Received. Bureau of Topographical Engineers, War Department Records, Record Group 77. National Archives, Washington, D.C. (Correspondence includes Egloffstein to Macomb, Hazzard to Macomb, Humphreys to Floyd, Humphreys to Macomb, Ives to Dimmock, Ives to Dorsey, Ives to Fisher, Ives to Newberry, Ives to Vail, Macomb to Abert, Macomb to Humphreys, Macomb to Leroux, Macomb to Wilkins, and Newberry to Macomb.) Copies in possession of author.

Macomb, J. N. "Map of Explorations and Surveys in New Mexico and Utah made under the Direction of the Hon. J. B. Floyd, Sec. of War, by Capt. J. N. Macomb, Topl. Engrs., assisted by C. H. Dimmick [sic], C. Engr. &c., 1860." Manuscript map. Record Group 77, W81, Roll no. 4, National Archives, Washington, D.C.

"Mules or other Public Animals, Santa Fé, N. M., June 1859, San Juan Expedn." Letterbook, 64. [Letters Received. Bureau of Topographical Engineers, War Department Records, Record Group 77.] National Archives, Washington, D.C. Copy in possession of author.

Newberry, John S. [Abridged Diary. July 13, 1859–September 28, 1859.] N unentered, 1861. Letters Received. Bureau of Topographical Engineers, War Department Records, Record Group 77. National Archives, Washington, D.C.

Newberry, John S., to Dr. Joseph Leidy. Correspondence. College of Physicians of Philadelphia.

Newberry, John S., to Spencer F. Baird. Correspondence. Record Unit 7002, Box 30. Smithsonian Institution Archives, Washington, D.C.

Oldham, Ann. Personal communication with author, July 18, 2007. Pagosa Springs Museum.

"San Juan River Survey: Astronomical and Barometrical Observation, 1859." [Bureau of Topographical Engineers, War Department Records, Record Group 77.] National Archives, Washington, D.C. Copy in possession of author.

"The United States in ac. with J. N. M. for San Juan Exploration." Letterbook, 74–75, [Macomb's Accounts for Third Quarter, 1859. Bureau of Topographical Engineers, War Department Records, Record Group 77.] National Archives, Washington, D.C. Copy in possession of author.

Wilkins, John D., Third Infantry, to "Officer Commanding Fort Defiance, New Mexico," July 8, 1859. Department of New Mexico Letters, vol. 10, 351. Record Group 98, National Archives, Washington, D.C. In Arrott's Fort Union Collection, Thomas C. Donnelly Library, New Mexico Highlands University.

Wilkins, Katherine. Personal communication with author, November 14, 2006. Virginia Historical Society, Richmond.

Published Sources

Anderson, Allen. *Map of the Military Department of New Mexico: Drawn under the direction of Brig. Gen. James H. Carleton.* Albuquerque, New Mexico: Horn & Wallace, 1864.

Army and Navy Register. Washington, D.C., March 23, 1889.

Aton, James M., and Robert S. McPherson. *River Flowing from the Sunrise: An Environmental History of the Lower San Juan.* Logan: Utah State University Press, 2000.

Barnes, F. A. *Canyonlands National Park: Early History and First Descriptions.* Moab, Utah: Canyon Country Publications, 1988.

———. "Early Explorations of Utah," *Canyon Legacy* 9 (Spring 1991): 2–9.

———. *The 1859 Macomb Expedition into Utah Territory.* Moab, Utah: Canyon Country Publications, 2003.

———. *Hiking the Historic Route of the 1859 Macomb Expedition.* Moab, Utah: Canyon Country Publications, 1989.

———. "Utah's Early Place in Paleontological History," *Canyon Legacy* 6 (Summer 1990): 9–14.

Bartlett, Richard A. *Great Surveys of the American West.* Norman: University of Oklahoma Press, 1962.

Beckwith, E. G. "Map No. 4. From the Coo-che-to-pa Pass to the Wasatch Mountains from Explorations and Surveys made under the direction of the Hon. Jefferson Davis, Secretary of War, by Capt. J. W. Gunnison, Topl. Engrs. assisted by Capt. E. G. Beckwith 3d. Artillery," in *Reports of Explorations and Surveys to Ascertain the Most Practical and Economical Route for a Railroad from the Mississippi to the Pacific Ocean, . . .*vol. 2. Washington, D.C.: Beverley Tucker, 1855.

Biedleman, Richard G. *California's Frontier Naturalists.* Berkeley: University of California Press, 2006.

Chenoweth, William L. "John Strong Newberry: Pioneer Colorado Plateau Geologist," *Canyon Legacy* 24 (Summer 1995): 2–3.

Cobos, Ruben. *A Dictionary of New Mexico and Southern Colorado Spanish.* Santa Fé: Museum of New Mexico Press, 1983.

Colton, J. H., & Co. *Territories of New Mexico and Utah.* New York: J. H. Colton, 1855.

Cope, E. D. "On a Dinosaurian from the Trias of Utah," *Proceedings of the American Philosophical Society* 16 (1877): 579–85.

———. "Report upon the extinct Vertebrata obtained in New Mexico by Parties of the Expedition of 1874, Chapter XI, Fossils of the Mesozoic Periods and Geology of Mesozoic and Tertiary Beds," in George M. Wheeler, *Report upon United States Geographical Surveys west of the One Hundredth Meridian, in charge of First Lieut. Geo. M. Wheeler, Corps of Engineers, U. S. Army, under the direction of Brig. Gen. A. A. Humphreys, Chief of Engineers, U. S. Army.* Vol. 4. Washington, D.C.: Government Printing Office, 1877.

Crampton, C. Gregory. *Land of Living Rock: The Grand Canyon and the High Plateaus: Arizona, Utah, Nevada.* New York: Knopf, 1972.

———. *Standing Up Country: The Canyon Lands of Utah and Arizona.* New York: Knopf, 1964.

Crampton, C. Gregory, and Steven K. Madsen. *In Search of the Spanish Trail: Santa Fe to Los Angeles, 1829–1848.* Layton, Utah: Gibbs Smith, 1994.

Cuch, Forrest S., ed. *A History of Utah's American Indians.* Salt Lake City: Utah State Division of Indian Affairs and Utah State Division of History, 2000.

Cullum, George W. *Biographical Register of the Officers and Graduates of the U.S. Military Academy, from 1802 to 1867.* Vol. 1. Rev. ed. New York: James Miller, 1879.

Daily Alta California (San Francisco, Calif.), June 13, 1859.

Daily Rocky Mountain News (Denver, Colo.), June 23, 1869.

Egloffstein, Frederick W. von. *Map of Explorations and Surveys, in New Mexico and Utah made under the direction of the Secretary of War by Capt. J. N. Macomb, Topographical Engineers, assisted by C. H. Dimmock, C. Engineer, 1860.* New York: Geographical Institute, Baron F. W. von Egloffstein, 1864.

Emory, William H. *Notes of a Military Reconnoissance, from Fort Leavenworth, in Missouri, to San Diego, in California, including part of the Arkansas, Del Norte, and Gila Rivers.* Washington, D.C.: Wendell and Benthuysen, 1848.

Etter, Patricia A. "The 1849 Diary of Stanislaus Lasselle," *Overland Journal* 9, no. 2 (1991): 3–33.

Froiseth, B. A. M. *Froiseth's New Sectional & Mineral Map of Utah: Compiled from the latest U.S. Government Surveys and other Sources.* Second ed. Salt Lake City, Utah: Froiseth, 1878.

Goetzmann, William H. *Army Exploration in the American West, 1803–1863.* New Haven, Conn.: Yale University Press, 1959.

———. *Exploration and Empire: The Explorer and the Scientist in the Winning of the American West.* New York: Knopf, 1966.

Gregg, Josiah. *A Map of the Indian Territory, Northern Texas and New Mexico, Showing the Great Western Prairies.* New York: Henry G. Langley, 1844.

Gregory, Herbert E. *The San Juan Country: A Geographic and Geologic Reconnaissance of Southeastern Utah.* U.S. Geological Survey Professional Paper 188. Washington, D.C.: Government Printing Office, 1938.

Guernsey, A. H. "Army Life on the Border," *Harper's New Monthly Magazine* 33, no. 196 (September 1866): 429–44.

Hafen, LeRoy R., and Ann W. Hafen. *Old Spanish Trail: Santa Fé to Los Angeles.* Glendale, Calif.: Arthur H. Clark, 1954.

Hamilton, Joseph Gregoire de Roulhac, and Mary Cornelia Thompson Hamilton. *The Life of Robert E. Lee for Boys and Girls.* Boston: Houghton Mifflin, 1917.

Hayden, Ferdinand V. *The Geological and Geographical Atlas of Colorado and Portions of Adjacent Territory.* Washington, D.C.: Julius Bien, 1877.

———. "Map of South West Colorado with parts of Utah, New Mexico, and Arizona," plate 37 in F. V. Hayden, *Ninth Annual Report of the United States Geological and Geographical Survey of the Territories, embracing Colorado and parts of adjacent Territories: being a Report of Progress of the Exploration for the Year 1875.* Washington, D.C.: Government Printing Office, 1877.

———. *Tenth Annual Report of the United States Geological and Geographical Survey of the Territories embracing Colorado and parts of adjacent Territories.* Washington, D.C.: Government Printing Office, 1878.

———. *United States Geological and Geographical Surveys of the Territories, Geological and Geographical Atlas of Colorado and Portions of Adjacent Territory.* Washington, D.C.: Julius Bien, 1877.

Heitman, Francis B. *Historical Register and Dictionary of the United States Army from its organization, September 29, 1789, to March 2, 1903.* Vol. 1. Reprint ed. Urbana: University of Illinois Press, 1965.

Holmes, W. H. "Report on the Geology of the Sierra Abajo and West San Miguel Mountains," in F. V. Hayden, *Tenth Annual Report of the United States Geological and Geographical Survey of the Territories, embracing Colorado and parts of adjacent Territories, being a Report of Progress of the Exploration for the Year 1876.* Washington, D.C.: Government Printing Office, 1878.

Huene, F. von. "Dystrophaeus viaemalae Cope in neur Beleuchtung," *Separat-Abdruck aus dem Neuen Jahrbuck für Mineralogie, Geologie und Palaeontologie* 19 (1904): 319–33.

Ives, Joseph C. *Report upon the Colorado River of the West.* Reprint ed. New York: Da Capo, 1969.

Jackson, Donald, and Mary Lee Spence, eds. *The Expeditions of John Charles Fremont.* 4 vols. Urbana: University of Illinois Press, 1970–84.

Jackson, W. Turrentine. *Wagon Roads West: A Study of Federal Road Surveys and Construction in the trans-Mississippi West, 1846–1869.* Berkeley: University of California Press, 1952.

Lange, Frederick, Nancy Mahaney, Joe Ben Wheat, and Mark Chenault. *Yellow Jacket: A Four Corners Anasazi Ceremonial Center.* Boulder, Colo.: Johnson Books, 1986.

Lucas, Spencer G., Adrian P. Hunt, and Kim Martini. "Newberry's Locality for Cretaceous Plant Fossils at Whetstone Creek, New Mexico," *New Mexico Journal of Science* 27, no. 2 (December 1987): 95–98.

Macomb, John N. *Report of an Exploring Expedition, from Santa Fé, New Mexico, to the Junction of the Grand and Green Rivers of the Great Colorado River of the West, in 1859, . . . with Geological Report by Prof. J. S. Newberry.* Washington, D.C.: Government Printing Office, 1876.

Madsen, Steven K. "Retracing the Spanish Trail: Across Colorado's San Juan Basin," *Spanish Traces* 2, no. 2 (Fall 1996): 1, 4–11.

———. "Retracing the Spanish Trail: Across the Colorado Plateau," *Spanish Traces* 4, no.1 (Spring 1998): 5–13.

———. "The 1859 San Juan Exploring Expedition along the Old Spanish Trail," *Spanish Traces* 12, no. 3 (Fall 2006): 1, 16–30.

McKinney, Kevin C., ed. *Digital Archive—Geological Report by J. S. Newberry and Map by J. N. Macomb from the Exploring Expedition from Santa Fé, New Mexico to the Junction of the Green and Grand Rivers of the Great Colorado of the West in 1859, with Descriptions of the Cretaceous Fossils Collected on the Expedition, by F. B. Meek.* [Reston, Virginia]: U.S. Department of Interior, U.S. Geological Survey, 2000.

McNitt, Frank, ed. *Navaho Expedition: A Journal of a Military Reconnaissance from Santa Fé, New Mexico to the Navaho Country made in 1849 by Lieutenant James H. Simpson.* Norman: University of Oklahoma Press, 1964.

Petersen, Jesse G. *A Route for the Overland Stage: James H. Simpson's 1859 Trail across the Great Basin.* Logan: Utah State University Press, 2008.

Peterson, John Alton. *Utah's Black Hawk War.* Salt Lake City: University of Utah Press, 1998.

Powell, William H. *List of Officers of the United States from 1779 to 1900 . . . . Compiled from the Official Records.* New York: L. R. Hamersly, 1900.

Pyne, Stephen J. *How the Canyon became Grand: A Short History.* New York: Viking, 1998.

Reeve, Frank D. "Early Navaho Geography," *New Mexico Historical Review* 31 (October 1956): 290–309.

Reinhartz, Dennis, and Gerald D. Saxon, eds. *Mapping and Empire: Soldier-Engineers on the Southwestern Frontier.* Austin: University of Texas Press, 2005.

Remley, David. *"Adios Nuevo Mexico": The Santa Fé Journal of John Watts in 1859.* Las Cruces, N. Mex.: Yucca Tree, 1999.

Robinson, John W. "Antonio Maria Armijo: New Mexico Trader to California Ranchero, *Spanish Traces* 11, no. 3 (Fall 2005): 17–30.

Roland, Charles P. *Albert Sidney Johnston: Soldier of Three Republics.* Austin: University of Texas Press, 1964.

Ruffner, Ernest. H. *Annual Report upon Explorations and Surveys in the Department of the Missouri: Appendix QQ of the Annual Report of the Chief of Engineers for 1876.* Washington, D.C.: Government Printing Office, 1876.

Schubert, Frank N. *Vanguard of Expansion: Army Engineers in the Trans-Mississippi West, 1819–1879.* [Washington, D.C.]: Historical Division, Office of Administrative Services, Office of the Chief of Engineers, [1980].

Şengör, A. M. Celâl. *The large wavelength deformations of the lithosphere: Materials for a history of the evolution of thought from the earliest times to plate tectonics.* Memoir 196. Boulder, Colo.: Geological Survey of America, 2003.

Simpson, James H. *Report of Explorations across the Great Basin of the Territory of Utah for a direct Wagon-Route from Camp Floyd to Genoa, in Carson Valley, in 1859.* Reprint ed. Reno: University of Nevada Press, 1983.

U.S. Congress. *Report of the Secretary of War*. Senate Executive Document 1, vol. 2, 36th Cong., 2nd sess., serial no. 1079, 1860.

U.S. Supreme Court. *State of N. M. v. State of Colo.*, 267 U.S. 30 (1925).

U.S. War Department, Bureau of Topographical Engineers. *Map of Utah Territory showing Routes connecting it with California and the East . . . From the Latest and Most Reliable Data*. Richmond, Va.: Ritichie and Dunnavant, 1858.

———. *[Map of the] Territory and Military Department of Utah, compiled in the Bureau of Topographl. Engrs. of the War Depart[ment] chiefly for Military Purposes, under the Authority of Hon. J. B. Floyd, Sec. of War*. [Washington, D.C.]: n.p., 1860.

U.S. War Department, Corps of Topographical Engineers. *Reports of Explorations and Surveys to Ascertain the Most Practicable and Economical Route for a Railroad from the Mississippi River to the Pacific Ocean, Made under the Direction of the Secretary of War, in 1853–56, According to Acts of Congress of March 3, 1853, May 31, 1854, and August 5, 1854*. 12 vols. Washington, D.C.: Beverley Tucker and George W. Bowman, 1855–61.

Weishampel, David B., Peter Dodson, and Halszka Osmólska, eds. *The Dinosauria*. Second ed. Berkeley: University of California Press, 2004.

Wheat, Carl I. *1540–1861, Mapping the Transmississippi West*. 5 vols. San Francisco, Calif.: Institute of Historical Cartography, 1957–63.

Wheeler, George M. *U.S. Geographical Surveys West of the 100th Meridian, Parts of Southern Colorado and Northern New Mexico*. Atlas Sheet No. 69. Washington, D.C.: n.p., 1882.

When Cultures Meet: Remembering San Gabriel Del Yunge Oweenge, Papers from the October 20, 1984, Conference held at San Juan Pueblo, New Mexico. Santa Fé, N. Mex.: Sunstone Press, 1987.

White, Charles A. "Biographical Memoir of John Strong Newberry, 1822–1892," in National Academy of Sciences, *Biographical Memoirs* 6 (1909): 1–24.

Wilbar, A. P. "Sketch of Public Surveys in New Mexico, 1860," in U.S. Congress. *Report of the Secretary of War*. Senate Executive Document 1, vol. 2, 36th Cong., 2nd sess., serial no. 1081, 1860.

Zwinger, Ann. ". . .a worthless and impracticable region. . . ," *Plateau* 52, no. 2 (June 1980): 25–32.

Websites

Arlington National Cemetery. "John Navarre Macomb, Jr., Colonel, United States Army," http://ww.arlingtoncemetery.net/jnmacomb.htm (accessed August 14, 2003).

Beattie, Kansas. "History of Beattie," http://www.marshallco.net/beattie/history1.html (accessed June 24, 2007).

"Bent, St. Vrain & Company," http://www.sangres.com/history/bentstvrain.htm (accessed May 10, 2007).

Buck, Francis. "Le Carnival de Venise, Quick Step: Composed and Arranged for Piano Forte and respectfully Dedicated to Captn. Charles Dimmock (of

Richmond, Va.).” Richmond, Va.: George Dunn, n.d., http://scriptorium.lib. duke.edu/sheetmusic/conf/conf00/conf0011/ (accessed May 17, 2006).

Catholic Encyclopedia on CD-ROM. “Frederick W. von Egloffstein,” http:// www.newadvent.org/cathen/05327.htm (accessed June 20, 2007).

“Charles Henry Dimmock + Elizabeth Lewis Selden,” http://www.dimick.org/ family.php?famid=F1805 (accessed December 28, 2007).

Civil War Pensions. “Frederick W. von Egloffstein.” Organization Index to Pension Files of Veterans who served between 1861 and 1900. (July 19, 1869.) Publication no. T289. National Archives, Washington, D.C., http://www. footnote.com/searchdocuments.php?query=Frederick+W.+von+Egloffstein &collection=1#7969122 (accessed April 21, 2008).

E. A. Poe Society of Baltimore. “Poe’s Lost Headstone,” http://wwweapoe.org/ balt/poegravs.htm (accessed May 17, 2007).

“Family of Marshall Davies Lloyd: John Navarre Macomb, Jr.,” http://www. gencircles.com/users/mlloyd/3/data/1038 (accessed September 15, 2004).

Guide to the John Strong Newberry Papers, 1898. Provenance Note 2005. Special Collections, George Washington University, Washington, D.C., http:// www.gwu.edu/gelman/spec/ead/ms0257.xml (accessed May 4, 2007).

Krygier, J. B. “Envisioning the American West: Maps, the Representational Barrage of 19th Century Expedition Reports, and the Production of Scientific Knowledge,” *Cartography and GIS* 24, no. 1 (1997) 27–50, http://go.owu. edu/~jbkrygie/krygier_html/envision.html (accessed October 31, 2006).

Matherne, Anne Marie. “Effects of Roads and Well Pads on Erosion in the Largo Canyon Watershed, New Mexico, 2001–02,” *U. S. Geological Survey Scientific Investigations Report 2006–5039*, http://pubs.usgs.gov/sir/2006/5039 (accessed May 5, 2007).

Mesa Verde National Park. “Park History: 1859,” http://www.nps.gov/archive/ meve/park_info/park_history.htm (accessed April 17, 2007).

National Museum of Natural History. “Theme II: Discovering and Understanding Life’s Diversity. Department of Paleobiology: Vertebrate Paleontology,” http://www.si.edu/ofg/Units/sorsnmnh.htm (accessed May 6, 2006).

[Naturalization Papers.] “Frederick W. von Egloffstein.” Soundex Index to Petitions for Naturalizations filed in Federal, State, and Local Courts in New York City, 1792–1906. Publication no. M1674. National Archives, Washington, D.C., http://www.footnote.com/searchdocuments.php?query=Frede rick+W.+von+Egloffstein&collection=1#7969122 (accessed April 21, 2008).

New Mexico Magazine. “New Mexico Magazine’s timeline of important dates,” http://www.nmmagazine.com/NMGUIDE/memorias4.html (accessed June 8, 2007).

Old World Auctions. “Lot #165—Map of Explorations and Surveys in New Mexico and Utah . . . ,” http://www.oldworldauctions.com/auction106/detail. asp?owa_id=2145212957 (accessed April 13, 2005).

Panse, Sonal. “The Robinhood of the Rio Grande,” http://www.buzzle.com/ editorials/5-8-2004-53894.asp (accessed December 29, 2007).

PBS: The West. "Juan Cortina (1824–1890)," http://www.pbs.org/weta/thewest/people/a_c/cortina.html (accessed December 29, 2007).

Rothermel, Charles T. and Company. "Francis Porter Fisher." *Portraits and Biographies of the Fire Underwriters of the City of Chicago.* Chicago: Charles T. Rothermel and Company, 1895, http://www.archive.org/stream/portraitsbiograp-00chas/portraitsbiograp00chas_djvu.txt (accessed May 23, 2009).

Selected Families and Individuals: John Strong Newberry, http://members.cox.net/paradiseoc1/pafg140.htm (accessed February 16, 2008).

Sorley, Merrow Egerton. *Lewis of Warner Hall: The History of a Family.* Baltimore, Md.: Genealogical Publishing, 1979, http://worldcat.org/wcpa/oclc/4953525 (accessed May 19, 2007).

United States Patent and Trademark Office. "Fredk. Von Egloffstein, of New York, N.Y.: Heliographic and Photographic Spectrum for Producting Line-Engravings. Specifications forming part of Letters Patent No. 51,103, dated November 21, 1865; antedated November 5, 1865," http://www.uspto.gov/patft/ (accessed December 27, 2007).

Weideman, Paul. "Fort Marcy Area Holds History," *(Santa Fe) New Mexican,* http://www.freenewmexican.com/sfguide/114.html (accessed May 31, 2007).

INDEX

227, 228, 229, 231, 232, 233, 235,
238, 239, 240, 241, 246, 249, 251;
Santa Fé to Taos Road, 39; Taos to
Santa Fé wagon route, 7
Santa Fé Plaza, 26, 32, 34, 38, 43n1,
145, 149
Santa Fe Trail, xx, 20, 23, 25, 26,
26n48, 102, 107, 133; Santa Fé
Road, 143, 179, 253
Santo Domingo, New Mexico, xxi,
94, 95, 131, 170, 171, 209, 226
Sarouaro, 130, 158, 219
Sauropod dinosaur bones, 8, 9, 82
Schubert, Frank N., xv
Secretary of War, 11, 11n12, 28, 125,
246
Sena, Jose, 43n1
Shiberetch Utes, 69, 71, 82, 82n76, 221
Ship Rock, or Needles, xix, 87, 206,
223
Sibley, Henry Hopkins, 28, 229;
Sibley tent, 28n54
Sicicavané (Tabeguache Ute), 174
Sierra Abajo, 65, 130, 161, 162, 163,
201, 203, 204, 219, 220, 221, 222.
See also Abajo Mountains
Sierra de la Plata, 58, 62n35, 218. See
also La Plata Mountains
Sierra de los Valles, xix, 91. See also
Valles Caldera
Sierra la Carriso, 58. See also Carrizo
Mountain
Sierra la Sal. See La Sal Mountains
Sierra Nevada Mountains, 4
Silver Mountains, 58
Simpson, James H., 4, 7n5, 113, 114,
225n1, 247
Smith, Caleb B., 116, 249
Smithsonian Institution, xv, xxi, 5,
8, 9, 17n31, 83, 108, 109, 237;
Museum of Natural History, xv
Sobutah. See Sowiette
South Wester (Missouri River steam-
boat), 19, 138–139
southern mail and stage, 29, 34, 102,

147, 148, 149, 174, 235
Souvetah. See Sowiette
Sowiette, 52, 54, 66, 67, 69, 154, 155,
156, 158, 216, 220
Spanish explorers, 45
Springfield, Missouri, 35
St. Francis Cathedral, Santa Fé, 33
St. Juan's Day, 34, 147
St. Louis, Missouri, 19, 134, 138, 179,
191
St. Vrain, Céran, 16n25, 179
St. Vrain, Vincent, 16n25

T
Tabuache (Ute band), 102
Taos Road, 39, 174
Taos, New Mexico, 7, 12, 16n25,
45n4, 251
Tecoloté, New Mexico, 25; cathedral,
136
Temuché (Capote Ute leader), 43,
54, 56, 58, 102, 151, 153, 155, 156,
174, 214
Tesuque, New Mexico, 43
The Needles, 77. See also
Canyonlands National Park
Thompson Park, 61
Tierra Blanca (White Land), 66, 130,
219, 220
Tomasonia. See Valdez, Nepomuceno
Tomosamia. See Valdez, Nepomuceno
Topographical Bureau, xix, 28, 32
Torrey, John, 109, 241
Tunecha Mountain. See Chuska
Mountain

U
Upper Colorado River, 115, 246
Upper Rio Grande Valley, 12, 38, 43,
95, 214
Upper San Juan River, 50, 62
USS Explorer, 4, 21
U.S. Army, xvi, 3, 4, 7, 16, 39, 54n18,
55, 98, 99, 103, 106, 113, 116, 117,
120, 149